Putting Psychology in its Place

Putting Psychology in its Place is an historical account of the kinds of role Psychology has played and continues to play in our society, from its nineteenth-century origins to the advent of Cognitive Psychology and the spread of counselling.

A variety of issues are explored in their historical context including how Social Psychology has been shaped by contemporary social issues, why psycho-analysis had such an impact, the uses psychologists have made of animals, the role of war in directing psychological research and changes in how the discipline has dealt with race and gender. Graham Richards proposes that Psychology cannot simply look at its subject matter objectively from the outside, but is involved in actively changing and even creating that subject matter – of which it is also a direct expression.

Putting Psychology in its Place is imaginatively written and accessible; it will prove to be an invaluable introductory text for students and anyone interested in the discipline.

Graham Richards is part-time Principal Lecturer at Staffordshire University. His previous publications include *Human Evolution: An Introduction for the Behavioural Sciences* (1987), *On Psychological Language* (1989) and *Mental Machinery, Part 1: 1600–1850* (1992).

Putting Psychology in its Place

An introduction from a critical historical perspective

Graham Richards

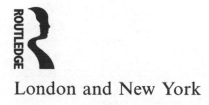

London and New York

First published 1996
by Routledge
11 New Fetter Lane, London EC4P 4EE

Simultaneously published in the USA and Canada
by Routledge
29 West 35th Street, New York, NY 10001

Reprinted 1998

© 1996 Graham Richards

Typeset in Times by Routledge
Printed and bound in Great Britain by
TJ International Ltd, Padstow, Cornwall

British Library Cataloguing in Publication Data
A catalogue record for this book is available from the British Library

Library of Congress Cataloguing in Publication Data
Richards, Graham.
   Putting psychology in its place: an introduction from a critical historical perspective/
   Graham Richards.
   Includes bibliographical references and index.
   1. Psychology–History–19th century. 2. Psychology–History–20th century. I. Title.
   BF95.R55 1996
   150' .9–dc20   95-41910
                                                                                    CIP

ISBN 0–415–12862–5 (hbk)
ISBN 0–415–12863–3 (pbk)

And if the world were black or white entirely
And all the charts were plain
Instead of a mad weir of tigerish waters,
A prism of delight and pain,
We might be surer where we wished to go
Or again we might be merely
Bored but in brute reality there is no
Road that is right entirely.

Louis MacNeice

This is just for Maura

Contents

Preface

The nature and aims of this book require a brief explanation. It is intended as a critical introductory overview of Psychology from a historical perspective. Some such overview is, I believe, necessary for anybody venturing into the discipline, particularly as A-level or undergraduate students. Numerous histories of Psychology being available, some statement of how this differs is in order. First, it seeks to use history as a basis for understanding the nature of Psychology as a cultural and intellectual phenomenon characteristic of late nineteenth- and twentieth-century Western cultures. Second, it attempts to incorporate some insights and approaches of recent history of science which have radically altered how the tasks and issues facing historians of science are conceptualised. In both respects it differs in orientation from histories published prior to the mid-1980s (see Chapter 1).

In a relatively brief text of this kind one difficulty is striking a balance between the conflicting needs to provide both factual information and broad interpretation of what these historical data mean. I have striven to do so, although perhaps more by see-sawing than stasis.

A statement of my general theoretical position was published in 1989 as *On Psychological Language and the Physiomorphic Basis of Human Nature*. While I would now couch some of this differently, my position is essentially unchanged. I have, however, become increasingly aware of the centrality of the 'reflexivity issue', of which more in due course.

This book largely derives from undergraduate courses on the history of Psychology which I have taught for many years. The approach taken evolved considerably over time. A major influence was through personal contacts made during the 1980s with those in the wider field of history of science to whom I am particularly indebted. My three years as Chair of the British Psychological Society's History and Philosophy Section (1991–94) were invaluable in numerous respects, including the moral support and intellectual stimulation of such stalwarts as Alan Costall, Clare Crellin, Jim Good, Sandie Lovie, Ullin Place, Carol Sherrard, John Soyland, Arthur Still, Elizabeth Valentine and Norman Wetherick. Also within the field of history of Psychology, my exchanges with Kurt Danziger, David Leary, Jill Morawski, Roger Smith and Robert Wozniak have been helpful in numerous ways. Mary and Geoff Midgley, my undergraduate mentors in the lamentably deceased Philosophy Department of the University of Newcastle upon Tyne, have continued to provide moral support and an example of intellectual integrity of more importance to me than they probably appreciate. Special thanks are due to the constant backing of John Radford, who first set me to teaching in this field, as well as to Marian Pitts and David Jary (Staffordshire University), John Hodge and Geoff Cantor (Leeds University) and Keith Sumner (Guildhall University) who have enabled me to continue to pursue my career in this field following early retirement from what was, from my standpoint, fast becoming an academic sinking ship. My many students over the years have also played their part in helping me to hone my ideas and I am ever grateful to them. The preparation of this book was greatly facilitated by support from the Renaissance Trust.

Finally, any credit must be shared with Maura whose loving support has never flagged.

Everything wrong with this book is my own fault – well, almost.

1　Psychology and history

The first thing likely to strike any new student of Psychology is probably its sheer diversity. Its sub-disciplines range from Physiological Psychology to Social Psychology, and the approaches adopted from experimental to philosophical. Also puzzling is that apparently near synonymous titles are given to different subjects, such as 'learning' and 'memory', 'reasoning' and 'intelligence'. Nor are the discipline's boundaries very rational: the dances of honey bees belong in Comparative Psychology, but nowhere are you likely to be required to study human dancing! That is the business of anthropologists – who also study kinship while psychologists study parenting. More disturbingly this diversity extends to the very goals and 'projects' of the discipline. Psychologists are far from agreed that their task is 'to predict and control behaviour'; many see it in rather opposite terms as enabling people to understand themselves sufficiently well that they can, among other things, resist attempts to predict and control them. And pondering on how this chaotic situation arose are historians of Psychology.

These latter are in an unusual situation. Most historians of science see themselves as belonging to a discipline called history of science, and would not claim to be contributing directly to the disciplines that they study. Most of Psychology's historians, by contrast, see themselves as also being psychologists. In the past they rarely had close dealings with other historians of science, although nowadays we tend to have a foot in each camp. Historians of Psychology adopt this position because they believe that their work bears directly on current disciplinary concerns, shedding light on a variety of crucial theoretical issues pertaining to that diversity mentioned at the outset, to the status of the discipline itself and to its relationship with its subject matter – hereafter referred to as 'psychology' with a lower-case 'p', reserving 'Psychology' (and 'Psychological') for the discipline itself.

Historians of Psychology thus see themselves as representing a self-reflecting facet of Psychology, as the discipline's introspectors, doing what is sometimes referred to as 'metapsychology'. Students often find it hard to grasp the point of this or see its relevance to their aspirations to become clinical, educational or industrial psychologists. It is therefore necessary to justify this claim that it is highly relevant for anyone wishing to understand Psychology (the discipline) and that it also sheds light on psychology (the subject matter).

We did not cast ourselves in this role until fairly recently. Until the 1970s most histories of Psychology, of which there are many, were written with rather different intentions. (Histories of Psychology in fact began appearing soon after it acquired a formal academic identity in the 1880s and 1890s.) One major reason for this is that Psychology long felt pressurised, especially in English-speaking countries, to prove its scientific credentials (an anxiety less acute than it once was). Psychologists interested in history therefore used history of Psychology as a way of furthering this cause. Their accounts had simple story-lines, unfolding Psychology's increasing commitment to scientific methods, and what it has accomplished by so doing. This invariably centred on a series of 'great men' and their theories or methodological innovations. By the 1940s most such histories were being written in the United States and aimed at the undergraduate market. These acquired a further role; in addition to proving Psychology's scientific credentials they also suggested to students that they were the direct intellectual heirs of Aristotle and Plato. A phrase which has now become a cliché, coined by the German psychologist Ebbinghaus, 'Psychology has a short history but a long past', was often invoked. Anybody who had ever written anything about psychological matters for whatever reason, and however they went about it, was retrospectively baptised as a psychologist before the fact. Ever since ancient Greece, it was claimed, the questions had remained constant, only the methods of answering them had changed. While rhetorically appealing, this does not actually bear close examination (see Chapter 2). Not all earlier histories of Psychology were of exactly these kinds: some sought in a scholarly way to elucidate how Western concepts of human nature had evolved; others, more partially, to show how the author's particular theoretical school was the true and logical culmination of this process.

While few contemporary historians of Psychology find these older approaches acceptable, it would be quite wrong to dismiss all the earlier works. Many are of exemplary scholarship, some still essential for the working historian. Nor are they devoid of valuable insights. What has happened is that we have belatedly caught up with a change that occurred in mainstream history of science during the 1960s, involving a rejection of these approaches in regard to the physical sciences and medicine. Several more or less denigratory terms are often used in this context and it will be helpful to identify them here. One is 'Whiggish', which originated in political history to describe the assumption that history was necessarily progressive ('progressivist' being a frequent synonym). It is now recognised that even in history of science this simple plot cannot do justice to the real complexities, that failures are as interesting and illuminating as successes. Our late twentieth-century global predicament renders it difficult in any case to still see science as an ever progressing, unalloyed benefit to humanity. Closely linked with this are the self-explanatory terms 'celebratory' and 'heroic'.

Another word often used is 'internalist', introduced by the sociologist Robert Merton in the late 1930s. As the limitations of heroic history began to be appreciated, it was felt that two possible tacks could be taken: either to concentrate purely on the development of a discipline's research, theories and discoveries in its own terms, or to look at how its fortunes were determined by economic and cultural factors. These were called 'internalist' and 'externalist' respectively. In the 1970s it was realised that these were not always separable, but sometimes interpenetrated in a thoroughgoing fashion. 'Internalist' has remained in use, however, both as a pejorative term for those who think that focusing exclusively on the internal history of a discipline is sufficient, and more neutrally for internally directed research undertaken within broader frameworks making no such claims.

Histories 'proving' that their author's theoretical position is the valid one are termed 'presentist'. It is never possible, of course, to write history from anything other than the 'present'; the interests, priorities and questions directing historical research inevitably arise within present cultural and intellectual climates. The 'presentist' error is in imagining our present perspective on the past to be the final one, enabling us to see the past 'objectively' and adjudicate with certainty on the merits and demerits of all past science. If we believe that our presently favoured theory has arrived at the truth, history becomes the heroic saga of how that truth was realised. But we can never transcend time in this way. What we can do is try to be open about how present interests are shaping our historical agenda.

The word 'heroic' is closely related to the so-called 'great man' approach to history. This sees historical events as primarily the result of the efforts of a succession of great men (and a few women), the rare benign or malevolent geniuses whose periodic appearance determines humanity's fate. While appealing to the schoolchild, this grossly distorts how history, including history of science, actually happens and is quite incompatible with taking 'external' factors into account. That there are and have been people whom we might legitimately call 'great' is not disputed, but they are not the only players and do not succeed single-handed. Explaining history in terms of the efforts of a handful of autonomous geniuses is tantamount to not explaining it at all, and in science conveys the erroneous impression of a simple yet mysterious division between these geniuses – apparently dwelling on a higher plane – and the rank and file labouring in their wake. The sheer impact of such figures renders it all the more important to scrutinise how they achieved their successes, and demystify, though not deny or denigrate, their accomplishments. For psychologists particularly it is surely of paramount interest to understand them as human beings rather than stay forever spellbound.

From what was said about earlier history of Psychology, it was (if not quite always) clearly guilty of most of these errors. But as already stated, history of Psychology is unlike most other areas of history of science in that its practitioners usually picture themselves as contributing to the very discipline that they are chronicling – and in the very act of doing so. To understand this claim we must say a little more regarding developments in history of science, philosophy of science and sociology of knowledge since the 1960s. One underlying trend in all these fields (the boundaries between which have become extremely blurred) has been towards the detailed examination of scientific practice. In pursuing this, in a variety of ways and at various levels of analysis, many have concluded that we can only understand the nature of science if we view it as the product of complex social processes. This has some serious implications when explored further because it means that no 'knowledge', not even scientific 'knowledge', has any final absolutely 'objective' status but is the product and expression of a specific cultural and historical context. Science too is embedded in the present. Without going further into this knotty issue, one spin-off has been that these fields have themselves acquired an increasingly 'psychological' character. Understanding 'scientific behaviour' raises questions relating to perception (e.g. how does one make sense of what one is seeing when nobody has seen it before?), cognition (e.g. how do scientists really create their theories and decide what their results mean?), personality (e.g. what motivates scientists to devote their life to a particular topic?), communication (e.g. how do scientists succeed or fail in getting their work accepted as valid? how are controversies resolved?) and group dynamics (how are scientific disciplines organised and managed?). Of course there are sociological and economic-level questions as well, but such psychological issues have become part and parcel of the current agenda.

What does this mean for Psychology? For a start it places it in a rather odd position *vis-à-vis* the other sciences because as the science of human behaviour its subject matter logically includes scientific behaviour. The numerous paradoxes arising from this cannot be addressed here, but it is important to appreciate that it casts Psychology in a quite ambiguous position *vis-à-vis* the natural sciences for, while trying to operate as a normal science, it is also on the outside looking in. Psychology as a discipline is perhaps in a similar self-reflecting relation to the rest of science as historians and philosophers of Psychology are to Psychology. The old question 'Is Psychology a science?' thus evades any easy answer; it is not even entirely clear any more quite what it means. This issue will keep recurring in the ensuing chapters.

This view of science as a product and expression of specific social contexts has, moreover, been developed into a way of looking at human behaviour and ideas in general, merging into the approach, adopted by many social psychologists over the last twenty years, known as 'social constructionism' – and thus represents a Psychological, or 'metapsychological', thesis in its own right. And now we at last get to the nub of the issue. Psychology itself must be one of the routes by which this process of 'social construction' operates. The history of Psychology thereby becomes one aspect of the history of its own subject matter, 'psychology'. The historian of Psychology is not only looking at the history of a particular discipline, but also at the history of what that discipline purports to be studying. Whereas in orthodox sciences there is always some external object of enquiry – rocks, electrons, DNA, chemicals –

existing essentially unchanging in the non-human world (even if never finally knowable 'as it really is' beyond human conceptions), this is not so for Psychology. 'Doing Psychology' is the human activity of studying human activity; it is human psychology examining itself – and what it produces by way of new theories, ideas and beliefs about itself is also part of our psychology!

For the historian of Psychology who is also a psychologist, the discipline's history is in itself therefore a psychological phenomenon. More specifically, we are looking at Psychology's role in the dynamic psychological process by which human nature constantly recreates, re-forms and regenerates itself, primarily in Western cultures. This sounds very grandiose, of course, and I would immediately concede that not all my colleagues see things in these terms. Nevertheless it is, I believe, logically necessary to acknowledge that Psychology has the complex 'reflexive' character being outlined here. To put it bluntly, Psychology is produced by, produces, and is an instance of, its own subject matter. What is more debatable is how seriously we should take this – whether it has genuinely important implications. One bottom-line lesson which I feel to be important is really a moral one: the psychologist is not outside the things that he or she studies, not an external 'objective' observer of the human psyche, but an active participant in the collective psychological life of their community, culture and, ultimately, species. This means that what psychologists say and do, the theories, images and models of the psychological that they devise and promote, have real consequences for everybody else. They are in an even weaker position than physical scientists to disclaim responsibility for what society does with what they produce, for even in producing it they are participating in this collective social psychological process.

Stated in these terms, the case may sound rather abstract and nebulous. This is why we need history of Psychology – to flesh out this situation in a visible, concrete fashion. In what follows, I hope to provide a more comprehensive picture of the enterprise that Psychology is engaged in than is usually given – one that takes account of its perplexing reflexivity and identifies more clearly its place in modernist culture, past and present.

There are easier justifications for the history of Psychology. One is simply that we cannot understand the present situation without knowing something about how and why it arose. Another is that it provides some check on needlessly repeating work that has been forgotten – something that psychologists are curiously prone to do. In this sense it might be seen as serving to maintain access to the discipline's long-term memory, preventing present-day psychologists from reinventing the wheel. A third would be that it extends our sampling, enabling us to track changes over time in how people perform on, say, a particular Psychological test. Each of these has some merit, but they all cast history in a sort of service role in relation to the rest of the discipline, failing to acknowledge that history has its own autonomous agendas which historians naturally see as being as important as anybody else's. In fact the incompatibility of the first and third of these with the approach espoused here is more apparent than real. Showing how and why the present situation arose is an intrinsic part of the present enterprise, as is the identification of psychological change over time. The second 'memory' role can, however, only be considered a subsidiary aspect of the historian's job, to be undertaken on a one-off basis with colleagues who have specific questions or concerns. This might well have incidental pay-offs – as well as averting total academic isolation!

Finally we need to consider a linguistic problem which arises directly from the reflexivity issue in the following way. Let us begin with the question: 'how are we able to talk about psychological phenomena?' The answer is not straightforward for we cannot actually define the words and expressions that we use in our 'psychological language' by pointing to the phenomena to which they refer. If language is to remain meaningful there must be public criteria for deciding whether it is being used correctly, yet psychological phenomena (and the psychological meanings of behavioural phenomena) are by definition private – you cannot directly observe my experience of pain, hate, bewilderment, colour, anxiety, etc. When we examine the words and expressions actually used in psychological discourse, however, we find that they nearly all appear to be metaphorical – and the exceptions (like 'sad', 'happy', etc.) are those with a large number of figurative synonyms (like 'depressed', or 'delighted', respectively). We are in effect saying 'I am like that' where 'that' refers to some public phenomenon or property. Moreover, we can go further, for what this in turn amounts to is that we structure and explain our private psychological experience in terms of how the public world is structured and explained in our culture. Insofar as we can actually communicate about the psychological it is therefore as a sort of internal reflection of the outside world. But is there anything *beyond* this reflection – something that is *really* going on independently of our efforts to describe it verbally? Well, there might be, and not all psychological communication is verbal anyway, but the point is that whatever *cannot* be communicated about is something that we cannot really be said to know about and is certainly not something that we could explore as a psychological phenomenon. We can only talk about that which we have a language for talking about – and as far as the psychological is concerned, we have no way of knowing what psychological phenomena are, no way of giving them meaning, except in terms of that language.

If this is so, then we are bound to accept (with whatever degrees of reluctance or glee) that *changes in psychological language signify psychological change in their own right*. This is clearly important for history of Psychology. At one level what we are studying is, quite literally, language – for it is only in this form that previous accounts of the psychological are available. In a direct and immediate fashion therefore, when psychologists introduce a new concept or theory about the psychological, they are engaged in *changing* it. It is at this linguistic level that the reflexive loops mentioned earlier, notably 'Psychology produces its own subject matter', are most tangibly manifested. To classify and explain the psychological in a new way is to be involved in changing the psychological itself. To think about oneself differently is to change oneself.

Contrary to some contemporary psychologists (such as Paul and Patricia Churchland), I do not believe that there is some independent psychological 'reality' beyond the language to which it refers with greater or lesser 'accuracy' – and which Psychology may eventually succeed in 'scientifically' capturing in a new technical vocabulary. This is not to be understood as saying that language is all there is but that psychological language is itself a psychological phenomenon – a psychological technique for both talking about other psychological phenomena *and* for giving them form and meaning. We all have innumerable private, 'psychological' experiences which we find impossible to 'put into words' – but this very fact makes us say things like 'I don't know what it meant', etc., we never know what to actually *do* with such experiences. We may try communicating them via another medium, like music or painting, but even then we cannot, by definition, say *what* has been communicated or know that we have succeeded.

Students often have great difficulty in grasping the consequences of this – that nobody prior to Freud had an Oedipus complex, that nobody before Pavlov and Watson was ever 'conditioned' and that nobody before *c*.1914 had a high IQ. What this means is that, however similar to such phenomena previous ones retrospectively appear to be, they were not terms in which the psychology of people prior to their introduction was actually structured. They had no psychological *reality*. The very act of introducing such concepts changed the situation by providing people with new terms in which to experience themselves – and only *then* can they be properly said to refer to really occurring psychological phenomena. The same point holds true for much of everyday psychological language ('folk psychology' as it is somewhat patronisingly called) – nobody 'went off the rails' before the advent of railways, nobody was 'on the same wavelength' before radio was invented, and further back, nobody could 'spell things out' before the invention of alphabetic writing. Identifying the psychological impacts of new psychological ideas as linguistically encoded should then occupy a high place in our priorities, for it promises further insights into the discipline's role in modern cultures over the last century and a half.

The purpose of this book is therefore to 'put Psychology in its place', to provide readers, especially those new to the discipline, with an overall picture of what kind of an enterprise it is and how it acquired its present cultural functions. But in keeping with my guiding philosophy I should stress that this is, in the end, my own particular view of it. Other historians and philosophers of Psychology, if undertaking a similar task, would undoubtedly produce accounts differing from it to a greater or lesser degree. It is not presented as the final word on the matter, but, like all other Psychological work, as a contribution to an ongoing process and its merits and flaws are matters for readers and critics to sort out.

BIBLIOGRAPHY

Further reading

Danziger, K. (1990) *Constructing the Subject: Historical Origins of Psychological Research*, Cambridge: Cambridge University Press. Highly acclaimed study of the reflexive nature of experimental Psychology.

Leahey, T.H. (1993, 3rd edn) *A History of Psychology: Main Currents in Psychological Thought*, Englewood Cliffs, N.J.: Prentice-Hall. Best full-scale general history currently available. *To be taken as further reading for most subsequent chapters.*

Richards, G. (1989) *On Psychological Language and the Physiomorphic Basis of Human Nature*, London: Routledge. Only one chapter of this is explicitly on history of Psychology but it presents my general 'metapsychological' position.

Smith, R. (1988) 'Does the History of Psychology Have a Subject?', *History of the Human Sciences* 1(2):147–77. Highly influential paper challenging the notions of historical continuity and disciplinary coherence as well as highlighting the functions served by traditional histories.

The only comprehensive bibliographical reference work is:

Watson, R.I. (1974, 1976) *Eminent Contributors to Psychology* (2 vols), New York: Springer. Vol.1 contains a bibliography of works by psychologists who died before 1970, vol. 2 contains a bibliography of secondary sources.

Classic history of Psychology

The following are among the most important of the many titles published.

Baldwin, J.M. (1913) *History of Psychology*, London: Watts. By one of the founders of American Psychology. Fairly brief and mainly focused on philosophy.

Boring, E.G. (1929, 2nd edn 1950) *A History of Experimental Psychology*, New York: Appleton-Century-Crofts. Single most influential account and an invaluable reference work. Made use of the concept of the *Zeitgeist* or 'spirit of the times' in addressing contextual factors.

Boring, E.G. (1942) *Sensation and Perception in the History of Experimental Psychology*, New York: Appleton-Century-Crofts. Spin-off from the previous work, similarly valuable for reference purposes.

Brett, G.S. (1912–21) *History of Psychology* (3 vols), abridged R.S. Peters (1953), London: Allen & Unwin. Primarily a history of the philosophy of mind, only reaching modern Psychology in the last volume. Peters' edition has a supplementary chapter attempting to bring it up to date.

Hearnshaw, L. (1964) *A Short History of British Psychology 1840–1940*, London: Methuen. The only pre-1980s monograph on British Psychology. Includes some institutional history.

Kantor, J.R. (1963) *The Scientific Evolution of Psychology Vol.1*, Chicago: Principia Press. 'Presentist' approach depicting behaviourism as the logical outcome of Psychology's development.

Klein, D.B. (1970) *A History of Scientific Psychology: Its Origins and Philosophical Background*, London: Routledge & Kegan Paul. Excellent on the philosophical roots of Psychology.

Murphy, G. and J.K. Kovach (6th edn 1972, 1st edn 1928 by G. Murphy only) *Historical Introduction to Modern Psychology*, London: Routledge & Kegan Paul. The most widely read general history from the time of first publication with a somewhat broader agenda than Boring.

Schultz, D. (1975) *A History of Modern Psychology*, New York: Academic Press. One of the last traditional histories.

Newer approaches

Ash, M.G. and R.W. Woodward (eds) (1987) *Psychology in Twentieth-Century Thought and Society*, Cambridge: Cambridge University Press. Important collection of papers filling out the cultural and contextual dimensions of the story.
Buss, A.R. (ed.) (1979) *Psychology in Social Context*, New York: Irvington. Marked the departure from internalism.
Leary, D.E. (ed.) (1990) *Metaphors in the History of Psychology*, Cambridge: Cambridge University Press. Stimulating collection of papers on the metaphorical nature of psychological discourse, although few contributors are really prepared to bite the bullet.
Murray, D.J. (1983) *A History of Western Psychology*, Englewood Cliffs, N.J.: Prentice-Hall. Departing somewhat from earlier approaches by broadening the agenda of topics covered.
Richards, G. (1987) 'Of What is the History of Psychology a History?', *British Journal for the History of Science* 20:201–11. Explores the implications of the ambiguities of the term 'psychology' as referring to both discipline and subject matter.
Richards, G. (1992) *Mental Machinery: The Origins and Consequences of Psychological Ideas: Part One 1600–1850*, London: Athlone Press. Attempts to rethink the pre-1850 period in the light of recent developments in the history of science and the nature of psychological language.
Robinson, D.N. (1995 3rd edn) *An Intellectual History of Psychology*, New York: Macmillan. Conservative but sophisticated and scholarly.
Rose, N. (1985) *The Psychological Complex: Psychology, Politics and Society in England 1869–1939*, London: Routledge & Kegan Paul. A telling sociological account, influenced by Foucault.
Rose, N. (1990) *Governing the Soul: The Shaping of the Private Self*, London: Routledge. Extends his previous work, focusing on Psychology's role as the source of 'technologies of subjectivity'.
Smith, R. (1992) *Inhibition: History and Meaning in the Sciences of Mind and Brain*, Cambridge: Cambridge University Press. An in-depth exploration of the ideological and cultural ramifications of the concept of 'inhibition' and the inseparability of its technical and its cultural meanings.
Soyland, J. (1994) *Psychology as Metaphor*, London: Sage.
Woodward, W.R. and M.G. Ash (eds) (1982) *The Problematic Science: Psychology in Nineteenth Century Thought*, New York: Praeger. Useful collection of papers opening up the origins of modern Psychology to contextual and constructionist scrutiny.

The major journals in this field are *The Journal of the History of the Behavioral Sciences* and *History of the Human Sciences*.

Additional references

Churchland, Patricia S. (1986) *Neurophilosophy: Toward a Unified Science of the Mind/Brain*, Cambridge, Mass. and London: MIT Press.
Churchland, Paul M. (1988, rev. edn) *Matter and Consciousness*, Cambridge, Mass.: MIT Press.

2 Before Psychology: 1600–1850

No discipline calling itself Psychology existed prior to the mid-nineteenth century. What we might clumsily call 'reflexive discourse' – discourse about human nature, 'mind' and the soul – has always existed, but, barring isolated exceptions, before 1800 this was not 'scientific' in any modern sense, let alone experimental. This is, on the face of it, surprising. In *The Advancement of Learning* (1605) and *Novum Organum* (1620), Francis Bacon had advocated a 'general science concerning the Nature and State of Man' at the outset of the 'Scientific Revolution'. Even so, by 1850 few experiments of a recognisably 'Psychological' kind are on record, and even non-experimental empirical research was sparse. In Britain even the word 'Psychology' was rare prior to the early 1800s, when the poet-philosopher Samuel Taylor Coleridge imported it from Germany (where philosophers had long used *Psychologie*). The significance of this absence must. be stressed since, as previously mentioned, Psychology was traditionally depicted as emerging seamlessly from earlier 'reflexive discourse', often starting with the ancient Greeks.

The line that the questions remain the same but the methods of answering them change is unsatisfactory, for had these earlier thinkers been asking the kinds of question that psychologists ask, devising the obvious empirical methods of answering them would have been easy. From at least 1700 they could have run rats through mazes, circulated questionnaires, seen how many trials it took to learn word lists, or invented instruments to measure reaction times – all methods typical of modern Psychology. The reason that they did not was that they were not asking these questions in the first place.

This is not to claim a complete lack of historical connection, only that their predecessors were not doing what psychologists began doing in the late nineteenth century, still less what they do today. They were not failing to answer the same questions, but asking different ones, about the nature of virtue, the relations between the immortal soul (if it existed) and the body, whether all our ideas came from sensory experience or whether some were innate and self-evident, what kind of a substance the mind was, how to master one's 'passions', or, at a cruder level, how character manifested itself in the face. In addressing these they frequently engaged in what looks like Psychological theorising, and were led to discuss topics like perception, the structure of the mind and even, occasionally, child development and animal behaviour. Such discussions set the terms in which psychologists began tackling the same topics, which is where the historical link lies. But caution is needed on reading too much into this: (a) these matters arose in the context of issues no longer figuring, at least in the same way, on Psychology's agenda, and (b) nobody treated such investigations as contributions to a single discipline, Psychology.

Many modern Psychological inquiries are occasionally anticipated in earlier works, but the connections (if any) between these and subsequent research are often obscure. Too often historians cast them as part of Psychology's history, even though they had little or no impact on the later work and were unknown to Psychology until the historian disinterred them. The interesting question that such anticipations raise is really why they did *not* have an impact, but to answer this would take the traditional historian in an unwelcome direction, highlighting the differences rather than the continuities between modern Psychology and previous work.

The easiest way of treating this period is in terms of prevailing disciplines and genres of 'reflexive discourse'. Unfortunately a whole swathe of these must be left aside here, including fiction, drama and poetry. These often provide valuable evidence about the psychological ideas of the times and how far new philosophical or physiological ideas about human nature had penetrated popular culture, but were not intended to extend knowledge about human nature as such. Even this proviso leaves a nigh-on unmanageable body of material. The most important genre was philosophy and as the eighteenth century progressed, physiology became increasingly influential. But while these traditionally dominate historical attention, there are numerous relevant works on education, language, aesthetics, madness, physiognomy, manners, and logic, for example, as well as volumes of, now mostly unreadable, theology. First, however, why did no discipline of Psychology materialise before 1850?

One obvious culprit is religion. During the 1600s theologians used the word 'pneumatology' for a supposed science or study of the soul. Relations between science and religion are always rather fraught, and one topic that theologians were very touchy about was any 'Baconian' approach which threatened their monopoly regarding the nature of the soul. This boundary was heavily policed during the Scientific Revolution. This is, ironically, very evident in the work of the French philosopher René Descartes in the 1620s–1640s who regularly figures as a hero because of his doctrine of 'mechanism' and his physiological speculations on 'reflexes' and how the body affects the mind. At the centre of his philosophy lies his famous distinction between mind and body. The body and material world consist of an extended substance governed by mechanistic laws amenable to scientific study. The mind, however, is an 'unextended substance' and can only be investigated by reason; it is thus *excluded* from the province of natural philosophy. Of course not everyone agreed with him, notably Thomas Hobbes, but the materialist opposition continued to argue in philosophical terms; they did not engage in Psychological research.

Second, throughout the period (though decreasingly so) it was unclear that Man (the term always used) was actually part of Nature, and thus in the province of science. This uncertainty was again religious – humans, having immortal souls, are semi-divine, partly above 'animate Nature'. Natural philosophy, however, is the study of Nature. To treat 'Man' scientifically was thus to risk accusations of heresy and, aside from the eighteenth-century radical French philosophers, few were prepared to risk it. Even physiologists, though happy to tackle sensation, balked at extending their theories to the mind itself. This doctrine also implied that the human mind was universally the same, that all humans were basically identical psychologically, even if there were differences in temperament, or due to environmental circumstances (before *c.*1790 'racial' differences were mostly explained either environmentally or by descent from different sons of Noah). Any philosophically derived 'laws of the mind' (e.g. those of 'association of ideas') were thus universal in scope, and if the reasoning by which they were derived was sound, further research was superfluous.

The question of 'Man's place in Nature', to use T.H. Huxley's phrase, was answered in terms of the long-standing idea of the Scale of Nature (*Scala Naturæ*), the Great Chain of Being, an ascending scale of perfection from bugs at the bottom to God at the top. Man, being part divine, bridged the gap between animals and angels, matter and spirit. The Angel–God gap was held to be immeasurable; otherwise, many believed, this scale was unbroken, although this presented difficulties. Towards the end of the eighteenth century this image underwent an important change. Whereas previously it had been static, representing the structure of an unchanging divinely ordered world, new ideas of progress, growing awareness of historical time and accumulating geological discoveries now gave it a dynamic dimension. Nature as a whole was progressing towards perfection, the Scale of Nature was, so to speak, being ascended over time. This laid the deeper foundations for subsequent evolutionary notions but did not immediately challenge 'Man's' semi-divine status. On the contrary it gave this more dramatic connotations.

Third, there is a problem about language, related to my remarks on this in Chapter 1, which may be simplified thus: new psychological ideas are generated, we saw, by reflexively applying metaphors from the public world. But the philosophy underpinning the Scientific Revolution involved a rejection of fanciful metaphors – scientists were to use only simple unambiguous language. Because the human mind was believed to be universally the same, existing psychological concepts were accepted uncritically as basically adequate. Philosophers like John Locke in the late seventeenth century restricted their psychological language to a few basic, seemingly unproblematic, terms like 'idea' and 'sensation'. The upshot was that this combination of the doctrine of universality and anti-metaphorical linguistic attitudes (shared, for different reasons, by all major schools of linguistic thought) inhibited the exploration *within disciplinary contexts* of the psychological potential of new scientific ideas. While new psychological ideas appeared, they usually did so, as always, as trendy metaphors – often from physiology or medicine. They were not introduced by would-be scientists of the mind utilising new ideas from science and technology in formulating new Psychological theories (as psychologists typically do, as we shall see). This is ironic because some, including Locke, recognised the fundamentally metaphorical nature of psychological language.

Fourth, which must suffice, many now argue that not until around 1800 did the notion of the individual mind as a unitary entity crystallise in Western thought. This is linked, they claim, to the rise of capitalism and economic individualism, and breakdown of earlier collective social structures. The discipline of Psychology is not therefore seen as possible prior to the nineteenth century because its subject matter was not yet thinkable as a unified object of investigation. This is a complex and contentious issue which, although we cannot further explore it here, is a major theme among contemporary historians of the human sciences.

TRADITIONS OF 'REFLEXIVE DISCOURSE' BEFORE 1850

While it is beyond the scope of the present work to provide a detailed account of this period, an overview of it is nonetheless necessary for an understanding of Psychology's point of departure.

The most significant genre was philosophy, of which three traditions were dominant during this period and each of these contributed significantly to the corpus of psychological concepts with which the first psychologists had to work:

- Rationalism, the label generally given to a lineage of French and German philosophers, the most important being Descartes, Malebranche (French), Spinoza (Dutch Jewish), Leibniz, Wolff, Tetens and Kant (German). Like all such labels it oversimplifies – any major philosopher's thought is in many respects unique. What unified them was a belief that basic metaphysical questions (e.g. the nature of existence, the origins and limits of knowledge, the nature of truth) can be answered by reason acting alone. If sufficiently logical and rigorous we can attain knowledge of such matters, the certainty of which actually surpasses anything based on our fallible senses.
- Associationism, generally considered to begin with John Locke (1689) and developed in Britain by Bishop Berkeley, the Scottish sceptic David Hume and David Hartley during the first half of the eighteenth century, to reach its final form in the work of James and John Stuart Mill in the nineteenth century. This also enormously influenced radical eighteenth-century French materialist philosophers such as Condillac, La Mettrie, D'Holbach and Helvetius. The central tenet of this school was that all psychological phenomena originated in atom-like or 'corpuscular' sensations which were built up into complex ideas by a few simple 'laws of association'.

- Scottish 'common-sense' realism. This began as a reaction against reductionist associationism, its leading exponent being Thomas Reid (1764).
During the period from 1764 to the 1840s this approach underlay much of
the work of 'Scottish Enlightenment' thinkers – David Hume being the main
exception. This school included Dugald Stewart, Adam Ferguson, Henry
Kames and Adam Smith and a host of lesser lights, Sir William Hamilton
being its final major figure in Scotland. These writers typically opted for a
compromise between rationalism and empiricism. On the one hand they
accepted the existence of innate faculties or 'powers', but espoused an
empirical *non*-reductionist approach to the identification and study of
these. In many respects the work of this school anticipated that of modern
Psychology more closely than either of the other two. For reasons to be
discussed in Chapter 4 it also came to dominate the indigenous American
'Mental and Moral Philosophy' tradition of the nineteenth century.
Curiously, however, it receives less attention than associationism and
rationalism in most histories. This neglect appears to be for three reasons.
First, none of its exponents was a philosopher of quite such stature as
Locke, Hume or Kant. Second, by the 1890s reductionism was seen as a
central scientific virtue so those wishing to stress Psychology's scientific
character preferred to cite the associationists as their favoured ancestors.
Third, the US 'Mental and Moral Philosophy' tradition was cast as the
establishment against which American 'new psychologists' of the 1880s and
1890s were rebelling.[1]

These three traditions created a legacy of often conflicting images of human
nature and psychological phenomena and how they should be studied. In
particular the relative importance of experience and innate factors, and of
empirical research, logical analysis or introspection as methods emerged as
central issues. These were not purely abstract debates but related to the cultural
settings in which the various schools flourished. In pre-revolutionary France
most philosophers were intent on undermining the still feudal *ancien régime*
and espoused strong materialist and anti-religious positions. For them an
associationist philosophy was the most congenial epistemological framework.
The Scots by contrast were eager to reconcile philosophy with Protestantism
and were at the same time keen to find a rational basis for studying human
society in the light of the dramatic changes accompanying the Industrial
Revolution. For them a non-reductionist but practical orientation seemed
most appropriate. The university-based German philosophers, in a feudal, but
non-centralised, culture as yet unaffected by the Industrial Revolution on a
large scale, were in the most ivory-towered position and inclined to adopt a

---

1 A note on terminology is in order here. 'Empiricism' is the doctrine that knowledge is derived
from experience, 'sensationalism' the doctrine that experience ultimately consists of atomistic
sensations (in all sensory modes), 'associationism' the doctrine that these sensations are
combined by a number of 'laws of association' to yield complex ideas and concepts. While
these clearly tend to go together, they are logically distinct; in particular empiricism does not
necessarily imply the other two.

purely intellectual mode of tackling philosophical issues which offered no threat to the ruling princes, electors and margraves of the various German states. Unlike the Scots and Germans few English philosophers were university-based, and unlike the French they were disinclined to extreme radicalism (although there were exceptions such as William Godwin). Nor were their religious allegiances as heartfelt as those of the Scots. Hostile to what they viewed as airy-fairy speculation, they saw associationism as the philosophy most in keeping with Newtonian natural philosophy. In fact there is very little English philosophy of much significance between Hartley (1749) and James Mill (1829). The associationism versus 'common sense' division is, I should add, perhaps clearer in retrospect than it was at the time. Thomas Brown's very influential *Lectures on the Human Mind* (1822), for example, straddled the divide quite impressively (although it has been co-opted into the associationist camp by most historians).

Conceptually each contributed to the emergence of Psychology. As far as rationalism is concerned, we need note the following: (a) Kant gave mind a more active role than it possessed in most rival systems, in which it passively obeyed quasi-natural laws; (b) Kant, particularly, disputed the logical possibility of a science of the mind – it was unquantifiable and beyond direct investigation; (c) rationalist philosophical analyses, being non-reductionist, provided a conceptually subtler account than those of reductionist associationists and materialists. These were clearly a mixed blessing for the prospects of a scientific Psychology. Following Kant, German philosophy reacted in two ways. First, some, such as Schelling, rejected his view that mind (or spirit) was unknowable 'in itself', and went to romantic idealistic extremes, rhapsodising about Man being the vanguard of a cosmic process by which the Absolute was realising itself. Although this 'transcendental idealism' had a number of positive features, stimulating renewed consideration of human nature in all its complexity, it was felt, somewhat unfairly, by most British and many French thinkers to be inflated windbaggery. Others, however, sought to circumvent Kant's rejection of the possibility of a scientific Psychology – Herbart and Lotze being the most eminent. It was from this strand, in combination with advances in physiology, that a discipline calling itself Psychology later established itself in Germany.

Associationism's legacy lay primarily in its reductionist mode of analysis. Although the original laws of association ('contiguity', 'contrast' and 'similarity') fell into disuse, the notion that learning and memory could be explained in fundamentally associationist terms persisted. From Alexander Bain onwards, many anglophone psychologists saw their task as involving the translation of associationist ideas into more scientifically sophisticated, often physiological, terms culminating in behaviourist learning theory.

The Scottish realist school's contribution was more diffuse. As well as their deeper role in the history of US Psychology, their catalogue of innate 'powers' of the mind long continued to provide a framework for organising the topics in general Psychological texts, while their practical orientation (including interest in child development and social psychological phenomena) adumbrated the possibility of an applied discipline of the kind that Psychology eventually became.

The foregoing sketch, in which little attempt has been made to discuss the details of the numerous philosophical systems included under this triad of umbrella terms, must suffice for present purposes. The point I wish to stress here is that none of these philosophical traditions is attempting to study psychology in a thoroughgoing 'natural philosophical' or 'scientific' fashion. The Scottish school occasionally comes close but even here there is little resembling 'research' as we now understand it.

For the beginnings of this we need to look at physiology which, by the late eighteenth century, was making serious headway in conceptualising biological processes. As it did so, psychological issues of various kinds soon assumed prominence. Most significantly, as the eighteenth century drew to a close there was growing debate about brain functioning. One important manifestation of this was Franz Gall's 'craniology', later known as phrenology. He claimed that functions were highly localised in different 'cerebral organs', the relative sizes of which indicated an individual's character and determined the shape of their cranium, from which their character could thus be read. It enjoyed a particularly sympathetic reception in Scotland where its list of functions closely matched the Reidians' 'powers'. Its foremost Scottish advocate was George Combe. Phrenology enjoyed great popularity as a 'scientific' approach to personality from *c.* 1810 until the early 1850s (a little longer in the United States) and influenced several pioneer psychologists (notably Alexander Bain, Herbert Spencer and the US educationist Horace Mann) during their early years, although they later abandoned it. In many respects it was a 'dry run' for Psychology. Traditionally dismissed as a naive pseudo-science by disciplinary historians, it is now understood to have played a vital contextual role in popularising the notion of a secular 'science of the mind', as well as pioneering what is now known as the 'functionalist' approach. Opponents, such as the French biologist Flourens, disputed localisation on experimental grounds, and eventually succeeded in discrediting the theory. (Associated with, though distinct from, phrenology was 'physiognomy'. The ancient notion that character could be read from the face was reformulated in Romantic terms in the late eighteenth century by the Swiss pastor Lavater.) Later the localisation theory returned to favour, but in a very different form (see Chapter 9).

Among other key discoveries was the differentiation between the afferent and efferent (or motor) nerves – those carrying information from sense organs to the brain and those controlling the muscles, accomplished independently by Charles Bell and the French physiologist Magendie by the 1820s and, a little later, the fuller development of the concept of reflex action by Marshall Hall in the 1830s and 1840s which put the issue of 'unconscious' action clearly on the map as well as possibilities of theorising about the biological basis of learning.

Finally, the experimental study of the senses, beginning with the early nineteenth-century work of E.H. Weber in Germany and lesser-known French researchers, had two important consequences: first, methodologically, it paved the way for Psychological experimentation, and second, it succeeded in bringing the experimental approach across the border from physiological topics to psychological ones, e.g. reaction times (RTs) and sensory thresholds (the area later called psychophysics). This laid the basis for Fechner's and Wundt's work in the 1850s, generally held to represent the birth of experimental Psychology. Mention must also be made of Johannes Müller, a German physiologist whose multi-volume handbook of human physiology (1834–40) brought together and evaluated the early nineteenth-century developments, serving as the primary reference work on the topic.

Such developments in physiology began, from around 1800, to make increasing inroads into philosophy's academic monopoly on psychological issues. By and large, however, direct confrontation was held at bay, neither camp wanting to see the other as an enemy. While philosophy and physiology may be seen as Psychology's major roots, it is vital to understand that other disciplines and interests were also involved. I will indicate just some of them.

Developmental Psychology has its deeper origins in the various ideas regarding education that flourished during this period. Two key figures are Locke, who published *Some Thoughts Concerning the Education of Children* in 1693, and the French philosopher Jean-Jacques Rousseau, one of the first 'Romantics', whose extraordinarily influential *Emile* (1762) described, in fictional form, his ideal of how boys should be educated. This is often taken as the founding text of 'modern', 'progressive' educational theory. At the end of the eighteenth century in Britain numerous books appeared on education (including education of women, and often written by women), drawing on Locke's and Rousseau's ideas, and occasionally those of other philosophers (e.g. Reid). It is this genre that mediates between philosophy and practice, trying to apply philosophical ideas on learning to the real world of education. Educational theory and pioneering educational projects flourished in mainland Europe after Rousseau – major names including Pestalozzi, Herbart and Froebel (see Chapter 13). In France the famous incident of the feral child Victor of Aveyron, taken under his tutelage by Itard, further stimulated interest in child development and the question of how far 'human nature' was a product of civilisation and how far it was inborn. While research into the significance of early educational writings for the history of Psychology remains fairly meagre, they indisputably stimulated public awareness of the potential practical relevance of philosophical ideas about the mind, thereby creating a climate in which demands for professional expertise on child development could develop. Thus, when Psychology did emerge, it was here that it found its first area of application.

An area in which innovatory psychological concepts were especially needed was the treatment of madness, always a singularly difficult, and often not very popular, task of medicine. From the mid-eighteenth century onwards the history of psychiatry acknowledges a great many 'pioneers' such as Pinel who released the lunatics from their chains at the Bicêtre (a large Paris asylum) after the French Revolution, Samuel Tuke who founded the humanitarian 'Retreat' at York, and J.C. Reil, a German psychiatrist who proposed radical therapeutic methods. Most psychiatric writers prior to the 1850s developed theories and/or classifications of mental illness and its symptoms which incorporated models of the structure of the mind, often containing original elements. Such notions as the psychosomatic nature of symptoms, the existence of an unconscious, the causative role of trauma, the super-ego/ego/unconscious division and many others are first aired, albeit hazily or in different terminology, at this time. We return to this in Chapter 8.

Finally we should note the numerous works on social philosophy and pioneer sociology. As social change accelerated during the eighteenth century and the effectiveness of religious authority declined, many, including Scottish Enlightenment thinkers such as Adam Smith, felt compelled to seek other bases for what they called 'civil society'. Implementing such a project usually involved formulating some new core notion of 'human nature', leading the Scots, for example, to adopt the principle of 'sympathy' as a social equivalent to 'gravity' in physics. It was a topic that combined concern with morality or 'virtue' with practical understanding of human social behaviour. A fine example of this is Smith's *Theory of Moral Sentiments* (1759), which contains many penetrating observations on social phenomena and what we would call 'attitudes'. His concerns clearly verged on those of Social Psychology. The 'utilitarian' image of human nature proposed by Jeremy Bentham, very different from Adam Smith's, was the one favoured by associationists. Most notorious was Mandeville's *Fable of the Bees: or, Private Vices, Public Benefits* (1723), a cynical satire in which the disastrous social consequences of a general outbreak of virtue were explored, an early version of the recurrent argument that humans are basically selfish and competitive. Other prominent social theorists of the period included Rousseau (who introduced the notion of the 'social contract'), Montesquieu, Adam Ferguson and William Godwin. The views of human nature offered by social philosophers cover the range from pessimism (Mandeville) to utopian optimism (e.g. Godwin), one popular image being 'the noble savage', inspired by explorers' accounts of the apparently idyllic lives of 'savages' (notably, in Captain Cook's case, Tahitians). This image, which influenced Rousseau, powerfully affected the Romantic movement which flourished from *c.*1780 to the 1830s. Finally, this period sees the first 'speculative histories' of the human race, outlining its progress from savagery to civilisation, including the origins of language – precursors of the subsequent, often only slightly less speculative, evolutionary accounts which have been produced since the mid-nineteenth century. Social philosophising necessarily involved authors in adopting some core, non-religious, notion of human nature, displaying their own 'human natures' in so doing. Clearly, in a case like this, the histories of Psychology and psychology become inextricable.

Other genres and schools of thought might easily be added: 'mesmerism', or 'animal magnetism' (popular from the 1770s to 1840s), the linguistics of James Harris, Horne Tooke, Lord Monboddo and the German, J.G. Herder, and various seventeenth-century works on 'the passions' and gesture. The lesson of all this, however, is that after *c.*1600 ideas about human psychology were changing in many different ways and on many fronts. Some underlying trends are discernible – a gradually mounting willingness to treat human nature as a phenomenon to be studied by 'natural philosophers' rather than philosophers and theologians alone, growing interest in processes of change and development, interest in the linkage between psychological and biological phenomena, and mounting concern with those practical matters such as education, mental illness, crime and even (in the case of phrenology) incipient 'personnel selection', which later provided Psychology with a market for its expertise. Methodologically, however, it is only in the early nineteenth century that, especially in German physiology, the experimental methods of physical science start being applied to psychological issues, while statistical methods of data analysis are largely absent until the 1880s.

Even by 1850 these varied interests and approaches had not cohered into a single discipline. They each tackled different kinds of question and operated with differing, if often related, conceptual frameworks. The word 'Psychology' was gaining wider circulation, but its meaning was more restricted than that which it has today, referring primarily to mental (or 'intellectual') philosophy. Something was needed to integrate all these realms of inquiry. That something was, as we will see in the next chapter, the rapid rise to ascendancy of evolutionary thought triggered by the work of Charles Darwin and Herbert Spencer in the 1850s. It was not, however, the absence of such an integrating theory alone that delayed Psychology's appearance; prior to the early 1800s it is also clear that European cultures had in fact no 'place' for such a discipline. Insofar as the cultural roles that modern Psychology plays were enacted at all (and many were not), they were dissipated across that variety of other disciplines that I have indicated here.

BIBLIOGRAPHY

Space precludes detailed references to the vast body of work referred to in this chapter. These are readily accessible in the 'Further reading' texts and numerous histories of philosophy.

Further reading

General

Hearnshaw, L.S. (1987) *The Shaping of Modern Psychology*, London: Routledge & Kegan Paul.
Klein, D.B. (1970) *A History of Scientific Psychology: Its Origins and Philosophical Background*, London: Routledge & Kegan Paul. Especially good on philosophy.
Richards, G. (1992) *Mental Machinery: The Origins and Consequences of Psychological Ideas, Part One: 1600–1850*, London: Athlone Press.

Physiology

Boring, E.G. (1942) *Sensation and Perception in the History of Experimental Psychology*, New York: Appleton-Century-Crofts.
Fearing, F. (1930) *Reflex Action: A Study in the History of Physiological Psychology*, London: Baillière, Tindall & Cox.
Neuberger, M. (1981; 1st German edn 1897) *The Historical Development of Experimental Brain and Spinal Cord Physiology before Flourens*, trans. and ed. Edwin Clarke, Baltimore: Johns Hopkins University Press.

Madness

See Chapter 8 references.

Education

While much has been written on the history of education, little seems to have been done regarding its role in Psychology's history. See Richards (1992) reference above, and Chapter 4 and Chapter 13 references.

Social philosophy and sociology

Bryson, Gladys (1945) *Man and Society: The Scottish Inquiry of the Eighteenth Century*, Princeton: Princeton University Press, reprinted (1968) New York: Augustus Kelley.

Language and linguistics

Aarsleff, Hans (1983, 2nd edn) *The Study of Language in England 1780–1860*, Minneapolis: University of Minnesota Press/London: Athlone Press.
Land, Stephen K. (1986) *The Philosophy of Language in Britain: Major Theories from Hobbes to Thomas Reid*, New York: AMS.

3 Founding Psychology
Evolution and experimentation

In the 1860s two developments occurred which supplied (a) an integrating framework for emerging types of psychological inquiry, and (b) scientific procedures for pursuing them. These were, respectively, the success of evolutionary thought associated with Charles Darwin and Herbert Spencer, and the appearance in Germany of the experimental methodologies identified with Gustav Fechner and Wilhelm Wundt, followed by the British development of parametric statistics. These will be considered in turn.

EVOLUTIONARY THOUGHT

Darwin's *Origin of Species* (1859) proposed the doctrine of 'natural selection' to explain organic evolution scientifically. Current forms of organic life including, by implication (although he was as yet unready to spell it out), humans, had evolved from previous life forms through aeons of time by a mechanism which appeared, in itself, quite blind. And these earlier forms left various legacies in their living descendants. Although Darwin convinced the majority of scientists of the validity of the evolution hypothesis, 'natural selection' was immediately attacked as insufficient (though not rejected as a factor), while some pre-existing evolutionary ideas were readily assimilated into it. It would be misleading to see 'evolutionary thought' and 'Darwinism' as synonymous. The 'natural selection' paradigm's eventual victory only came in the 1920s. In particular it was unclear (even to Darwin) that inheritance of acquired characteristics ('Lamarckian inheritance') could be rejected. Evolution's major populariser was Herbert Spencer, whose evolutionary *The Principles of Psychology* in 1856 was followed from the 1860s by numerous hefty volumes expounding his 'synthetic philosophy' – a grandiose vision of evolution as an inexorable cosmic process in which matter became progressively more heterogeneous and complex. The history of nineteenth-century evolutionary thought – a vast, multi-faceted topic – has received attention from a multitude of writers, particularly since 1960. For present purposes a fairly small number of central evolutionary ideas can be identified which supplied the unified theoretical framework that Psychology needed:

- Humans were descended from primates and could thus be considered zoologically. They were no longer semi-divine and beyond the remit of science.
- 'Spontaneous variation': the raw material for natural selection was the occurrence in each generation of random variations. (The 'gene' concept later clarified this, but lack of genetic understanding handicapped evolutionary theory until the 1920s.)
- Recapitulation: this idea, introduced by German biologist Ernst Haeckel, held that each individual recapitulates in its development from conception to maturity the evolutionary stages through which its species has passed. Often summed up as 'ontogeny reflects phylogeny', this was termed the 'biogenetic law'.
- 'Degeneration': if natural selection is suspended, 'unfit' organisms survive and reproduce, the quality of the population declines and 'degenerate' lines are established, subverting the usual evolutionary process which guarantees 'survival of the fittest' (Spencer's, not Darwin's, phrase).
- Although not strictly required by Darwinian theory, evolution was, perhaps inevitably, seen as essentially progressive. In the human case organic evolution had been succeeded by 'social evolution' – an 'ascent' from savagery via barbarism to modern industrial civilisation. This image was influentially promoted by the American L.H. Morgan (1877).

These notions galvanised interest in human nature on a wide range of fronts. To summarise briefly:

1 They encouraged the investigation of the evolution of 'mind' and how far human characteristics were present in rudimentary form in 'lower' animals or, conversely, how far humans retained 'lower' traits. This stimulated the comparative study of human and animal behaviour now known as 'Comparative Psychology'. One aspect of this was a fascination with 'instincts'. The concept of 'instinct', long used to refer to divinely implanted innate patterns and categories of behaviour, was given a far harder scientific meaning and significance. A major figure in developing this theme was Darwin's protégé George Romanes, followed at the century's end by Lloyd Morgan (see Chapter 14).
2 They focused attention on the diversity of the human stock as the raw material from which future generations would be 'naturally selected'; this underlay Francis Galton's pioneer studies of individual differences and the development of statistical procedures for analysing them.
3 Recapitulation gave new significance to the child as a route for looking back in time and tracking the evolution of humankind. Important figures in this include James Sully, G. Stanley Hall and Wilhelm Preyer (see Chapter 13).
4 The structure of the nervous system could now be understood in terms of older and newer components, the brain itself evolving by successive additions to the brain-forms of lower organisms. Spencer's influence was considerable here, because his theory proposed that 'associations', if

sufficiently strong, could forge new, heritable, nervous connections. This integrated the environmentalist position of the leading associationist philosophers (principally James and John Stuart Mill) with the hereditarian implications of developments in physiology and neurology.

5 The notion of degeneration gave the investigation of human nature an added urgency, as well as an explanatory framework, in dealing with such social issues as crime, madness, 'idiocy' and alcoholism. Galton figures prominently here as the founder of 'eugenics', another influential savant being the Italian criminologist Lombroso.

6 The evolutionary image of human history as progressing through various stages (an idea rooted in eighteenth-century 'speculative histories') could also be applied to social behaviour, e.g. Gustav Le Bon saw crowds as collectively regressing to a more primitive mentality (see Chapter 12).

7 Finally, most late nineteenth-century psychologists espoused the evolutionary perspective as their general theoretical framework. In the United States these included William James and James Mark Baldwin, in Britain G.H. Lewes, in France Theodore Ribot and Gabriel Tarde, and in Germany non-Wundtians such as Karl Groos. There were some exceptions to this, however, notably James Ward (who was influenced by Wundt) and G.F. Stout, who adopted more philosophical orientations.

The diverse studies of children, animals, physiology, social behaviour and madness were thus unified as aspects of a single project: exploring the implications of the evolutionary perspective for human nature. We return to its impact on these fields in the relevant subsequent chapters. Inevitably this resulted in a tendency towards nativist 'instinct' explanations, but also advanced the 'functionalist' approach. By 'functionalism', what is meant by psychologists is basically that a psychological phenomenon can be explained by identifying its survival value for the organism. This in itself need not entail nativism, however, since it can refer to the adaptational value of, say, learned responses, in relation to the organism's current environment. The term also carries the mathematical connotation of x being a function of y, i.e. in some way systematically co-varying with it. This too is incorporated into its Psychological meaning: a response might be said to be a function of the occurrence of some stimulus. It is, however, one of those weasel words carrying somewhat different meanings in different contexts (in which it resembles the even more weaselish 'structuralism'). In the event, English-language Psychology texts up to 1900 are dominated by those written from an evolutionary perspective. Its role in Psychology is one aspect of evolutionary thought's broader cultural impact as reinforcing, for example, such beliefs as the 'naturalness' of competitive capitalism and the natural superiority of the white 'races'. Galton's 'eugenics' concerns were the principal manifestation of this in Psychology.

A further figure who cannot be omitted is the Scot Alexander Bain. While he was never a fully committed evolutionist, his two earliest books, *The Senses and the Intellect* (1856) and *The Emotions and the Will* (1859), comprehensively surveyed psychological issues from an empirical perspective, incorporating the latest physiological findings. Often labelled an 'associationist', Bain's thought also retained elements of the Reidian tradition. His approach was not experimental, rather he strove to systematise and classify psychological phenomena. Although he wrote numerous other works these were his most influential, and revised versions continued in use as textbooks until the 1890s. In 1876 he founded the journal *Mind*, the major forum for Psychological papers until the end of the century when specialist Psychology journals began to appear (*Mind* specialising in philosophy thereafter).

EXPERIMENTAL METHODOLOGY

The role of evolutionary thought is absolutely crucial to the birth of modern Psychology (and 'psychology' too in fact), but was underplayed by earlier disciplinary historians by contrast with the rise, in Germany, of an experimental methodology. They chose to stress Psychology's scientific credentials by emphasising German experimentalism's vital role in gaining Psychology a foothold among the natural sciences. Its origins lie in a meeting between physiological studies of the senses, notably E.H. Weber's, and philosophical concerns with refuting Kant's arguments that scientific Psychology was impossible. The work marking the advent of experimental Psychology is generally taken as Gustav Fechner's 1859 *Elemente der Psychophysik*, 'Elements of Psychophysics'. Here, building on Weber's work, he investigated the relationship between changes in stimulus magnitude as objectively measured and as experienced. Weber had already discovered that the 'just noticeable difference' (j.n.d.) – i.e. the amount of change necessary for a change to be perceived – was a function of the size of the stimulus, e.g. a half-inch increment in length is easily spotted if the initial length is an inch, but not if it is 50 feet. What Fechner succeeded in doing was to derive a unit, based on the sensory threshold ('limen') for any sensation to be experienced at all, which could be used to quantify experienced, as against objectively measured, magnitude. With this he derived the 'Weber–Fechner Law', a generalised formula for relating perceived to objective changes in stimulus magnitude. Although this 'law' has, to a limited extent, withstood the test of time, it was the three experimental procedures he employed that had the most long-term impact and still continue to be used. These procedures, the 'method of constant stimuli', the 'method of limits' and the 'method of average error' (their names vary), are described in most textbooks as well as in histories such as Boring (1950). Fechner's aim was in fact philosophical – he thought he was helping to solve the mind–body problem. His legacy, however, was to bequeath to posterity the subdiscipline 'Psychophysics'.

Soon after this, Wilhelm Wundt, usually cast as Psychology's 'founding father', began his systematic experimental studies of consciousness using experimental introspection. He believed that this methodology was only applicable to psychophysical phenomena such as sensation, reaction times and attention, holding that thinking, language, personality, social behaviour and the like belonged to the humanities (in German, the *Geisteswissenschaften*) rather than sciences (*Naturwissenschaften*). The date of 1879 is normally given for the establishment of the first Psychological laboratory, by Wundt at Leipzig. Wundt's experiments involved not 'subjects' but 'observers', trained to introspect objectively on what passed in their consciousness during the experiment. (For a recent full account see Danziger, 1990.) Wundt's older contemporary Herman Helmholtz, one of the century's most eminent scientists, in whose Heidelberg laboratory Wundt was an assistant for thirteen years, also published fundamental work on perception and hearing (see Chapter 10).

Wundt's significance rests largely on his creation of the experimental laboratory and the fact that this attracted numerous American postgraduate students, who on returning home in the 1880s and 1890s eagerly developed his methods in new directions. Wundt is an interesting and controversial figure. His experimental Psychology, for which the English-speaking world remembers him, is only a fraction of his colossal output. He wrote extensively on philosophy and logic and capped a long career by producing a twelve-volume *Völkerpsychologie* ('Folk Psychology'), of which only Volume 1 (on language) was translated into English. As it transpired, Wundt's disciples, notably the English-born E.B. Titchener who emigrated to the United States, failed to permanently establish his introspective methodology beyond Germany, and his American ex-students soon abandoned the most Wundtian features of his Psychology. Even in Germany the following generation broke away from his doctrines. Most notably, the Würzburg school of Külpe, Marbe, Ach and K. Bühler, while introspectionist, rejected his view that all conscious contents were reducible to elementary processes of sensation and established the role of what they called 'conscious attitudes' in determining experience in experimental situations (to simplify grossly a highly complex theoretical issue). Other German-speaking philosophers and psychologists including Mach, Stumpf, Dilthey and Brentano also disagreed with Wundt on numerous theoretical grounds, besides those adopting the evolutionary approach. Wundt's eminence partly stems from the fact that Boring, Psychology's most influential historian, was Titchener's student. Since 1970 Boring's version of Wundt has been seriously contested; disagreement over what he actually believed and how important he really was still persists. Certainly in Germany experimental Psychology spread to other universities no faster than elsewhere, and the first autonomous Psychology degree was not offered until the Nazi period. For English-speaking psychologists it is, I think, fair to observe that Wundt has unduly dominated our picture of late nineteenth-century Psychological thought.

For the historian, Wundt's place in Psychology's history provides an interesting case-study. Since the discipline itself, guided by its historians, has accepted him as its heroic founding father, this must be accepted as a *psychological* fact in its own right as far as generations of psychologists are concerned. Yet current historical research on how he acquired this role reveals a rather muddier picture. Unlike Newton, Lavoisier, Darwin or Einstein, Wundt left no enduring legacy at either the theoretical level or by way of empirical discoveries. Why, then, his long-standing eminence? Yes, he *did* succeed in establishing an academic presence for experimental research on psychological topics and produced weighty textbooks and theoretical works on the subject. Beyond that, however, his eminence appears to derive more from the symbolic significance that he acquired for others than from the success of his Psychology. The discipline *wanted* a founding father with good experimental scientific credentials, and his American ex-students naturally revered him as their most influential teacher even while subsequently abandoning most of what he taught them. This tangled ongoing debate at least demonstrates how difficult, perhaps impossible, it is to differentiate between the contributions of actor and audience to an historical achievement.

More influential methodologically in the long run was the British statistical tradition launched by Galton and Pearson, rooted in earlier work by the Belgian statistician Quetelet, and continued by Spearman, Burt, Winch, Yule and R.A. Fisher. This has dominated modern experimental Psychology and psychometrics, yielding all those t-tests, correlation coefficients, ANOVAs (analyses of variance) and such which have plagued so many students' lives. It arose in the context of evolutionary concerns, more specifically in the need to measure variation within populations regarding hereditary traits. From the start, Galton's statistical methods had a dual purpose: first, to enable researchers to quantify the degree and nature of data variation, but second, they seemingly provided a tool for investigating the extent to which heredity was operating. Initially Galton focused on family pedigrees to establish how far eminence ran in families and was therefore, he believed, hereditary. He soon moved on to ponder the respective roles of 'nature and nurture' (effectively initiating this perennial debate), while his eugenic concerns demanded techniques for describing and comparing populations as a whole (see also Chapter 11).

The rapid development of statistics around 1900 provided psychologists with precisely the kind of quantitative tools they hankered after as necessary for their scientific credibility. A synergistic relationship developed: new statistical techniques opened up new research possibilities, while psychologists' heightened aspirations spurred the development of new statistical techniques adequate to the tasks that they sought to undertake. The two primary directions that this took were (a) measuring individuals on traits with regard to their standing in the population (or a sub-population) as a whole (psychometrics), and (b) comparing how groups (either the same group or different groups) performed under different experimental conditions. In the former, statistics became the primary research instrument in its own right, providing both techniques for designing psychometric tests and the tool by which the very things to be measured could, it was believed, be reliably identified or discovered. In the latter, while enabling the quantification of how 'significant' experimental results were, the statistical techniques available also guided the design of the experiments themselves (see Chapter 11).

By 1900 methodological issues had become the major priority for mainstream academic psychologists in the United States and Britain, while theoretical issues had become less urgent. The majority still worked within a broad evolutionary framework, but experimentalists (if not psychometricians) were shifting their attention to the 'nurture' side of things. What seemed most important was accumulating quantifiable empirical data on matters hitherto rarely subjected to scientific investigation: memory, learning, child development, fatigue, emotion and such. Data first, theory second, was the overriding attitude. And while previously the mind or 'consciousness' was seen as the discipline's subject matter, the study of behaviour was making increasing inroads, supplementing if not replacing the mind itself.

So far this chapter has adopted a fairly 'internalist' approach, concentrating on theoretical and methodological factors *within* the tradition of Psychological inquiry which enabled it to integrate intellectually (if not yet institutionally) under a single disciplinary label. Even so, hints have been made of factors beyond these. It is time to take a closer look at them.

It is a simple fact that virtually all those involved in creating Psychology were white middle- and upper-class males, sharing the values and attitudes of their gender and social class. A few observations about this group may be made immediately. First, they saw themselves as being at the peak of humanity not only economically and culturally but, increasingly, in evolutionary terms. Second, they were acutely aware that they were responsible for managing societies of unprecedented size and complexity – again seen as the pinnacle of humanity's evolutionary development. Third, they really did see women and non-whites as intellectually deficient and possessed of various innate traits unfitting them for destinies other than domestic or menial (see Chapters 15 and 16). When scientifically minded men of this character turn to study their fellow humans, their approach must inevitably be coloured by the attitudes, values and priorities associated with such a position, and it is surely not somehow deeply 'anti-scientific' to try to take this into account.

From this hierarchical world-view their attitude was essentially managerial. The appeal of Psychological expertise lay in its promise that those possessing it would be able to manage more effectively the populations under their control. This 'management of individuality', as Nikolas Rose calls it, should not be mistaken for ruthless oppression, rather it took the form of extreme paternalism, albeit with preparedness to take harsh decisions regarding the recalcitrantly unmanageable. Psychological expertise would enable them to educate the young efficiently, diagnose and deal with harmful deviancy and pathology, inform their policies towards, and treatment of, various social groups and subject populations, and enable them to direct those they governed into the most fitting walks of life, as well as improving industrial efficiency by a better understanding of phenomena such as fatigue and attention. It was this potential applicability of psychological expertise that provided Psychology's underlying cultural momentum, moving it ever further from traditional philosophical concerns with the nature and structure of consciousness or the mind. Instead, from Galton onwards, it progressively gravitated towards developing practical expertise. Over and above any intrinsic scientific flaws, Wundtianism simply had little to offer such a project.

This agenda was reinforced by the cultural meanings that rapidly accrued to evolutionism. From their lofty height men like Galton, Spencer and Lombroso surveyed the tumultuous scene beneath with some apprehension. The foundations were in real or potential danger of being undermined by the proliferating lower orders, inferior human stock, who seemingly outbred their superiors. This threatened not just a historically transient ruling class or economically privileged clique but civilisation itself, the entire human evolutionary achievement. Humanity's very future was at stake. Thus the eugenic and degenerationist thinking of Galton and many like him across Europe profoundly affected their conception of the task of Psychology. We will see in later chapters how this infused Psychology's initial views of madness, women, children and 'race'.

An intriguing feature of the situation as far as the relationship between Psychology and psychology is concerned is the prominence of an image of human nature which was actually quite new: beneath our civilised veneers lurks a 'beast within'. The social position of the class to which Psychology's founders belonged was thus reflected in their image of the structure of the psyche. Enlightened reason had to control and manage the lurking instinctual and bestial forces of irrationality. As well as in numerous other cultural forms, we can find this in turn-of-the-century Psychological writings ranging from the French psychologists Tarde and Le Bon to Freud himself, with his entirely negative view of the unconscious. In this climate opposition thought naturally turned increasingly to the celebration of the irrational and 'primitive' (e.g. in painting and music).

A further, less obvious consequence of these developments was that Psychological writers became blind to certain insights into the reflexivity of the enterprise which had, to a limited extent, been achieved by earlier philosophers. The foundational position of Psychology in relation to the natural sciences for example – the fact that scientific thinking and behaviour must logically be part of the subject matter of any would-be science of thinking and behaviour – was lost from view as the imperative to prove its scientific credentials intensified. This was an insight central to Hume, for example, as well as the contemporary American 'Mental and Moral Philosopher' Noah Porter. One error of Psychology's founders was to confound the Olympian mode of consciousness produced by their social class position with 'scientific objectivity' itself. Only they, it seemed, could see the entire picture 'objectively' from their exalted position. All below were to some degree incapable of 'objectivity'. Only the ruling paternal eye really understood. This position was sustainable precisely because their evolutionary perspective enabled them to see their situation as a natural one, rooted ultimately in biology, rather than the product of purely social and historical forces. If they were on the top, this of itself *proved* their essential superiority.

This is not to say that Psychology's rise was entirely due to 'top-down' factors of this kind. If the ruling classes saw such a discipline as potentially assisting them in discharging their paternal managerial duties to the national family, faith in science was spreading at the grassroots too. It was to this that phrenology owed its success, and the subsequent acquiescence of the populace to psychological testing needs to be understood in the light of gradual mass familiarisation with quasi-scientific phrenological and physiognomical personality analyses since the beginning of the nineteenth century. Aspirations towards better education, control of criminality, improved understanding of mental distress and the like were shared by everyone enthused by modern 'scientific' industrial culture or experiencing the problems that it brought in its train. In this respect masters and subjects were in accord. But as to which side *they* were on – psychologists were as yet unconscious of any conflict of interests.

There was, however, an underlying tension. To be useful Psychology would have to be applicable. This implied that expert *environmental* intervention in psychological affairs would eventually be effective in determining the course of events. On the other hand, the prevailing evolutionary framework was fundamentally *hereditarian* or 'nativist', implying that environmental influences could have a limited psychological effect at best. This has been an axis of controversy ever since. Broadly speaking, professionals whose job is descriptive and diagnostic, such as psychometricians in the Galtonian tradition, have tended to be 'nativist'. If you are claiming to measure someone's 'Intelligence', for example, you will be unfavourably disposed to the prospect of this changing significantly next week or next year because of environmental influences. Those whose jobs are interventionist, by contrast, have tended to be 'nurturists', since such jobs would be pointless unless they believed that their environmental interventions were likely to be effective. The immediate lesson of this here is that it suggests that their theoretical orientations are not likely to be unaffected by the kinds of 'external' pressures on psychologists (with which they will tend to identify anyway) to direct their efforts towards those goals prioritised by their own class and culture. In the nineteenth century these tended towards managerial description, classification and diagnosis within hereditarian evolutionist assumptions; in the twentieth century this has been supplemented, though not displaced, by interventionist and self-liberatory goals, for which environmentalist orientations are more congenial.

CONCLUSION

Psychology's late nineteenth-century debut is a distinctively 'modern' development. It involved creating images of human nature consistent with, and reflecting, life in the new industrial–scientific cultures. Evolutionary thought provided a rich 'modern', 'scientific' way of viewing the world and humanity's place within it which yielded the first and perhaps most profound of such images. The experimental methodology introduced by Wundt similarly represented an appropriately radical departure from the past in how human nature should be studied, even if his own introspective approach proved inadequate. In late twentieth-century retrospect these developments clearly carried a heavy price, especially in the case of evolutionary thought. However valid its core hypothesis, the cultural meanings that it acquired rapidly constrained evolutionary thought, especially about humans, within the class, 'race' and gender-specific interests of those promulgating it. Women were less evolved than men, Africans less evolved than Europeans, criminals the degenerate offspring of tainted stock, and within each of us lurked a bestial savage striving to shake off reason's shackles.

It was not to be in Europe, however, that Psychology first succeeded in establishing itself institutionally as an autonomous academic discipline but in the United States. Why and how it did so is the topic of the next chapter.

BIBLIOGRAPHY

Further reading

Evolutionary thought

Boakes, R. (1984) *From Darwinism to Behaviourism*, Cambridge: Cambridge University Press. On Comparative Psychology.
Richards, R.J. (1987) *Darwin and the Emergence of Evolutionary Theories of Mind and Behavior*, Chicago: Chicago University Press.
Young, R.M. (1970, 1990) *Mind, Brain and Adaptation in the Nineteenth Century*, Oxford: Oxford University Press. The best account of the physiological Psychology side of the story.

Wundt and German Psychology

Boring, E.G. (1929, 2nd edn 1950) *A History of Experimental Psychology*, New York: Appleton-Century-Crofts.
Danziger, K. (1990) *Constructing the Subject: Historical Origins of Psychological Research*, Cambridge: Cambridge University Press.
Rieber, R. (ed.) (1980) *Wilhelm Wundt and the Making of a Scientific Psychology*, New York: Plenum Press. For the 'revisionist' debate on Wundt.

Primary texts

For full bibliographic data see 'Further reading' texts.

Major early psychological works espousing evolutionism

Child development

Chamberlain, A.E. (1900) *The Child: A Study in the Evolution of Man*.
Darwin, C. (1877) 'A Biographical Sketch of an Infant', *Mind*, 2.

Groos, K. (1901) *The Play of Man*.
Hall, G.S. (1904) *Adolescence* (2 vols).
Preyer, W. (1888) *The Mind of the Child* (vol.1).
Sully, J. (1895) *Studies in Childhood*.

Animal behaviour

Darwin, C. (1872) *Expression of the Emotions in Man and Animals*.
Groos, K. (1896, English edn 1898) *The Play of Animals*.
Lloyd Morgan, C. (1894) *Introduction to Comparative Psychology*.
Lubbock, J. (1882) *Ants, Bees and Wasps*.
Romanes, G.J. (1882) *Animal Intelligence*.

Individual differences

Galton, F. (1883) *Inquiries into Human Faculty*.
See also:
Fancher, R. (1985) *The Intelligence Men: Makers of the IQ Controversy*, New York: Norton.

Physiological Psychology

Carpenter, W.B. (1874) *The Principles of Mental Physiology*.
Ferrier, D. (1876) *The Functions of the Brain*.

General theory

Baldwin, J.M. (1902) *Development and Evolution*.
James, W. (1890) *Principles of Psychology* (2 vols).
Lewes, G.H. (1874–9) *Problems of Life and Mind* (5 vols).
Spencer, H. (1855) *The Principles of Psychology*.

Social Psychology

Le Bon, G. (1896) *The Crowd*.
Ward, L. (1892) *The Psychic Factors of Civilization*.

Mental illness and other forms of 'deviance'

Galton, F. (1869) *Hereditary Genius*.
Lombroso, C. (1876) *L'Uomo Delinquente* ('The Delinquent Man').
Lombroso, C. and W. Ferrero (1895) *The Female Offender*.
Maudsley, H. (1892, 5th edn) *Responsibility in Mental Disease*.
Wilson, A. (1910) *Unfinished Man*.

Wundt and Fechner's major works

Fechner, G. (1859) *Elemente der Psychophysik*.
Wundt, W. (1862) *Beitrage zur Theorie der Sinneswahrnehmung*.
Wundt, W. (1863) *Lectures on Human and Animal Psychology*, trans. J.E. Creighton and E.B.Titchener 1896.
Wundt, W. (1874) *Grundzüge der physiologischen Psychologie*.
Wundt, W. (1896) *Grundriss der Psychologie*.
Wundt, W. (1900–20) *Völkerpsychologie* (10 vols).

Other major German texts

Brentano, F. (1874) *Psychologie vom empirischen Standpunkt* .
Ebbinghaus, H. (1885) *Memory: A Contribution to Experimental Psychology* (English
  trans. 1913, reprint 1964).
Helmholtz, H. von (1863) *Die Lehre von den Tonempfindungen.*
Külpe, O. (1893, English edn 1893) *Outlines of Psychology.*
Mach, E. (1885, English edn 1906) *The Analysis of Sensations.*
Müller, G.E. (1878) *Zur Grundlegung der Psychologie.*
Stumpf, C. (1883, 1890) *Tonpsychologie* (2 vols).

French Psychology

Binet, A. (1888) *Études de psychologie expérimentale.*
Ribot, T. (1873) *English Psychology.*
Ribot, T. (1883, 2nd edn) *Diseases of Memory.*
Ribot, T. (1886) *German Psychology of Today.*
Taine, H. (1871) *On Intelligence.*
Tarde, G. (1890) *Les Lois de l'imitation.*

Additional reference

Morgan, L.H. (1877) *Ancient Society or Researches in the Lines of Human Progress
  from Savagery through Barbarism to Civilization.*

4 William James and the founding of American Psychology

WILLIAM JAMES (1842–1910)

Just as philosophy is sometimes said to consist of footnotes to Plato, it might similarly be argued that in some respects modern American Psychology is a series of footnotes to William James's two-volume masterpiece *The Principles of Psychology* (1890). To understand James's historical role it is necessary to consider briefly his life and personality – his own 'psychology'. He was the eldest son of a rich New England family, his father being a keen follower of the eighteenth-century Swedish mystic Swedenborg. After William came Henry, the novelist, whose wider fame excels William's own. Third came Alice, now remembered as a diarist and something of a feminist heroine. Two younger brothers, Wilkie and Garth, had less eminent lives. One feature of their childhood was that their father led them a wandering, albeit affluent, life, criss-crossing Europe (and the Atlantic) numerous times. His educational ideas were somewhat eccentric. While keen for his children to gain a wide knowledge of life, science and culture, he had a horror of them ever committing themselves to specific careers. As soon as one of them showed real interest in a topic he tended to discourage them from pursuing it too deeply and shunted them onto something else. Knowing about chemistry was fine; wanting to become a chemist was not.

It was an intellectually stimulating life-style, gaining the eldest children early mastery of French and German, but it was also confusing and disruptive. By his late teens William was suffering serious emotional problems and displaying numerous psychosomatic symptoms. In the terminology of the day he was clearly 'neurasthenic' – we would now say neurotically anxious and depressed. He dropped out of Harvard where he had been studying medicine and comparative anatomy, and tried painting, at which he had considerable skill, then abandoned that too. In 1865 he journeyed up the Amazon with the great zoologist Louis Agassiz, fell ill, concluded that zoology was not his forte either, decided to be a philosopher and returned worse than ever. By 1869 he was a virtual invalid and only in 1872, when he was 30, did he really start pulling his life together. Psychodynamic theorists would see his prolonged incapacitation as an ultimately creative 'moratorium' period, but only someone in his socially privileged position could get away with it. Eventually he qualified as a doctor at Harvard Medical School (although he never practised), becoming an Instructor at Harvard in 1875.

During the early 1870s James and a friend, C.S. Peirce (future founder of 'pragmatism'), honed their philosophical skills in the brilliant, but eccentric, evolutionist Chauncey Wright's 'Metaphysical Club' in Cambridge, Massachusetts. In 1876, three years before Wundt's Leipzig laboratory was founded, James began giving instruction in physiological Psychology, using a small demonstration laboratory which Americans sometimes invoke as the first Psychological laboratory, although it was not experimental and little more than a large cupboard. He was promoted to Assistant Professor of Physiology. In 1878, the year of his marriage to Alice Gibbens, he began writing the *Principles*, and in 1880 switched to Assistant Professor of Philosophy, becoming full Professor in 1885 only to change titles once more, in 1889, to Professor of Psychology. Ironically, after 1890, his interests moved increasingly towards philosophy, particularly the advocacy of pragmatism, and he invited the German anti-Wundtian Hugo Munsterberg to take over the experimental side. (University College London acquired most of Munsterberg's equipment for the first English Psychology laboratory.) In 1901–2 he returned to Psychology in his famous Gifford Lectures at Edinburgh, published as *The Varieties of Religious Experience*; otherwise his last years were devoted to philosophy.

Throughout adulthood James continued the wandering habits of childhood, only once spending six years continuously in the United States. He was a personal friend or acquaintance with nearly all the leading academic and literary figures of his day (contacts often facilitated by his charming brother Henry who had settled in Europe).

One way of reading James's career is to see him as resolving the question of 'what shall I be?', rendered so acute by his father's educational strategy, by becoming a professional mind, an expert on what it was like to be conscious. And very good at it he was too. The mature William James was an attractive personality, open-minded, tolerant of paradox and inconsistency – which he sought to articulate rather than hide – and ever sympathetic to the psychological troubles of others. His open-mindedness is evident in his continued interest in psychic research long after it ceased to be fashionable.

Why was James initially so disturbed? I have indicated some personal reasons already, but these served to render him peculiarly conscious of the wider underlying anxieties of the post-Darwin era. The 'determinism vs. free will' debate, intensified by the successes of contemporary deterministic science, particularly preoccupied him in his early twenties. A reading of the French philosopher Renouvier showed him a way out – and he resolved, he says, as his first free act, to believe in free will. The philosophy of pragmatism, which Peirce and James (along with John Dewey) later developed, was very much aimed at rescuing the notion of free will in human affairs. This in itself casts James in an ambiguous light as far as scientific Psychology is concerned, for his commitment to the adequacy of science to account for human nature was less than wholehearted.

A final background point needs to be made to set James in perspective. The New England culture in which he grew up (and which his father embodied) was deeply infused by the earlier nineteenth-century movement known as New England Transcendentalism, a later American version of Romanticism, of which the leading figures had been Ralph Waldo Emerson (who had dandled the infant William on his lap), Henry Thoreau and Nathaniel Hawthorne. The legacy of this is, I believe, fairly clear in James's own writings. The *Principles* is acknowledged as a literary masterpiece, and often echoes the style of Emerson's essays.

The reason that James is so significant is partly that his position is so obviously ambivalent regarding Psychology, and that the ambiguities and paradoxes he raised have remained with the discipline ever since (see Allport, 1943). Unlike most American 'founding fathers' he was uneasy about mounting the 'science' bandwagon. Yet he was as cosmopolitan a thinker as it was possible to be, in touch with all contemporary developments in philosophy, Psychology and physiology and sufficiently on the ball to review Freud and Breuer's paper on hysteria in 1893, the year of publication. The *Principles of Psychology* itself is a highly ambiguous work. Wundt allegedly exclaimed on reading it: 'It's literature, it's beautiful, but it's not Psychology!' (in German of course). Much of it had earlier appeared in journal form, hence many of the ideas it contained were already known to his contemporaries. In some ways it was the high point of the older introspective philosophical approach, but it comprehensively surveyed and integrated the new scientific Psychological information available from Germany, France, Britain, Italy, Russia and North America. In this latter role it served as a point of departure, both goad and challenge, for the succeeding generation even when rejecting its underlying orientation. Such unity as it possesses is not that of a scientific theory, but more a matter of stylistic consistency and 'voice', the personality or 'psychology' of James himself. Let us then consider some of its contents.

Although I cannot cover them in any depth, among the most enduringly influential chapters were the following:

1   Chapter IX   The Stream of Thought
2   Chapter XXV   Emotion
3   Chapter X   The Self
4   Chapter IV   Habit
5   Chapter VII   Methods and Snares of Psychology
6   Chapter XVI   Memory

The stream of thought

This expounds one of James's best-known ideas, the stream of thought or, as it became more widely known, the stream of consciousness, notion. His basic argument, one he sees as refuting rigid determinism, is that because every experience changes the organism, it never has the same experience twice – for on the second occasion on which the same stimulus is presented the organism itself is different. No psychological state recurs in precisely the same form. If we try to capture the course of consciousness, five basic points emerge which, though possibly obvious, need to be spelled out:

(a) every thought belongs to a personal consciousness;
(b) within that consciousness thought is always changing;
(c) it is 'sensibly continuous' – we do not experience any gaps in it;
(d) it always appears to deal with objects independent of itself;
(e) it selects from these all the while.

Pursuing these points (especially b and c), he observes that consciousness does not appear 'chopped up in bits' – 'It is nothing jointed; it flows. A river or stream are the metaphors by which it is most naturally described... .Let us call it the stream of thought, of consciousness, or of subjective life.' The character of this 'stream' and the difficulties we have in introspectively grasping it are then spelled out, deploying a variety of further metaphors, e.g. the bird's life 'of alternate flights and restings' used to capture the distinction between 'transitive and intransitive' passages of consciousness (it is transitive ones that are peculiarly recalcitrant to introspection), and the bamboo stalk with its joints, analogous to sudden events which change, but do not break, the continuity of consciousness. Among other things this argument raised serious problems for associationism, which becomes just one more metaphor for certain features of the stream, not the full story. This idea had considerable influence, for example James Joyce's *Finnegans Wake* has been seen as an attempt to trace this stream in all its detail, while it also helped to popularise the psychoanalytic notion of 'free association' – with which it sometimes got confused.

Emotion

This chapter contains the James–Lange theory of emotion (Karl Lange, a Danish psychologist, having proposed something similar), one of the few relatively hard hypotheses that James proposed. It demonstrates his ability to argue convincingly for an initially implausible idea – that rather than emotions determining bodily reactions, the reverse is the case. Like the English psychologist McDougall a little later, he saw instincts and emotions as inextricably linked: 'every object that excites an instinct excites an emotion as well' but emotions fall short of instincts in 'terminating in the subject's own body' instead of entering into 'practical relations with the exciting object'. In brief he argues that 'we feel sorry because we cry, angry because we strike, afraid because we tremble' (vol. II, p. 450). The following passage indicates how difficult it is to differentiate Psychology and 'psychology':

In rage, it is notorious how we 'work ourselves up' to a climax by repeated outbreaks of expression. Refuse to vent a passion and it dies. Count ten before venting your anger, and its occasion becomes ridiculous. Whistling to keep up courage is no mere figure of speech. On the other hand, sit all day in a moping posture, sigh and reply to everything with a dismal voice, and your melancholy lingers. There is no more valuable precept in moral education than this, as all who have experience know: if we wish to conquer undesirable emotional tendencies in ourselves, we must assiduously, and in the first instance cold-bloodedly, go through the outward movements of those contrary dispositions which we prefer to cultivate. The reward of persistence will infallibly come.... Smooth the brow, brighten the eye, contract the dorsal rather than the ventral aspect of the frame, and speak in a major key, pass the genial compliment, and your heart must be frigid indeed if it do not gradually thaw!

(vol. II, p. 463)

This conveys not just a Psychological theory of the emotions, but at least two other levels of meaning: (a) echoes of how he himself finally overcame his prolonged moping, sighing and melancholy 'dispositions' by an act of will, and (b) a typical late nineteenth-century piece of moral discourse, representative of the 'psychology' of the times – an extended exhortation to 'count to ten before losing your temper, pull yourself together, straighten your back, stop frowning!'

Another quotable passage is this:

Prof. Sikorsky of Kieff has contributed an important article on facial expression of the insane to the Neurologisches Centralblatt for 1887. Having practised facial mimicry himself a great deal, he says: When I contract my facial muscles in any mimetic combination, I feel no emotional excitement, so that the mimicry is in the fullest sense of the word artificial, although quite irreproachable from the expressive point of view. We find, however, from the context that Prof. S's practice before the mirror has developed in him such a virtuosity in the control of his facial muscles that he can entirely disregard their natural association and contract them in any order of grouping.

(vol. II, p. 465)

This surely tells us more about the state of psychiatry in Kiev than it does about the expression of emotion!

The James–Lange theory has not fared well, and there was a long consensus that certain animal experiments by Walter Cannon had disproved it. Even so, it is difficult not to feel that James was onto something. The phenomenology of emotion is often consistent with his doctrine – following a bump in the car, we feel fine, then realise that our legs are trembling and that we are actually in a state of shock, or we think we are displaying great *sang froid* in dealing with some upsetting incident until, on meeting a friend, we discover ourselves bawling our eyes out. Again, try grinning miserably or cheerfully scowling.

The self

James's discussion of the 'self' launched a topic that later figured centrally in Social Psychology (e.g. G.H. Mead's studies in the 1930s and current work on how we construct our self-image). James's fellow pioneer James Mark Baldwin (1897) also tackled it. He begins by distinguishing between the self 'as known', i.e. as an object of knowledge (the 'empirical ego' or 'me'), and the self as 'knower' (the 'I', the 'pure' or 'transcendental ego') which cannot be scientifically investigated. This distinction is actually a version of one going back to Kant (and indeed to Buddhism). It transpires that there is a hierarchy of empirical selves: 'the material me', 'the social me' and 'the spiritual me'. On further examination there are innumerable social selves, virtually a different one for every acquaintance and type of situation. My 'self' extends to my belongings, my favourite football team perhaps, or my country. All that with which I feel a personal identification or sense of belonging is an aspect of 'me' – if it is damaged, lost, fails or whatever, I feel it as my own loss or failing. There is also a nice little equation:

$$\text{Self-esteem} = \frac{\text{Success}}{\text{Pretensions}}$$

The other chapters I will mention more briefly. That on habit lays the groundwork for the early work on learning by Edward Thorndike (done in James's basement) which led him to formulate the Laws of Effect and Exercise. It contains some powerful sermonising on habit as the 'enormous fly-wheel of society' which keeps 'the miner in his darkness, and nails the countryman to his log-cabin and his lonely farm through all the months of snow; it protects us from invasion by the natives of the desert and the frozen zone' (vol. I, p. 121). Again, the Psychological and 'psychological' seem to fuse. He is far less at odds with associationism here than in the 'Stream of Thought' chapter.

The 'Methods and Snares' chapter is particularly important, though more difficult than most of the others, in containing an influential account of the introspective method. Notably he draws attention to one very dangerous 'snare': 'the psychologist's fallacy' – a tendency to confuse the 'idea' that one is reporting with the object of the idea (also known as 'stimulus error'), this arising because we use the same words for both. The idea of a wall is not built up from ideas of bricks. In dealing with phenomena such as emotion, however, this distinction becomes more obscure The psychologist must avoid confusing 'his own standpoint with that of the mental fact about which he is making his report'. For James, introspection is still *the* primary method of Psychology, but I feel that this chapter unwittingly elucidates the sheer difficulty of valid introspection for those less remorselessly introspective than James himself. Some current writers (e.g. Jill Morawski) see this argument (which was widely accepted) as a means by which the first psychologists outflanked the 'reflexivity' problem: in effect it claimed that psychologists could, by their training, achieve a distinctive mode of objective professional consciousness from which to view consciousness itself. The chapter also contains an entertaining account of the new German experimental methods (James says that they could never arise in a nation capable of being bored) which explicitly articulates his deep ambivalence towards experimentalism and the 'pendulum and chronograph philosophers'. He knows that the discipline's future lies in this direction and, as mentioned, appoints Munsterberg for just this purpose, but temperamentally he has no feel for it (even though he happily cites reports of experimental findings).

Finally, the 'Memory' chapter introduces the distinction between short-term or 'echoic' memory and secondary or long-term memory (STM and LTM), including an interesting discussion on the duration of STM and how long the 'rearward portion of the present space of time' extends. James gave it an upper limit of twelve seconds but Baldwin (reviewing the book) disagreed, arguing for four seconds at most.

Taken overall, the *Principles* played a major role in setting the agenda of issues for the next generation of 'functionalist' psychologists, although it was far from the only textbook available. James sets his ideas in a broad evolutionary framework in which the basic function of mind is to gain knowledge. It covers nearly the whole field, although some areas such as animal and Developmental Psychology are absent (but it does contain the famous comment that a newborn baby's life is 'one great blooming, buzzing confusion' (vol. I, p. 488), with which few would now agree).

To sum up: James's contribution to Psychology was a central but complex one. His own deeper aims were to rescue free will, to set limits on rigid determinism, and, like his 'Mental and Moral Philosophy' predecessors, to promote Psychology as a route for morally beneficial self-knowledge and understanding. Yet he is fascinated by the findings of contemporary empirical research, citing and quoting a vast array of contemporaries whose work fuels his own creative thought. Whatever he finds 'introspectively', he is keen to reconcile with the latest findings in physiology, German Psychophysics, or French clinical studies of double consciousness. It is a cliché to say that people are 'transitional' or that their thought combines new and old, but in James's case it is for once deeply true. The traditional aspects of his work (introspection, moralising, self-conscious use of literary style, personal distaste for experimentation) genuinely contrast with its original aspects (orientation towards scientific evidence, preparedness to rethink basic issues, acceptance of an evolutionary perspective, and curiosity about hitherto neglected or unfashionable phenomena and topics). He was indeed a brilliant introspector, and excellent at evoking such 'vague' borderline phenomena as having something on the tip of the tongue or how attitudes change with age. Equally, it remains a moot point how far James belongs to the nineteenth century or the twentieth. Although a fairly near contemporary of Freud – very much a twentieth-century figure – his overt long-term influence has been far less. And yet it is surprising how American Psychology periodically indulges in a spell of re-reading and reassessing James. For Americans he is a cultural hero as well as a psychologist, their first major home-grown philosopher. 'Nothing human is alien to me' – James certainly strove to exemplify this ancient adage in his own life and thought, even if his cultural setting and privileged position meant that some human things remained invisible to him.

In historical retrospect James seems to loom in stature far above his contemporaries in American Psychology. At the time, however, charismatic and central though he was, his standing as a scientific psychologist of the new school was a matter of debate. Let us now step back and look at how the 'New Psychology', as it called itself, became established so successfully and rapidly in the United States between 1880 and 1900.

THE FOUNDING OF 'NEW PSYCHOLOGY' 1880–1900

Most pre-1980s accounts tend to accept uncritically the pioneers' claims to represent a revolutionary break with the past, with nothing done in the United States prior to their own endeavours being of much value. Recent writers have begun to contest this picture. Ever since the early nineteenth century American universities and colleges had imposed on their students a compulsory course of 'Mental and Moral Philosophy'. The reason for this was that these institutions (invariably having denominational affiliations, most frequently Presbyterian) felt it necessary to counter the materialist and atheist arguments of many leading European thinkers by demonstrating the consistency of Christianity with philosophy and logic. They had good grounds for anxiety as around 1800 there had been major campus riots by avowedly atheist students (including Bible-burning and arson). The philosophical tradition which most college presidents (who taught such courses) adhered to was the Scottish 'common-sense' school which dominated the 'Mental and Moral Philosophy' curriculum prior to the 1880s, although German idealism and some French philosophers also had a presence. The traditional image is of Mental and Moral Philosophers as hidebound, dogmatic and anti-scientific, one writer variously describing the Scottish school as 'a great cloud', 'a frigid wave', a 'kind of Protestant scholasticism' (Davis, 1936). The 'New Psychology' was cast as a liberating break from the stranglehold of this sterile force.

Recently a number of us have been doing that daunting thing – reading the forbidding tomes produced by this despised school. The organisational and institutional factors involved in the shift from Mental and Moral Philosophy to Psychology have also come under scrutiny. We are now beginning to appreciate that even in the 1860s a number of US writers, including some Mental and Moral Philosophers, are starting to address contemporary European developments such as the evolution question. During the 1870s there were numerous indications of movement and leading establishment figures were writing books that, while admittedly pious, were far from anti-scientific and dogmatic. Even more interestingly, several pioneer New Psychologists were inspired by, or were protégés of, leading Mental and Moral Philosophers. Three notable cases are: G. Stanley Hall, first inspired by John Bascom (now virtually forgotten); James Mark Baldwin, a protégé of the most eminent Mental and Moral Philosopher, James McCosh; and George Trumball Ladd, recruited to Yale by the notoriously conservative Noah Porter. Institutionally, the post-Civil War period saw a rapid expansion of US tertiary education, with numerous secular universities, such as Johns Hopkins, being founded, accompanied by growing pressure for postgraduate-level teaching, hitherto absent in the United States, and a decline in the college president's authority. My own view is that while Psychology established itself as a replacement for Mental and Moral Philosophy under these changing conditions, there were some important respects in which it continued to play a similar 'moral education' role. Furthermore, many textbooks published as 'Psychology' between 1880 and 1900 closely resemble their predecessors in agenda and structure, even if they are more secular in approach and more 'scientific' in tone. In other words, there were fairly high levels of continuity between old and new in several respects, and the 'New Psychology' revolutionary rhetoric was frequently more an expression of aspiration than achievement – not until the present century was the 'revolution' really accomplished. German and British influences were indeed crucial, but such influences were discernibly at work from the 1860s.

We may now turn to those, besides James, most involved in the rise of the 'New Psychology': G. Stanley Hall, James Mark Baldwin, John Dewey, George Trumball Ladd, E.B. Titchener, James McKeen Cattell and E.W. Scripture. While these are the best known, there were numerous others whom we cannot discuss here such as Morton Prince, E.C. Sanford, Joseph Jastrow and, the only two women figuring significantly, Mary Whiton Calkins and Margaret Floy Washburn. (Some sociologists, notably Lester Ward, would warrant inclusion in a comprehensive account.) It must be stressed that while succeeding in presenting a fairly united front to the outside world, this group disagreed among themselves regarding most matters of importance such as the role and nature of experimentation, 'pure' versus 'applied' conceptions of Psychology's goals, whether or not behaviour as well as consciousness was part of their agenda, and how Psychology and Philosophy were – or should be – related.

Organisationally, the prime mover of the 'New Psychology' was G.S. Hall (who had done a doctorate under Wundt), founder of the American Psychological Association (APA) as well as Psychology departments at Johns Hopkins and Clark universities and numerous journals (most importantly the *American Journal of Psychology* (1887) and *Pedagogical Seminary*, later *Journal of Genetic Psychology* (1891)). His primary area of interest was Developmental Psychology, espousing recapitulationism and initiating the first large-scale programme of empirical research. His *magnum opus* was the two-volume *Adolescence* (1904). In 1910 he invited Freud, Jung and other psychoanalysts to the Clark University twentieth anniversary celebrations, providing them with their first opportunity to expound the doctrine in the New World. Hall was undoubtedly an opportunist and a highly effective political animal in promoting Psychology's interests between 1880 and 1910, capable of trimming his sails to the prevailing wind when necessary (e.g. variously claiming that Psychology was entirely secular or affirming its doctrinal respectability according to the audience being addressed). His emphasis on child development was well calculated to highlight the new discipline's practical value. His last major psychological work was *Senescence* (1922).

James Mark Baldwin was, like Hall, an ardent evolutionist and founded the Toronto and Princeton laboratories. Unlike Hall he was a keen laboratory experimentalist, but it was his *Mental Development in the Child and the Race* (1894) and *Social and Ethical Interpretations of Mental Development* (1897) that were his most influential Psychological works. A prolific writer, he shifted increasingly towards philosophy although he remained Professor of Psychology at Johns Hopkins until 1908. In 1894 he co-founded the *Psychological Review* with Cattell to compete with the *American Journal of Psychology*. Theoretically his most significant contributions were his innovations in evolutionary theory and the groundwork that he laid for subsequent Developmental and Social Psychology studies of the 'self'. This last is now receiving renewed attention from historians.

The keenest advocates of Wundtian Psychology were the English *émigré* Titchener (at Cornell) and Scripture (at Yale), both Leipzig veterans. Titchener carried the Wundtian introspectionist flag (calling his approach 'structuralism') until his death in 1927, but was virtually the only US-based psychologist to do so beyond *c.* 1900. His textbooks were, none the less, highly influential in promoting undergraduate laboratory-based courses. Titchener's Wundtianism is generally considered to have parted from the original by recouching it in terms more akin to British associationism than that had been. Though theoretically marginalised, he remained highly respected within the discipline and theoretical differences did not prevent friendly relations with the behaviourist J.B. Watson, for example. Scripture's US career was less successful. Following an almighty row with his superior, G.T. Ladd, at Yale regarding the department's experimental orientation he left, eventually becoming an expert on speech disorders, based for a time in London, and ending his career as Professor of Experimental Phonetics in Vienna. His *Thinking, Feeling, Doing* (1895) was the first thoroughly experimentally oriented textbook, while the similarly pitched *The New Psychology* (1897) is partly responsible for this term's use as a name for the founding movement as a whole.

Cattell, another of Wundt's ex-students, was based at Columbia, where he founded a laboratory. After an initial phase of psychophysical research, his interests turned to individual differences, Educational Psychology and testing (see Chapter 11). After 1900 his main forte became that of a journal founder and editor (most importantly of *Science, American Naturalist* and *American Men of Science*). As a pacifist opponent of the war he lost his Columbia post in

1917, but continued promoting the discipline's interests in the applied field and was president of the 1929 Ninth International Congress of Psychology. In 1981 his early diaries and letters (1880–8) were published, providing interesting insights into his Wundt years.

Dewey played an early role in the 'New Psychology' by virtue of his 1886 *Psychology*, considered by Boring to be the first English text promoting the new approach aside from the Englishman James Sully's *Outlines of Psychology* (1884). It was, however, hardly radically different in agenda from the 'Mental and Moral Philosopher' Bascom's *The Science of Mind* (1881). His eminence is more due to his later formulation of a version of pragmatism with which to advance the applicable 'functionalist' view of Psychology as against the German approach. His 1896 paper 'The Reflex Arc Concept in Psychology' was a profound, if often misunderstood, attack on the objective reality of the stimulus/response distinction. At Chicago he was instrumental in establishing the distinctive Chicago functionalist tradition. His associations with G.H. Mead and the sociologist W.I. Thomas at this time (1894–1904) were of particular importance. Later he became an eminent educational philosopher and embodiment of the liberal–progressive US intellectual tradition.

Ladd's significance for Psychology rests largely on his early textbooks and establishment of Psychology at Yale. His original interests in physiological Psychology and experimentation were soon ousted by philosophical and theological concerns. Theoretically he is generally included in the early functionalist evolutionary camp, but played little direct role in furthering the Applied Psychology project which derived from this.

The preceding sketches do barely more than identify the leading *dramatis personae* in the story. Nevertheless they may indicate how diverse in character the US founders in fact were. O'Donnell (1985) has provided the most extensive re-examination of this founding phase currently available and from his pages emerges a picture of constant feuding and dissent among these figures and their associates. He is also downbeat about the significance of the flurry of Psychology laboratories which appeared during the 1880s and 1890s, seeing them as having a pedagogic initiatory role rather than a productive research one.

How, then, *did* Psychology establish itself so rapidly and successfully in the United States? While to some extent the jury is still out on this question, a few closing observations on the issue may be offered:

1   Expansion and organisational changes in the US university and college system provided an institutional opportunity for the new generation of aspiring psychologists unmatched anywhere in the Old World. They were able to co-opt the existing Mental and Moral Philosophy curriculum and convert it into a more secular discipline which could be harnessed to the wider progressivist cultural aspirations for a scientifically managed technological society.

2 The 1880–1900 phase is one during which the 'purist' European concept of Psychology as a 'science of the mind' was rapidly being squeezed (though not eliminated) by an evolution-influenced functionalist concept of the discipline as a potential producer of marketable expertise. This shift is apparent not only between psychologists but in the careers of individuals such as Dewey, Munsterberg and Cattell, with James's *Principles* (1890) serving as a kind of fulcrum.

3 The usual image of a group of like-minded experimentally oriented revolutionaries collaborating to forge modern US Psychology is none the less deceptive. The existence of the APA as an umbrella organisation facilitated the promotion of a public image of unity but behind the scenes, as previously mentioned, these figures were at loggerheads on all the fundamental issues. America was, however, big enough to contain this diversity and as the numbers of Psychology graduates grew, along with methodological variety, US psychologists themselves soon functionally adapted, turning their discipline's inherent pluralism into an asset.

BIBLIOGRAPHY

Further reading

Allport, G. (1943) 'Productive Paradoxes of William James', *Psychological Review* 50: 95–120. The whole issue is devoted to James.
Boring, E.G. (1929, 2nd edn 1950) *A History of Experimental Psychology*, New York: Appleton-Century-Crofts.
Brozek, J. (ed.) (1984) *Explorations in the History of Psychology in the United States*, London: Associated University Presses.
O'Donnell, J.M. (1985) *The Origins of Behaviorism: American Psychology 1870–1920*, New York: New York University Press. This is essential reading.
Psychological Science (1990), 1(3). Issue devoted to James on the centenary of publication of *Principles*; numerous authors on different topics.

William James's principal works

Psychology

James, William (1890) *The Principles of Psychology* (2 vols), New York: Henry Holt.
James, William (1892) *Psychology: Briefer Course*, London: Macmillan.
James, William (1899) *Talks to Teachers on Psychology*, London: Longmans Green.
James, William (1902, reprint 1960) *The Varieties of Religious Experience*, London: Fontana.
James, William (1908) *Human Immortality*, London: Dent.

Philosophy, etc.

James, William (1896) *The Will to Believe and Other Essays*, New York: Longmans Green.
James, William (1907) *Pragmatism*, New York: Longmans Green.
James, William (1910) *A Pluralistic Universe*, New York: Longmans Green.

James, William (1926) *The Letters of William James* (2 vols), ed. Henry James, London: Longmans Green.

Selected secondary references

Allen, G.W. (1967) *William James: A Biography*, London: Hart-Davis.
Cotkin, G. (1990) *William James: Public Philosopher*, Baltimore: Johns Hopkins University Press.
Dooley, P.K. (1974) *Pragmatism as Humanism: The Philosophy of William James*, Chicago: Nelson-Hall.
Feinstein, H.M. (1984) *Becoming William James*, Ithaca: Cornell University Press. Excellent psychological study of James's formative years.
MacLeod, R.B. (ed.) (1969) *William James: Unfinished Business*, Washington, DC: American Psychological Association. Papers on aspects of James's psychological work.
Perry, R.B. (1935) *Thought and Character of William James* (2 vols), Boston: Little, Brown. Classic review of James's life-work.
Poirier, R. (1988) *The Renewal of Literature: Emersonian Reflections*, London: Faber. Locates James in a distinctive Emersonian literary tradition.
Richards, G. (1991) 'James and Freud: Two Masters of Metaphor', *British Journal of Psychology* 82: 205–15. Issue contains other papers first given at a 1990 BPS Symposium on the centenary of *Principles* by G. Bird and E.R. Valentine.

Other pioneer American psychologists

Pre-'New Psychology'

Major secondary sources on this are the following:

Davis, R.C. (1936) 'American Psychology 1800–1885', *Psychological Review* 43(6): 491–3. Out of date, but useful.
Fay, J.W. (1939) *American Psychology Before William James*, New Brunswick, N.J.: Rutgers University Press. Still the only comprehensive account.
Roback, A.A. (1952, rev. edn 1964) *History of American Psychology*, New York: Collier.

Major works by founders of the 'New Psychology'

Full bibliographic data in 'Further reading' texts.

Baldwin, J.M. (1894) *Mental Development in the Child and the Race.*
Baldwin, J.M. (1897) *Social and Ethical Interpretations of Mental Development.*
Baldwin, J.M. (1902) *Development and Evolution.*
Dewey, J. (1886) *Psychology.*
Dewey, J. (1896) 'The Reflex Arc Concept in Psychology', *Psychological Review.*
Hall, G. Stanley (1904) *Adolescence* (2 vols). Most of his early work was in journal paper form, notably in his own *Pedagogical Seminary.*
Jastrow, J. (1901) *Fact and Fable in Psychology.*
Ladd, G.T. (1887) *Elements of Physiological Psychology.*
Ladd, G.T. (1898) *Outlines of Descriptive Psychology.*
Sanford, E.C. (1898) *Course in Experimental Psychology.* First appeared in *American Journal of Psychology,* 1891.
Scripture, E.W. (1895) *Thinking, Feeling, Doing.*
Scripture, E.W. (1897) *The New Psychology.*

Titchener, E.B. (1898) *A Primer of Psychology.*
Titchener, E.B. (1901–5) *Experimental Psychology* (4 vols).

Additional references

Boring, E.G. (1948) 'Masters and Pupils among American Psychologists', *American Journal of Psychology* 61: 527–34 (reprinted in E.G. Boring, 1963, *History, Psychology, and Science: Selected Papers*, ed. R.I. Watson and D.T. Campbell, New York: Wiley). Summarises the academic lineages of the first US psychologists, although tends to ignore connections with Mental and Moral Philosophy.

Cattell, J. McK. (1981) *An Education in Psychology: James McKeen Cattell's Journal and Letters from Germany and England 1880–1888*, ed. M.M. Sokal, Cambridge, Mass.: MIT Press.

Richards, G. (1995) '"To Know Our Fellow Men To Do Them Good" American Psychology's Enduring Moral Project', *History of the Human Sciences* 8(3): 1–24.

5 Behaviourism

US Psychology's founding phase culminated in 1913 in the movement called 'behaviourism', the impact of which extended well beyond those identifying themselves as behaviourists. While experimental Psychology was well established by 1910, the forms that this took varied and research reports remained unstandardised. Basic psychophysics aside, it was difficult to compare findings of different researchers or replicate experiments. Much experimental work of the post-1900 period was explicitly 'functionalist', a label adopted by Dewey's Chicago colleague J.R. Angell. A fairly eclectic approach, this persisted as the central mainstream position of US experimental Psychology until the Second World War, avoiding most traditional philosophical issues in favour of adaptational accounts of both mental phenomena and behaviour – often in Applied Psychology contexts. 'Behaviorism' – to adopt its American spelling – may be seen as an extreme form of this functionalism. Its enduring effect was as much methodological as theoretical, although it was largely as a theoretical-level movement that it was launched. In this chapter we will look at three aspects of behaviourism: (a) how J.B. Watson, its founder, envisaged 'behaviorism' in 1913, (b) the variety of forms that it subsequently took, and (c) the difficulties that led to a weakening of its influence after 1945.

WATSON'S 'BEHAVIORISM' OF 1913

In the early 1900s US culture was pervaded by an almost utopian enthusiasm about its destiny (quite literally – the concept of America's 'manifest destiny' was widespread). It saw itself engaged in creating the first truly modern technological industrial civilisation and was thus highly future-oriented and primarily concerned with the practical utility of science and technology. Watson, a temperamentally rebellious young man from humble South Carolina roots, fully shared this aspiration. Unfortunately we cannot deal here with his earlier academic career, but suffice to say that, by 1913, he was very discontented with the state of the discipline on several counts:

1 He had little sympathy with its continuing philosophical (as he saw it) concerns with the nature of consciousness and the mind–body problem (he

would have liked, he wrote, to bring up students 'in ignorance of the entire controversy'). These, he believed, kept Psychology bogged down in intractable metaphysical debates of little practical consequence.

2   Closely linked to this was his commitment to a positivist view of science as only capable of studying overt, visible, measurable phenomena. Since consciousness, or 'the mind', was not amenable to such scrutiny it could not be investigated scientifically. We can really only study behaviour.

3   He had been greatly impressed by contemporary biological work, notably that of Jacques Loeb, whose *Comparative Physiology of the Brain and Comparative Psychology* (1901) advanced a highly reductionist approach to psychological questions as ultimately answerable in physiological terms. Watson felt that, by comparison, experimental Psychology (with a few exceptions in applied areas) was still floundering in an amateurish way and that its standards of both conceptual and methodological rigour were poor.

4   He believed that Psychology was too human-centred. A central point of reference here was the rapidly developing discipline of genetics. Just as genetics was concerned with the general phenomenon of heredity, not with heredity in one species, so Psychology, Watson argued, should be concerned with behaviour in general. And just as geneticists were confining their empirical research to a single convenient species – the fruit fly – so psychologists could adopt the white rat. Geneticists were not interested in the fruit fly as such, simply using it as a representative 'reproducing organism' with which to investigate genetics in general. So the white rat could serve as a convenient 'behaving organism' to study behaviour in general. This argument, even if we can now see it as seriously flawed, was certainly not a stupid one.

5   Finally, he was increasingly unhappy with the hereditarian bias in Psychology (the legacy of its commitment to evolutionary thought). The reasons for this are somewhat complex but one major factor is that Watson was seeking scientific techniques for, to use his own phrase (ritually repeated by psychologists ever since), 'predicting and controlling behaviour'. This of course stemmed from his belief in science as a provider of practical knowledge. As already noted, if you wish to change and control behaviour you will naturally come to downplay the importance of immutable genetic factors. Here Watson was really only taking functionalism to its logical conclusion in seeking adaptational explanations for psychological and behavioural phenomena. It has also, however, been suggested that he misunderstood a classic experiment by the geneticist Johanssen, which he mistakenly interpreted as showing that environmental factors were the major determinants of behaviour. Whatever the truth, while Watson initially accepted a role for heredity, albeit limited, this became attenuated in time to a belief that 'unlearned' behaviour is restricted to a few physiologically governed reflexes.

These dissatisfactions come to a head in his manifesto paper 'Psychology as the Behaviorist Views It' of 1913. I do recommend this to the reader – it is fairly short and almost polemical in style, so easily manageable. He attacks Psychology at all levels: its methods, its language, and the tasks it sets itself. By the end it is clear that, for Watson, Psychology is really an adjunct to biology, its findings serving to illuminate the organism's biological structure – or as he puts it, they 'become functional correlates of structure and lend themselves to explanation in physicochemical terms'. Methodologically there is great need for uniformity in procedure and reporting of results – and the results that interest the behaviourist are such things as learning curves and rapidity of habit formation. Introspection is totally out.

The problem for Watson at this stage is how to tackle higher-order phenomena like thinking and language. He feels confident, however, that in due course these will become amenable to behaviourist methods and suggests that, in principle, thinking could be understood as 'subvocal speech' – speech of course being an overt behaviour. This proved one of the least tenable of his doctrines and is fraught with fairly obvious difficulties.

Watson's paper served to rally a number of younger psychologists, such as R.M. Yerkes, A.P. Weiss, W.S. Hunter and M. Parmelee for whom it seemed to point the way to the discipline's future (although its initial impact has perhaps been exaggerated). A contemporary, Max F. Meyer, had independently arrived at much the same position, although he has tended to be overshadowed. The experimental study of learning, pioneered by Thorndike in the 1890s, rapidly dominates their central research. When the Russian physiologist Pavlov's work came to Watson's attention, Watson eagerly assimilated his theoretical concepts. The initial success of Watson's project rested in large part on the perception by fellow American psychologists that he had finally succeeded in hauling Psychology firmly into the natural sciences. His rejection of mentalistic concepts and insistence on restricting attention to overt behaviour seemed to mark the discipline's final abandonment of philosophical concerns as well as reflecting the dominant positivist view of the nature of science. We can only scientifically study observable phenomena: feelings, emotions, mental images, fantasies and the like, being subjective and only accessible to the single individual experiencing them, are thus beyond our concern. All that matters is overt behaviour. We can of course study what people say that they experience (because speech is a form of behaviour), but this is a different level of inquiry from studying their experiences as such. It must be stressed, since the point is often misunderstood, that behaviourists did not claim that such mental phenomena were non-existent. They did, however, believe that they had no scientific significance and that overt behaviour could be explained without considering them.

Behaviourism rapidly evolved a technical language incorporating that of Pavlovian theory, comprising terms like stimulus, response, reinforcement (positive and negative), conditioning (classical and operant) and habit strength. As it happened, however, the theoretical unity that Watson aspired to introduce was relatively short-lived, behaviourist theorising soon taking a variety of directions. While these divisions lacked the emotional intensity of those surrounding the Freudian tradition they nevertheless concerned fairly fundamental issues. It is to these that we turn next.

THE VARIETIES OF BEHAVIOURISM

Behind the rapid divergence lay the fact that Watson himself left academic life following a divorce scandal in 1920, having had an affair with, and subsequently married, Rosalie Rayner (his co-worker in the infamous Little Albert study in which an infant boy was conditioned to fear a fluffy rabbit). This cost him his job at Johns Hopkins University (where he had succeeded James Mark Baldwin – also dismissed over a sex scandal) and he joined the advertising agency J. Walter Thompson, to become highly successful in applying behaviourist principles to advertising. Academic behaviourism thus lacked a figure who could play the dominating role that Freud always played for psychoanalysis. The divergences were of several kinds:

- Some remained unhappy about excluding internal events and simply looking at overt S–R (stimulus–response) relations. Without wishing to readopt mentalistic concepts they sought ways of reincorporating these. The major figure in this respect was E.C. Tolman, who had been impressed by the Gestalt psychologists' holistic approach (see Chapter 6). His research led him, for example, to conclude that organisms acquired a 'cognitive map' of their surroundings merely by moving around it, by a process that he called 'latent learning'. He came to refer to such internal factors as 'intervening variables' and 'hypothetical constructs' (the distinction between which would require too lengthy an exegesis for inclusion here). Instead of S–R alone we now had S–O–R models ('O' meaning 'organism'). Underlying this, Tolman was primarily concerned with developing a behaviourism that could handle purposiveness, and evade the over-reductionist character of Watson's original version, by then under fierce Gestaltist attack. Clark Hull also strove to incorporate the internal in a highly elaborate, algebraicised theory which I will mention again shortly. Hull introduces concepts such as 'fractional anticipatory goal response', for example.
- Some of the divergency simply arose from extending behaviourism to other topics than learning. Thus Karl Lashley, a neurophysiologist, adopted the behaviourist framework in his brain-functioning research. He claimed that brain functioning was only localised in very broad terms, large tracts of the brain showing what he called 'equipotentiality' – they could be utilised to serve a great many functions and to take over those of which part had been removed (see Chapter 9). This of course fitted in nicely with Watson's environmentalism. From the mid-1930s he began to challenge the adequacy of behaviourism, but until then his behaviourist physiological Psychology

was a powerful and authoritative factor in maintaining the movement's prestige. In a different direction lay G.H. Mead's 'social behaviourism', concerned with the social construction of the self. This was miles away from Watson's ideas on what Psychology should be and there is much controversy about what precisely Mead meant by calling his approach 'behaviourist'.

- Another dimension of divergence was in terms of theoretical complexity. The polar opposites here are B.F. Skinner and Clark Hull. Skinner's approach became virtually atheoretical, purely concerned with empirically studying the shaping of behaviour by reinforcement contingencies, with no attention at all to supposed internal events and no elaborate theory construction. Hull's theory, on the other hand, was a highly ambitious attempt at producing a 'hypothetico-deductive' theory with postulates, theorems and quantification. His algebraic system included such symbols as sOR for 'momentary behavioural oscillation' and sUR for 'unlearned receptor–effector connection', and could generate equations such as $J = s\underline{E}R_d = D \times V_2 \times K \times sHR \times 10^{-.15d} \times V_1$ ('the influence on reaction potential reduction caused by the delay in reinforcement'). Be thankful that you are not entering the discipline in the 1960s (or worse, 1950s) when we were still expected to master the rudiments of this!

There is now wide agreement that the almost baroque theory that Hull developed sat unconvincingly with the rat-learning experiments on which it was based. Nevertheless some Hullian terminology entered the general vocabulary of the discipline. The late B.F. Skinner fared much better. His single-subject operant conditioning methods proved extremely versatile and he was able, to some extent, to produce the goods in terms of applicable techniques for predicting and controlling behaviour. Skinner was, however, a much subtler and more complex thinker than he initially appeared to most of the present author's generation during the 1960s and 1970s. His views on language, for example, are, on re-examination, proving to be more consistent with the modern linguistic philosophy account than was once thought. By the time he died Skinner seemed to be a lone survivor of a fast-fading approach, but already his reputation seems to be rising again. His own integrity in restricting his discourse to the terminology of his own system led, I think, to some misunderstanding, particularly during the 1960–80 phase when he was demonised as the archetypal amoral dehumanising manipulator, an image that his behaviourist utopian novel, *Walden Two* (1948), did little to dispel.

Despite this internal variety, only sketched here, there was for a long time a feeling that behaviorism represented the most advanced 'paradigm' for experimental Psychology. Whether it ever dominated the discipline to the extent that is often claimed is doubtful. In Woodworth's standard college textbook *Experimental Psychology* (1938), for example, only around 20 per cent of the text is clearly behaviourist in its concerns. The majority of working researchers between the two world wars were more eclectic functionalists, still inclined to judiciously include 'experience' alongside 'behaviour' as part of

Psychology's subject matter. But, as said at the outset, its impact extended beyond theory to affect the whole manner in which research was conducted and reported. After Watson there was no return to the personalised, discursive and idiosyncratic journal papers of the pre-1910 period. By the 1950s the tide was turning against behaviourism. A number of issues were arising with which behaviourists could not deal adequately, or at any rate as adequately as their rivals. (Skinner is the main exception here, partly precisely because he was not interested in theory-building.)

THE DECLINE OF BEHAVIOURISM

Although the presence in America of exiled European psychologists constituted a background challenge to behaviourism, I will refer here only to two core difficulties.

The 'organisation of behaviour' problem

According to classical behaviourism, complex behaviour involves associatively conditioning each successive component item to its predecessor. By the 1950s it was apparent that this simply cannot explain many higher-order human behaviours like piano playing or, even more obviously, language learning. Building these up by laboriously creating associative chains would simply take more time than anyone has available. As we will see in Chapter 7, this was the weak point in behaviourism's armour on which the new cognitive psychologists like George Miller focused. It was also addressed in D.O. Hebb's highly influential *Organization of Behavior* (1949), a post-war attempt at synthesising the contending behaviourist and Gestalt schools of thought in the light of advances in neurology. The cognitivist attack was boosted by the fact that in designing computers to perform complex actions the first generation of programmers had come up with much better ideas about how such outcomes might be neurologically implemented. The superiority of the new Cognitive Psychology in dealing with the organisation of complex behaviour dealt behaviourism a most damaging blow.

The return of instincts

The second difficulty arose from the new ethological research into animal behaviour by people like Konrad Lorenz and Nico Tinbergen, which called into question behaviourism's doctrinaire environmentalism. While earlier instinct theorists had dealt with instincts such as aggression, hunger, sex and the like, this new generation gave the instinct concept a much more specific meaning. This is discussed in Chapter 15; suffice to say here that in the light of the new ethology it was fairly obvious that behaviourism had been seriously misled by pinning its faith on the white rat.

Watson's initial rationale, that we could use the white rat as a convenient 'behaving organism' for studying behaviour as such, contained a hidden logical error. The very reason that the white rat was so convenient to use was that it happened to be a highly adaptive animal: pretty omnivorous, capable of adjusting to new environments rapidly, and very generalised (as zoologists call it) in its behaviour – in short *because* its behaviour was highly environmentally determined. To invoke findings on the white rat as evidence of the primary role of environment in determining behaviour was thus to beg the question (a fallacy known technically as *petitio principi*) – a three-toed sloth, a Galapagos tortoise or a lobster would yield a very different picture, but that of course is the reason that one cannot use them in the first place! Behaviourists initially responded by expanding the number of species that they used (and Skinner had always had a penchant for pigeons). But further scrutiny revealed that even in the white rat there were in-built constraints on the associations that it could learn. All species, it transpired, were 'prepared' and 'counterprepared' to learn, or not to learn, certain kinds of behaviour. Conditioning a pigeon's pecking response to enable it to obtain food by pecking a button is easy, but try conditioning its wing-preening to food and you are in trouble – it is 'counter-prepared'. Rats, on the other hand, can learn that a food is noxious in a single trial even though the negatively reinforcing consequences of ingestion are considerably delayed – they are 'prepared'. Neither phenomenon is explicable without invoking innate factors.

Eventually, even among those operating within the behaviourist tradition, it became clear that extreme environmentalism was untenable and that heredity played a crucial role in determining, and setting constraints on, animal behaviour. The 'nature–nurture' debate had, however, acquired important political connotations by the 1960s. Unfortunately behaviourists were, in this regard, caught wrong-footed as they were being popularly cast as dehumanising technocrats serving the 'system' in its oppressive schemes. Thus while environmentalism was at this time the, so to speak, 'politically correct' position, behaviourism, the most radically environmental school of all, failed to benefit. 'Politically correct' environmentalism was more sociological in character, focusing on the social environment and social psychological levels in order to combat such things as racism and sexism . Even while environmentalist, behaviourism was unable to benefit much from the prevailing pro-environmentalist cultural climate. But on the other hand, neither could it withstand the criticisms of the new 'nativist' ethologists (who, ironically, were able to partially evade the consequences of their prima-facie 'incorrectness' – at least until the mid-1970s – for reasons outlined in Chapter 15). Skinner, it is true, acquired a certain cult following as a result of *Walden Two*, while behaviour therapy, and 'token economy' regimes in juvenile custodial institutions, continued to develop fairly pragmatically, but the core area of behaviourist learning theory had lost its 'paradigmatic' position by around 1965.

THE IMPACT OF BEHAVIOURISM

What was behaviourism's broader impact? Popular culture has, surely, two main images of the psychologist. The most widespread is the psychoanalyst intent on discovering hidden meanings and messages in innocently intended behaviour. The other, however, is the white-coated scientist running rats round mazes and discovering numerous cunning ways to control behaviour – which of course derives from behaviourism. Like all Psychological theories, behaviourism acquired a popular meaning beyond its practitioners' control. In behaviourism's case it promoted the image of 'human being as maze-bound rat': somewhere, experts in behavioural control are subtly affecting our lives using scientific techniques of which we know not. (Even worse, we may believe that somewhere there exists a body of expertise on 'mind control', 'brainwashing' and the like, of which the unscrupulous can take advantage.) It is an apt, not entirely misleading, metaphor for late twentieth-century urban life. Also, we can now say things like 'I feel as if I've been conditioned' – meaning that somewhere along the line we have, unknowingly, been got at. For Watson, of course, the very notion of 'feeling that you've been conditioned' would have been a contradiction in terms since the term 'conditioned' could, by definition, only refer to overt behaviour. (See Chapter 14 for behaviourism's specific impact on Developmental Psychology.)

Philosophically, behaviourism's rise coincided with, and was seen as harmonising with, that of logical positivism and 'operationalism', a school of philosophy of science which insisted that only concepts definable in terms of verifiable public phenomena were really meaningful. To enter into this topic here would require a book-long digression; as far as it bears on behaviourism itself the best initial account is B.D. MacKenzie (1977). Among other things, MacKenzie argues in depth that Watson's move was more extreme than was strictly required by positivist doctrines. Even so, in its halcyon days behaviourism was welcomed by figures as philosophically astute as Bertrand Russell.

Was Watson a manipulator or a liberator? The answer to this is genuinely unclear. It is easy enough to find alarmingly manipulationist statements in his writings, but equally explicitly he saw himself as breaking the shackles that bound humanity in 'steel bands' of superstition, myth and folklore, and was an advocate of sexual, but not 'libertine', freedom. Like Skinner he saw an understanding of behaviourist principles as a route by which people could free themselves from unwanted habits and desires. As an aspiring technology of behavioural control and prediction, behaviourism's advocates, casting themselves as pure scientists, might have claimed that, like all scientific knowledge, it could be used for both good and ill, and that this decision was society's responsibility. In the end, however, our mistake is perhaps to suppose that behaviourism was meant to be a philosophy of life (though for Watson and Skinner personally it clearly approached this). It was not. To begin with at least it was an attempt at creating a technology by which behaviour could be controlled and behavioural problems rectified.

CONCLUSION

Behaviourism served an important historical function for Psychology in moving it *methodologically* into the realm of the natural sciences – really in a sense by insisting that psychologists actually *behave* like scientists. The *theoretical* price paid was an abandonment of concern with many genuinely profound philosophical and theoretical questions about Psychology's status and nature which had previously preoccupied the discipline, and commitment to a reductionism which many felt deeply unsatisfying and which seemed to throw out the baby with the bath water. For about four decades – from 1913 to the early 1950s – behaviourism made the running in American experimental Psychology, although, as indicated, it was never an entirely homogenous doctrine. As a theoretical movement it eventually foundered on the twin rocks of the problem of how complex behaviour was organised and the inadequacy of its extreme environmentalism. Not all hands were lost in this foundering, however; on the contrary, numerous survivors have managed to continue aspects of the behaviourist project in less dogmatic fashion. In any case, as with all Psychological theories, behaviourism's impact is a psychological fact in its own right and the concepts and images of human nature that it yielded have, for better or worse, irreversibly entered our culture.

ADDITIONAL POINTS

Watson's own 'psychology' was in many ways highly conflicted. Anyone wishing to explore this topic in depth should read one of his biographies. For example, he is theoretically anti-emotion but in practice highly emotional (as a brief browse through his writings shows), he dismissed imagery as unimportant but suffered a life-long fear of the dark which he was unable to remove by behaviourist means, etc.

The Russian 'reflexology' school of Pavlov and Sechenov represented a somewhat analogous development in Russia (and after 1917, the Soviet Union) to the rise of behaviourism in the United States. Pavlov, primarily a physiologist, was vital to behaviourism's success by virtue of his research on canine conditioning which supplied much of its theoretical framework. Pavlov is generally granted heroic status in histories of Psychology and accounts of his work are easily accessible. It is significant that both societies were in the throes of idealistically trying to create a scientific, technological, modern mass culture, albeit from opposing ideological bases, and that in both Psychology took up the task of devising the appropriate techniques of behavioural control.

BIBLIOGRAPHY

Further reading

Buckley, Kerry W. (1989) *Mechanical Man: John Broadus Watson and the Origins of Behaviorism*, New York: Guilford Press. The most recent biography.
MacKenzie, B.D. (1977) *Behaviourism and the Limits of Scientific Method*, London: Routledge & Kegan Paul.
O'Donnell, J.M. (1985) *The Origins of Behaviorism: American Psychology 1870–1920*, London: Associated University Presses.
Schwartz, B. (1989, 3rd edn) *Psychology of Learning and Behavior*, New York and London: Norton. For the current state of play in behaviourist Psychology this comprehensive contemporary textbook is the best starting point.
Smith, L.D. (1986) *Behaviorism and Logical Positivism: A Reassessment of the Alliance*, Stanford, Calif.: Stanford University Press.
Smith, R. (1992) *Inhibition: History and Meaning in the Sciences of Mind and Brain*, Cambridge: Cambridge University Press. See especially chapters 3 and 5 on Russian work.
Watson, J.B. (1913) 'Psychology as the Behaviorist Views It', *Psychological Review* 20: 158–77; reprinted in W. Dennis (ed.) (1948) *Readings in the History of Psychology*, New York: Appleton-Century-Crofts.

Major behaviourist books

For full bibliographic details see 'Further reading' texts.

Guthrie, E.R. (1935, rev. edn 1952) *The Psychology of Learning*.
Guthrie, E.R. (1938) *The Psychology of Human Conflict*.
Hunter, W.S. (1919, rev. 3rd edn 1928) *Human Behavior*.
Lashley, K.S. (1960) *The Neuropsychology of Lashley: Selected Papers of K.S. Lashley*, ed. F.A. Beach, D.O. Hebb, C.T. Morgan and H.W. Nissen, New York: McGraw-Hill. As Lashley's work was nearly all in journal form, this is the most accessible source.
Mead, G.H. (1934) *Mind, Self and Society from the Standpoint of a Social Behaviorist*.
Meyer, Max F. (1921) *The Psychology of the Other One*.
Parmelee, M. (1913) *Science of Human Behavior*.
Tolman, E.C. (1932) *Purposive Behavior in Animals and Men*.
Watson, J.B. (1919) *Psychology from the Standpoint of a Behaviorist*.
Watson, J.B. (1924) *Behaviorism*.
Watson, J.B. (1928) *Psychological Care of Infant and Child*.
Weiss, A.P. (1925) *A Theoretical Basis of Human Behavior*.

Later behaviourists

For full bibliographic details see 'Further reading' texts.

Hilgard, E.R. (1940, with D.P. Marquis; rev. edn G.A. Kimble 1961) *Conditioning and Learning*. The standard textbook.
Hilgard, E.R. (1948, 2nd edn 1956, 3rd edn 1966 with G.H. Bower) *Theories of Learning*. The standard textbook.
Hull, C.L. (1943) *Principles of Behavior*.
Hull, C.L. (1951) *Essentials of Behavior*.
Hull, C.L. (1952) *A Behavior System*.
Skinner, B.F. (1938) *The Behavior of Organisms*.
Skinner, B.F. (1948) *Walden Two*.

Skinner, B.F. (1953) *Science and Human Behavior.*
Skinner, B.F. (1957) *Verbal Behavior.*
Skinner, B.F. (1959, enlarged edn 1961) *Cumulative Record.* A collection of major journal papers.
Skinner, B.F. (1971) *Beyond Freedom and Dignity.*
Spence, K.W. (1956) *Behavior Theory and Conditioning.*
Stevens, S.S. (ed.) (1951) *Handbook of Experimental Psychology.*

See also:

Koch, S. (ed.) (1959) *Psychology: A Study of a Science.* Vol. 2 contains several (sometimes final) theoretical statements by major figures.

Russian behaviourism

For full bibliographic details see 'Further reading' texts.

Pavlov

Asratyan, E.A. (1949, English edn 1953) *I.P. Pavlov: His Life and Work*, Moscow. Interesting not only for what it says about Pavlov but also for its relentless ideological tone.
Frolov, Y.P. (1937) *Pavlov and his School: The Theory of Conditioned Reflexes* .
Frolov, Y.P. (1937) *Fish Who Answer the Telephone and Other Studies in Experimental Biology.* Popular account of contemporary Russian research on conditioning.
Gray, J.A. (1964) *Pavlov's Typology: Recent Theoretical and Experimental Developments from the Laboratory of B.M. Teplov*, intro. H.J. Eysenck. Explores the application of Pavlovian theory to personality.
Ivanov-Smolensky, A.G. (trans.1954) *Essays on the Patho-Physiology of the Higher Nervous Activity according to I.P. Pavlov and his School*, Moscow. Won the 1949 Stalin Prize.
Pavlov, I.P. (1927, reprint 1960) *Conditioned Reflexes: An Investigation of the Physiological Activity of the Cerebral Cortex.*
Pavlov, I.P. (1928) *Lectures on Conditioned Reflexes: Twenty-five Years of Objective Study of the Higher Nervous Activity (Behaviour) of Animals.*

The first English account of the psychological relevance of Pavlov's work appears to be the following:

Yerkes, R.M. and S. Morgulis (1909) 'The Method of Pawlow (sic) in Animal Psychology', *Psychological Bulletin* 6: 257–73.

Sechenov

Sechenov, I.M. (1960) *Selected Physiological and Psychological Papers*, ed. K. Koshtoyants, Moscow. Sechenov (*fl.* 1860s–1880s) is generally considered to be the 'father' of Russian Psychology and a major influence on Pavlov.

Bekhterev

Bekhterev, V.M. (1917, 4th edn 1928) *General Principles of Human Reflexology.* Pavlov's main rival.

Further secondary sources

Burnham, J.C. (1968) 'On the Origins of Behaviorism', *Journal of the History of the Behavioral Sciences* IV(2).

Cohen, D. (1979) *J.B.Watson: The Founder of Behaviourism*, London: Routledge & Kegan Paul.

King, W.P. (ed.) (1930) *Behaviourism: A Symposium*, London: SCM Press.

Watson, J.B. and W. McDougall (1928) *The Battle of Behaviorism*, London: Kegan Paul, Trench & Trübner.

6   Gestalt Psychology

Coincidentally with behaviourism's rebellion in the United States, another very different rebellion, Gestalt Psychology, occurred in Germany. We may at the outset identify one underlying difference: behaviourism sought to become more scientific by emulating the behaviour of natural scientists, Gestalt psychologists by adopting the most advanced theoretical ideas of contemporary physics. Unlike behaviourists they neither ignored consciousness nor reduced psychological phenomena to atomistic elementary units such as S–R connections – moves that they felt were profoundly mistaken. In this chapter I will outline some of the central concepts developed by the three major Gestalt psychologists, Max Wertheimer (the movement's founder), Wolfgang Köhler and Kurt Koffka, who were, as far as one can tell, in complete accord. I will then discuss its fate and some other figures associated with the school.

First, to set the scene: German psychologists and philosophers were far from united in accepting Wundt's essentially reductionist approach to the nature of mind and his doctrines were strongly disputed (see Chapter 3). One topic in particular continued to fox both Wundtians and anti-Wundtians alike – the perception of form. The Austrian Graz school was especially concerned with this. The problem is captured in Von Ehrenfehls' observation that we can recognise a tune regardless of key, tempo or instruments – the form persists although all the elements have changed. This resisted solution from a 'bottom-up' direction and seemed to imply that the brain somehow contained innate forms to which it matched stimuli – hardly credible, given the variety of forms that we can identify.

At first sight this appears to be a recondite technical question – how can we account for form perception within an analytical theoretical framework? This, however, is but the tip of the iceberg of the far more profound issue of 'meaning' itself, and the appropriateness of scientific reductionism for an understanding of the mind. It is clear from their writings (particularly Koffka,1935) that Gestaltists viewed current events very differently from the future-oriented Americans. Although the movement started in 1911, they were soon working in the heartland of Europe in the grim aftermath of the First World War and saw their culture as under serious threat. Reductionist

Psychology of the behaviourist as well as Wundtian type was, moreover, part of that threat since it eliminated all consideration of human values:

> Meaning and significance could have no possible place in such a molecular system: Caesar's crossing the Rubicon; certain stimulus–response situations; Luther at Worms: so many others; Shakespeare writing *Hamlet*; Beethoven composing the Ninth Symphony; an Egyptian sculptor carving the bust of Nephretete, would all be reduced to the stimulus–response schema.
>
> (Koffka, 1935, p. 26)

They thus cast themselves as defenders of meaning and culture against a rising tide of arid and philistine scientific reductionism – a situation exacerbated by the wider anarchy engulfing Europe at the political, military and economic levels. It is essential, I think, to remember this, and it is rarely made clear in history texts.

If opposed to reductionism, they were not opposed to science itself; on the contrary, they were closely associated with the leaders of modern physics: Wertheimer was a lifelong friend of Albert Einstein and Köhler had studied under Max Planck, inventor of quantum theory. Unlike Watson they suffered few personal doubts about either their own scientific credentials or those of their project, and were thus less concerned with methodology as such. They did not feel driven to prove that Psychology could be a science, as they felt securely part of 'science' already. Ironically this counted against them in the long run.

Now let us consider a few of their central concepts. In doing so, the way in which they reconceptualised form perception will emerge.

1 *Field*. Their single most important move was to adopt the new approach, pioneered by Einstein, known as 'field theory'. This concept of 'the field' lies at the heart of all Gestalt theory. What, though, is a 'field'? Traditionally, to simplify drastically, scientific explanation had taken the form of identifying the linear cause–effect sequences which determined phenomena. Field theoretical physics, by contrast, reconceptualised the problem by viewing phenomena as arising from a network, or field (*Feld*), of forces – gravity and electromagnetism, for example. Linear sequences are replaced by 'fields' with an overall structure or form – thus iron filings scattered around a magnet align themselves with the form of the magnetic field. The Gestaltists therefore saw their task as identifying those fields of forces that determine behaviour and mental phenomena, and the laws governing these. Psychological phenomena could be said to occur at the intersection of several kinds of 'field' – biological, perceptual, environmental and so on. Approaching things in this way enabled the retention of 'mental' phenomena as a central topic – for the structure of conscious phenomena is one outcome or product of these interacting force-fields, which they in turn reflect as iron filings around a magnet reflect the magnetic field. It also meant that reductionism could be avoided, for it was essentially a holistic

approach. This last is an important point and provided their solution to the form-perception question: *rather than seeing wholes being built up from parts, the structure of the whole will determine what the parts are, should one analyse it*. And certain phenomena only exist at this level: if two dots are placed alongside one another we immediately have the relational property of left-and-rightness – there is no way of determining whether a dot is the left or right dot by scrutinising it ever more closely in isolation. In short, the adoption of the field notion – which, as is clear from Koffka (ibid.), they did not see as a mere metaphor but as a route for incorporating Psychology into the unified discourse of the sciences – promised to enable them to tackle issues of value, meaning and consciousness in a truly scientific manner.

2 *Isomorphism*. This is a concept adopted from the branch of mathematics known as 'topology' which is concerned with the properties of different forms rather than with quantification. In topology two forms are, technically, 'isomorphic' if one can be mapped onto the other (thus the forms *s*, *c* and *l* are isomorphic with each other, as are *p*, *b*, 9 and *d*). This was deployed by Gestalt psychologists to link conscious experience with physiological-level phenomena, and is closely associated with the field concept. Putting it briefly, their doctrine of isomorphism is that conscious, 'phenomenological' experience is isomorphic with underlying physiological processes. The classic example was the phenomenon of apparent movement (the 'phi-phenomenon'), now familiar from neon signs, etc. Nothing has moved in the outside world, but we experience movement. Wertheimer suggested that this was because something was happening at the physiological level 'isomorphic' with the movement – perhaps the leakage of current between two poorly insulated circuits. Köhler eventually developed an elaborate theory of the brain as operating in terms of constantly fluctuating electrical fields isomorphic in structure with conscious experience. Although a clever move, this doctrine proved one of their weakest points as, from the 1940s, findings from neurological brain research proved incompatible with it.

3 *Prägnanz*. In exploring their field approach the Gestaltists claimed to have discovered or identified a general principle, *Prägnanz*, governing the structure of psychological phenomena, namely that they are always organised in the neatest, tightest, most meaningful way. We lack a precise English equivalent for this (although it is related to the word 'pregnant' as in 'the situation is pregnant with possibilities'). This general principle was elucidated further by a number of 'laws of *Prägnanz*' (although these could not exhaust the meaning of the general principle itself). Most fundamentally, *some* organisation always occurs, however random the stimuli – we hear pulsation in white noise, we see figures in haphazard markings on a wall, etc. These 'laws' became the most widely known of Gestalt theory's ideas, especially, though not exclusively, as applied to perception. Others include the following:

(a) Figure/ground distinction. We always experience one part of the overall stimulus array as a figure against a background. If information is ambiguous we experience continuous oscillation as in the well-known Maltese cross, Necker cube or face/vase figures. The figure/ground distinction applies to all modalities. In hearing we identify the sound of someone speaking as a 'figure' against a 'ground' of other noise. Our selectivity in doing this often becomes apparent in tape-recordings of lectures or discussions: when playing them back we hear all sorts of noises – coughs, doors closing, lifts, traffic – of which we were originally unaware.

(b) Contrast and closure. We tend to ignore or override minor breaks in a figure (closure), but if they are sufficiently significant we exaggerate their scale (contrast). Contrast, more generally, includes the tendency to exaggerate perceptible differences between stimuli (e.g. in adjacent areas of light and darkness, what looks grey alongside a very white area will look bright white when set against a black area). There are a multitude of illustrations of this to be found in books on perception. 'Closure' also manifests itself over time in our need to finish 'unfinished business'. This produces the 'Ziegarnik effect' – we recall interrupted, unfinished tasks better than completed ones (reported by Lewin's student B.V. Ziegarnik in 1927 in the main Gestalt journal *Psychologische Forschung*).

(c) Constancy. What they called 'well-articulated' forms tend to resist change, particularly if familiar – thus even when viewed in different lights and from different angles we still 'see' the same form persisting. We do not become baffled when we see a saucer edge-on. Without constancy our perception of the world would be highly chaotic, shifting from moment to moment as objects appeared from different angles. This is also closely related to the next 'law'.

(d) Transposition. We are, for example, able to recognise letters of the English alphabet regardless of stylistic variation (e.g. F, F, F, *F*) even if they retain hardly any 'elements' in common with the usual letter forms (as when depicted as shadows on three-dimensional forms of the letters). We recognise a familiar face whether presented in a photograph, a painting, in the flesh or as a cartoon, in profile or face-to-face. This is a very important aspect of the Gestalt argument – relationships are more important than parts. In relation to recognition of tunes this phenomenon, as already noted, played a major early role as it was especially difficult to account for in terms of the 'bottom up' approaches previously adopted.

There are numerous other 'laws' but these should suffice to convey the message. While perception became a central topic for Gestalt theorising (as learning had for behaviourists), it was not restricted to this. The idea that the field structure of the situation played a major role in learning was the theme of one of the most famous Gestalt experimental programmes – Köhler's experiments done on Tenerife during the First World War (where the British had interned him). He demonstrated first that chickens could learn that a reward was in the lighter or darker of two boxes (i.e. they had learned a relationship, not a single S–R association), but then undertook experiments on chimpanzee problem-solving. The best remembered of these are Sultan's realisations that he could obtain bananas by pulling them into his cage with a stick, or stacking up boxes when they were hanging beyond reach. The point of these experiments was to show how the solutions occurred when the subject, as it were, mentally reorganised the structure of the situation – which could be aided, for example, by laying the stick pointing towards the banana rather than at right angles to it. This sudden 'insight learning' (the 'aha!' experience as it is sometimes called) proved a considerable challenge to behaviourist learning theory.

In their later work the Gestaltists, especially Wertheimer, concentrated increasingly on cognition and problem-solving, exploring how a problem's presentational structure facilitated or hampered its solution. As an illustration of this, Wertheimer retold an anecdote about the mathematician Gauss. When Gauss was an infant in the kindergarten the teacher instructed the class to add up 1+2+3+4+5+6+7+8+9+10. Little Gauss immediately shot his hand up and gave the correct answer of 55, explaining that as 1+10 is 11, 2+9 is 11 etc., there are five pairs of 11 and 5 × 11 is 55. Instead of attempting to solve the problem sequentially as posed, he had first reorganised its structure. Among the influential cognitive research undertaken from a Gestalt perspective was that of K. Duncker on factors affecting problem-solving. This involved presenting subjects with hypothetical problems (e.g. 'how can you apply high-intensity X-rays to an internal tumour without damaging intervening tissue?') and asking them to 'think aloud' as they tried to solve them. Again these highlighted the need to reorganise the elements in the situation if a solution was to be achieved. It is fair to say that Gestalt Psychology in many ways laid the groundwork for modern Cognitive Psychology, although we will see in Chapter 7 that cognitivists radically altered the terms in which thinking was addressed.

What then happened to Gestalt Psychology? Koffka went to the United States in the 1920s but maintained strong links with his colleagues, so until the early 1930s the school was able to make considerable headway as a scientific alternative to behaviourism, even, to some extent, in the United States (as we saw in the case of E.C. Tolman). Nazism forced Wertheimer and Kurt Lewin into exile (both being Jewish), Köhler (almost uniquely among non-Jewish German psychologists) quitting in solidarity. (Within Germany the theory was taken over by Wolfgang Metzger who reformulated its holistic approach to endorse Nazi doctrines.) They eventually found academic posts but were unable to adjust easily to the US context, although their ideas greatly influenced Social Psychology, particularly via the work of Lewin. Solomon Asch, who performed the famous conformity experiments, also strongly endorsed the Gestalt approach (see Asch, 1952). In a way, however, they were partly victims of their success – their best insights were readily incorporated into mainstream thought while, as just indicated, their approach to cognition was overtaken by the post-war generation of US cognitive psychologists. At the theoretical level their central doctrine of psychophysiological isomorphism was refuted by neurophysiologists, while their 'field theory' approach in general proved difficult to sustain, less clearly the single most advanced mode of scientific thinking, than had earlier seemed to be the case. There was no Gestaltist Skinner to carry the flag further and by Köhler's death in 1967 the movement had long ceased to exist as an identifiable school. Its anti-reductionism and insistence on addressing values and meanings was nevertheless continued by the humanist school, one of whose leaders, Abraham Maslow, studied under Wertheimer in the early 1940s in New York at the New School of Social Research.

Closely associated with, though not exactly a member of, the Gestalt school, Lewin also had some success in the United States in developing his own 'topological' approach, which incorporated the field concept. During the 1940s Lewin applied this to topics ranging from personality to learning and group dynamics. Again the central message is that behaviour can only be understood in terms of the total field or 'life-space' of the behaving entity, be it an individual, group or organisation. Lewin developed various methods of representing and analysing this 'life-space' and its dynamics, as well as exploring the methodological implications of such an approach. Gestaltism's long-term effect on US Social Psychology was to ensure that a phenomenological and holistic theoretical strand continued alongside the dominant empiricism of most post-war attitude theorists. This began to bear fruit somewhat later during the 1960s (see Chapter 13).

The school was often criticised for alleged experimental sloppiness and thus castigated as 'unscientific' – this is an error, as it was rather that they had a different, more relaxed concept of what being scientific meant. My personal view is that Gestalt Psychology was in many respects far more sophisticated and creative than behaviourism. Of course it backed the wrong horse at a deeper theoretical level, but this was a highly excusable – and in the event a quite productive – error. Its legacy to the studies of perception, cognition and Social Psychology should not be underestimated even though it often remains unacknowledged. And finally, of course, we must remember that their demise as a school was primarily due to historical circumstances beyond their control. This is even truer of their many German contemporaries (like Wilhelm Stern or Karl and Charlotte Bühler), unassociated with specific 'schools', who, as far as the English-speaking world is concerned, have been largely forgotten .

It is possible that some readers are now rather baffled as to why I have not mentioned Fritz Perls' Gestalt therapy. The word 'Gestalt' is probably now better known in this connection than any other. In fact there is hardly any connection at all between Gestalt Psychology and Gestalt therapy. In some ways they are quite opposite in temper – Gestalt Psychology is among the most rigorously cerebral of Psychological doctrines, whereas Gestalt therapy was very much a reaction against intellectualism and stressed the emotional and irrational. Perls' use of the term refers to the therapeutic procedure itself in which the client is required to focus clearly on some aspect of their experience or situation, etc., as a 'figure' and address its psychological meaning. This also involves the Gestaltist notion of 'closure' or 'completing unfinished business' (e.g. the therapist might take the role of a deceased parent to enable the client to express finally all the things that they wanted, but were unable, to say to that parent). While there are some affinities between them in their use of such notions as 'figure/ground' and 'closure', these are deployed quite differently in Gestalt therapy. Fritz Perls himself was not closely associated with the German Gestalt school, and although his first book (written in South Africa) is dedicated to Wertheimer, his major theoretical point of reference was Freud.

What does the story of Gestalt Psychology tell us about Psychology itself? One important point that emerges is the difficulty of successfully transferring theoretical perspectives between cultural contexts. Unlike the physics of their famous colleagues, the Psychology of the Gestaltists did not fare well beyond the German-speaking culture in which it had arisen (and the collapse of which caused its enforced exile). This suggests that, scientifically sophisticated though they were, their Psychology was rooted in the 'psychology' of their culture in a way in which contemporary German physics was not. How they viewed their task and subject matter was simply different in some central respects to the views prevailing in the United States. This did not mean that their ideas were rejected, quite the contrary, but that they became refashioned and assimilated in a rather piecemeal manner into US Psychology. Something similar happened to psychoanalysis (see Chapter 8). A second point is that Gestalt research yielded several popular iconic representations (now quite divorced from its theory) of 'what Psychology is about': Köhler's apes, the 'figure/ground' distinction, the stimulus material used in their perception studies, and some of Duncker's experiments, for example, continue to appear in textbooks or adorn their covers. Even if the theory was in the end rejected by anglophone Psychology, its products thus remain part of the discipline's 'self-image'. Finally, Gestalt Psychology provides an unusually explicit example of the way in which Psychology derives its ideas from elsewhere (in this case from physics). While this often only involves exploring a new metaphor, in this case it was a quite conscious attempt at incorporating Psychology into the 'unified universe of discourse' of physical science – 'field' was *not* just a metaphor. In this respect its failure is perhaps especially instructive – for those who want instruction – regarding the difference in nature between Psychology and the physical sciences.

BIBLIOGRAPHY

Further reading

Asch, S.E. (1952) *Social Psychology*, Englewood Cliffs, NJ: Prentice-Hall. See especially chapter 2.
Koffka, K. (1935) *Principles of Gestalt Psychology*, New York: Harcourt Brace. See especially chapters 1–3 for a comprehensive statement of the Gestalt approach.

Köhler, K. (1917, English edn 1925, reprint 1957) *The Mentality of Apes*, Harmondsworth: Penguin. Essential reading for anyone wishing to explore the character of Gestalt research further.

Sokal, M. (1984) 'The Gestalt Psychologists in Behaviorist America', *American Historical Review* 89: 1240–63. Very useful, and quite amusing.

Major Gestalt texts

Duncker, K. (1926) 'A Qualitative (Experimental and Theoretical) Study of Productive Thinking (Solving of Comprehensible Problems)', *Journal of Genetic Psychology* 33: 642–70.

Duncker, K. (1945) 'On Problem-solving', trans. Lynne S. Lees, *Psychological Monographs* 270.

Koffka, K. (1928) *The Growth of the Mind*, London: Kegan Paul, Trench & Trübner.

Köhler, W. (1938) *The Place of Value in a World of Facts*, London: Kegan Paul, Trench & Trübner.

Köhler, W. (1940) *Dynamics in Psychology*, New York: Liveright.

Köhler, W. (1947) *Gestalt Psychology*, New York and Toronto: Mentor Books.

Lewin, K. (1935) *A Dynamic Theory of Personality*, New York: McGraw.

Lewin, K. (1936) *Principles of Topological Psychology*, New York: McGraw.

Lewin, K. (1951, reprint 1964) *Field Theory in Social Science*, New York: Harper.

Petermann, B. (1932) *The Gestalt Theory and the Problem of Configuration*, London: Kegan Paul, Trench & Trübner. Influential critique of Gestalt Psychology. Petermann remained in Germany, becoming Professor of Psychology and Pedagogy at Göttingen in 1939, and keenly promoting Nazi racial doctrines.

Wertheimer, M. (1945, enlarged edn 1959) *Productive Thinking*, New York: Harper. Key text on the 'cognitive' aspect.

On Lewin, see also:

Hall, C.S. and G. Lindzey (1957) *Theories of Personality*, New York: Wiley, chapter 6.

Also cited:

Perls, F.S. (1947) *Ego, Hunger and Aggression: A Revision of Freud's Theory and Method*, London: Allen & Unwin.

7 Cognitive Psychology

It is appropriate to move directly from Gestalt to Cognitive Psychology, for the past quarter century the most prominent school in experimental Psychology. Like behaviourism, this arose in the United States, although British figures such as Kenneth Craik and the late Donald Broadbent were involved, while Alan Turing's work – notably his 'Turing Machine' and 'Turing Test'[1] concepts – were also a background factor. It would be quite wrong to imagine that psychologists previously ignored cognition. As we saw, the Gestaltists paid it much attention, while in 1923 Charles Spearman had published *The Nature of 'Intelligence' and the Principles of Cognition* and in Switzerland Jean Piaget began studying the cognitive development of children in the 1920s. One could go back further to papers by Binet from the 1890s, Jardine's forgotten *Elements of the Psychology of Cognition* (1874), and even Spencer (1855). Traditional philosophy, moreover, commonly treated logic and cognition as nearly synonymous (e.g. Boole, 1854). Why, then, did Cognitive Psychology appear so revolutionary in the 1950s – a view maintained by its present-day historians? Certainly it was not the choice of cognition as a subject matter that was new. The answer is twofold:

- Cognitivism was seen as breaking behaviourism's hold on experimental Psychology, supplanting it as the most productive theoretical orientation. This view has been keenly promoted by cognitivism's advocates. In retrospect the 'rebellion against entrenched behaviourism' story appears to have been somewhat exaggerated (see Chapter 5), although it has some validity for the US situation at least.
- More genuinely revolutionary was the adoption of a new set of theoretical concepts, a new technical language. Cognitive psychologists were thinking about thinking in a quite novel way. It is on this that I wish to concentrate.

---

1 The Turing Test. You are faced with two keyboards (or equivalent) by which to communicate with an unseen source – one linked to a human, the other to a machine. If after your conversation you cannot tell which is which, the machine has passed the 'Turing Test'. This has attracted enormous debate and is a central point of reference for debates on machine consciousness.

To begin somewhat obliquely, by the late 1930s technology was approaching current levels of complexity, especially in radio, television and aero-engineering. The Second World War intensified this with inventions such as radar, the need to co-ordinate radar with air defences, problems posed by night flying, and finally the Manhattan Project. One feature of these innovations was the ever-escalating level of mathematical calculation involved, stimulating the development of ever more versatile calculating machines. Another consequence was that design problems regarding control and integration of complex technical systems were brought to the fore. From this setting, in which technology, mathematics and theoretical concern with design principles were interwoven, the concepts emerged that would underlie Cognitive Psychology. Note that these were not initiated by psychologists but by electrical engineers like Claude Shannon, mathematicians like Norbert Weiner and J. von Neumann, and logicians such as Turing. The invention that finally integrated these strands was of course the electronic computer, the first versions of which date from the late 1940s, with the 1948 invention of the transistor rendering computers, as we now know them, possible. From this came three central ideas which were to alter the conceptualisation of cognition: information, feedback and programming.

1   *Information*. Although the term 'information' is recorded from 1387, prior to *c*. 1940 the notion of measuring it would have seemed absurd (although a statistical usage by R.A. Fisher appeared in 1925). In 1948 Shannon of MIT endowed 'information' with a precise technical meaning enabling it to be quantified (a development that had been brewing since the 1930s). In retrospect his move looks simple: information can be measured in terms of the uncertainty that it eliminates. Adopting 'binary logic', this is formally convertible into the question of how many yes–no decisions are required to specify the information. As a simple illustration: to specify a given square on an 8×8 chess board we need to ask six yes–no questions of the form 'is it in the top half?'/'is it in the left half?' (each of which halves the remaining possibilities). In information theory terms this means that specifying a square requires six 'bits' (for 'binary digit') of information. Mathematically developing this insight soon took things into more complex realms, but the core conceptual point is actually quite straightforward. Converting this into hardware terms was easy: yes–no (1/0 in binary), was equivalent to on/off states of electrical switches.

   Using information theory one could start discussing things like 'channel capacity', 'storage capacity' and 'noisy signals'. One important innovation was the notion of 'redundancy', meaning 'surplus' information. If a 'signal' only contains the precise minimum of information, any interference will render it meaningless; additional 'redundant' information ensures successful transmission despite a degree of degradation. Thus in written English many letters are, strictly speaking, redundant. In small advertisements these are often eliminated to save space: 'desirable semi-detached house with 3 bedrooms, 2 reception rooms and a small garden' becomes 'des. semi 3 beds 2 recep. sm. gard'.

This notion of measuring information first entered Psychology in psychophysics and RT studies: it became possible, for example, to study RT as a function of the information in a stimulus array – how much longer does it take to react to one of eight possibilities than to one of four, one of two or in the absence of any choice? Other kinds of question rapidly followed. What is the information capacity of STM? How is information most effectively memorised or presented? What are the channel capacities for various sensory modalities? How fast is information of different kinds processed? Many such questions – never even askable before – soon came onto the agenda and were often of direct practical importance (e.g. in relation to instrument design). The upshot was to recast the study of cognition as the study of human information-processing.

2 *Feedback.* E.C. Tolman had, we saw, striven to incorporate 'purpose' into behaviourist theory. But this was difficult. The puzzle, prior to the 1940s, was that 'purposiveness' was apparently incompatible with scientific determinism – it suggested that something later in time could cause something earlier in time, which is counter to the unidirectionality of time and the very notion of cause–effect sequences – a cause cannot come after its effect. To say that you are studying to get a degree three years hence seems to imply that an event three years ahead is causing your present behaviour. Purposive or 'teleological' explanations had thus been systematically eliminated from physical science over the previous two centuries. Tolman introduced various technical expressions to try to circumvent this but none caught on. At this point, in the early 1940s, technology provided what looked like a nonmysterious solution – the notion of negative feedback. The term 'feedback' is first recorded in 1920 in the sense of feedback through microphones, when a microphone picks up output from its amplifier and we get that familiar 'howl' effect. The first usage in the sense with which we are concerned occurs, according to the *Oxford English Dictionary*, in 1943. Credit for realising its potential belongs to Norbert Weiner, who created a new discipline, cybernetics (from a Greek word meaning 'rudder', related to 'governor'), to promote its exploration.

Weiner had spotted the theoretical significance of some devices long familiar as gadgets for controlling the operation of machines such as steam engines. The earliest example, from ancient Greece, was a method for rigging a ship's rudder to maintain it on a constant course: should it veer to port, the rudder counteracted this by moving it to starboard and vice versa. Steam engines incorporated a 'planetary valve', invented in the eighteenth century, which maintained the engine at constant speed – if it accelerated, the balls on the valve were thrown wider which closed down the throttle, and if the engine slowed, the opposite happened, opening up the throttle. In each case what happens in formal terms is that the system's output is 'fed back' in such a way as to return it to a desired state. Now this greatly resembles purposiveness – the boat keeps heading for Athens, returning on course when diverted; the steam engine strives to maintain a particular speed despite momentary variations. But there is nothing mysterious about this; it is achieved by a simple 'feedback loop'. Weiner differentiated between positive and negative feedback. The howling amplifier is an example of positive feedback, where the feedback loop increases the divergence in output yet further. This is not necessarily bad: theories of human evolution, for instance, frequently postulate positive feedback loops between such things as brain size, access to nutritional foods and intelligence. More immediately significant, however, is the negative feedback loop which counteracts divergence, maintaining the system in a desired state (e.g. the homeostatic biological mechanisms for keeping temperature constant, adjusting vision to changing light levels, etc.). During the 1950s numerous small cybernetic robots were built ('cybernauts') to demonstrate how apparently 'purposive' behaviour could be artificially achieved.

The relevance of this for Psychology was obvious: purposive behaviour was no longer mysterious, but could be studied using the notion of feedback. But what was it that was being 'fed back'? What else, but information. The psycho-physiological system could be conceptualised as one which processed information about both the external environment and its own current state and output via feedback loops (some sensory, some neuromuscular etc.). So the image of human-as-information-processor incorporated the concept of feedback as a central feature. But there is still one feature missing. Information must somehow be *represented,* be it about a required internal end-state or about the world outside and the organism's transactions with it.

3　*Program.* Again, there were technical antecedents: in late eighteenth-century France complex looms were devised (known as Jacquard looms after their inventor) incorporating numerous frames. They were controlled by a chain of perforated wooden blocks passing through the loom, the pattern of holes determining which frames would rise and fall. This was exactly analogous to the punched tape or card later used for programming computers. These wooden blocks were perhaps the first 'software'.

Since the Middle Ages hosts of dancing or musical 'automata' had been constructed by inventors and engineers. These involved building into the machine some kind of unfolding sequence of instructions such as the pins on a music-box cylinder. Unlike the blocks on a Jacquard loom, however, they could not be rearranged. These may be thought of as the original 'hardware' programmes.

With the advent of computers, 'programming' acquired major significance. The first usage in this sense is indeed from a 1945 report on the ENIAC computer (the first modern 'electronic' computer built). For psychologists the concept proved immediately useful, for it seemed to be strictly analogous to the concept of a 'plan': we could now handle complex higher-order behaviour in terms of programs or plans which the organism 'ran through' – and these could be nested within one another and on any time-scale.

Programming, as indicated, occurs at two levels. First, at the 'hardware' level of the system's design it governs the system's structure and the repertoire of operations that it can perform. This includes how it will process information input from outside and may involve a wide range of feedback mechanisms. Second, there is the 'software' level, the means by which information is inputted into the system, instructing it to run through its repertoire of operations in a certain way. If learning to read is a 'hard-programming' educational phase, books are a form of 'software'. Acquiring one's native language is very closely linked with brain maturation and almost literally involves programming the 'hard-wiring' of the brain areas involved in language use.

This core group of concepts, along with numerous subsidiary and related ones, provided a new framework, drawn from outside Psychology, in terms of which topics like thinking, memory, learning, neurological organisation and the like could be tackled. (The analogy between electrical circuits with their on/off switches and the nervous system's on/off synapses had already been advanced in the mid-1940s.) The task now was to embark on a research programme that would explore the implications of this – what we know as Cognitive Psychology. Ultimately I suppose we could see it as an exploration of the 'human as computer' metaphor – although it ranges somewhat more widely than that. Humans are information-processing systems operating according to complex sets of programs derived from a variety of sources – from genetic to social – and sustained in this by sophisticated self-monitoring 'feedback' capacities. Though a very abstract way of couching things, this seemed to leave the door open for most of the phenomena that psychologists might wish to study. (It eventually returned to such philosophical chestnuts as the nature of consciousness and the mind–body relationship.) Ultimately it remains debatable whether 'purposiveness' can really be completely translated into feedback and programming terms, but undoubtedly the perceived possibility of doing so broke a major conceptual log-jam.

The first indications of the impact of this new approach, within what was then termed the 'Psychology of thinking', appear in works such as Bruner, Goodnow and Austin (1956) – a study of what (somewhat debatably) they called 'concept formation'. The majority of the book concerns a research programme using a special pack of eighty-one cards varying across three values on each of four features: colour (red, green, black), shapes (discs, squares, crosses), number of border lines (one, two, three), number of shapes (one, two, three), the subject being required to identify a target 'concept' (e.g. 'all cards with two shapes and one border'). While clearly cognitive in spirit this work did not, however, widely deploy the new technical concepts. These were more clearly in evidence in Miller (1956), his now classic paper on the information capacity of STM. Two years later Newell, Shaw and Simon

(1958) introduced their 'General Problem Solver' program which, it was claimed, had found a new, more elegant proof for one of the theorems in Whitehead and Russell's *Principia Mathematica*. This launched the artificial intelligence (AI) project which has flourished unabated ever since. In the same year Donald Broadbent began using information-processing flow charts (Broadbent, 1958). From this point the cognitive movement accelerated rapidly, its founding phase being sealed by a work that we should discuss in a little more detail.

PLANS AND THE STRUCTURE OF BEHAVIOR BY G.A. MILLER, E. GALANTER AND K. PRIBRAM (1960)

Although cognitivism had been developing for over a decade this work provided the first systematic and comprehensive statement of its perspective, and was really cognitivism's manifesto. The central argument is that human behaviour can best be understood in terms of the nesting and clustering of 'plans' – programs of action through which the organism runs in order to reach its goals. Whereas the central unit in behaviourism had been the S–R connection, these authors propose what they call the TOTE (test–operate– test–exit) unit. The TOTE unit is a simple feedback loop. Suppose that I am hammering a nail – first I 'test' the situation (is it straight?), then I 'operate' (hit the nail), then I test again (is it in far enough?), and if it is, I then 'exit' – there may of course be several test–operate sequences before exiting. But this whole unit will probably be a sub-component in a larger plan – I am nailing a strip of wood to the wall into which I intend to screw some hooks. Earlier on, this plan involved a trip to a DIY store to buy the materials and will end when I 'exit' after testing that the hooks bear the weight of the family coats. At which point I may realise that a glass door-panel will bang into the last hook! This will modify my hook-mounting plan such that in future it includes a TOTE unit representing 'check against swinging doors', to be implemented before nail-banging starts.

One reason that this alternative to S–R was so powerful was that it could handle complex behaviours – pianists playing a rapid arpeggio do not learn this by associating each note to the previous one, rather they run through an 'arpeggio program' (and note the similarity between musical notation and the punched-tape kind of programming technique). Another aspect of this is one that Miller explored in some detail – how we organise information by 'chunking' it; music-hall 'perfect memory' entertainers had long ago devel-oped techniques of memorising large amounts of information in this way, and indeed these go back to classical times. It also has a fairly close relationship with Gestalt ideas on structuring of problems so that they can be solved in the most efficient way.

The book had great success, pulling together recent developments in linguistics (notably Noam Chomsky's work), neurology, memory, problem-solving research and even hypnosis, to show how they were amenable to the cognitive approach. As it happened, the TOTE unit itself did not establish itself as a technical term, primarily because other expressions proved more useful as Cognitive Psychology expanded throughout the 1960s. Nevertheless, the book is widely acknowledged as signalling the point when the academic tide finally turned in cognitivism's favour.

One measure of the maturation of a new theory or school is the appearance of undergraduate college textbooks. In 1967 Ulric Neisser's *Cognitive Psychology* appeared, fulfilling this role for cognitivism, although he back-tracked somewhat from the pure information-processing model, stressing the selective and synthesising aspect of human processing which artificial systems lacked. In the mid-1970s Neisser became far more sceptical, but for the time being his textbook was read as confirming cognitivism's broad potential and for the next twenty years it effectively made the running in mainstream experimental Psychology, closely allied with AI studies and, increasingly, with neurophysiology. The work of later figures such as Fodor, Kahnemann, Marr (see Chapter 10), Pylyshyn, Minsky and, in Britain, Wason, Johnson-Laird and Boden cannot, unfortunately, be surveyed here. They have variously extended cognitivism to the study of such things as syllogistic reasoning (Wason and Johnson-Laird), creativity (Boden), the 'modularity' model of mind (Fodor) and perception (Marr). Within cognitivist theorising there is now a theoretical debate concerning the relative merits of 'computational' and 'connectionist' approaches, and considerable excitement about 'parallel distributed processing' (PDP) models. For these issues readers should consult one of the numerous recent textbooks.

What should be noted is how a movement that began as offering a new theoretical framework for studying higher mental processes gradually developed into something with a far more comprehensive semi-philosophical character. By the 1980s writers such as Paul and Patricia Churchland were claiming to have virtually solved such perennial issues as the 'mind–body problem' and, in effect, casting 'cognitive neuroscience' as the panacea for all human ills. Are we beginning to discern a pattern here? As with psycho-analysis, behaviourism and Gestalt Psychology for example, Psychological schools of thought seem prone to expanding from the relatively restricted scientific issues that serve as their starting points into putative philosophies of life.

Cognitive Psychology's arrival was engineered quite self-consciously by a relatively small group of American psychologists, most centrally G.A. Miller, J. Bruner, H.A. Simon and their co-workers. In Britain Broadbent was active from the start, while non-psychologists like Shannon and von Neumann played a continuing role. Even so, others were moving in the same direction, some of whom became identified as cognitive psychologists once the move-ment was established. Chomsky was always invoked as an ally because of his theory of the deeply programmed nature of grammar and opposition to behaviourist accounts of language (notably Skinner's). George Kelly's 'perso-nal construct theory' has a strong cognitivist character, while Osgood et al.'s

The Measurement of Meaning (1957) was moving in a cognitive direction also, despite the retention of much Hullian terminology. Festinger's 'cognitive dissonance theory' (see Chapter 12) and Ellis's 'rational–emotive therapy' were catching the same wind. Bruner soon 'rediscovered' Piaget and incorporated Piagetian Psychology into American cognitivism.

By the 1980s cognitivism was so intertwined with AI research and neurophysiology that, to many devotees, links with the rest of Psychology seemed tenuous. As they saw it, especially in the United States, the rest of Psychology had gone 'soft' and was under the joint thumbs of humanistic Psychology and social constructionist, feminist-influenced Social Psychology. Due in part to the fact that a succession of APA presidents were drawn from the latter camps a split developed, and in some universities Psychology was divided between 'cognitive science' and social science or social studies departments. This has not widely happened in the United Kingdom, but tensions are there.

From my own viewpoint Cognitive Psychology represents a very major example of how novel technologies and scientific discoveries can change how we think about ourselves. Perhaps it should go without saying that cognitivism's success has both reflected and reinforced a 'contextual' climate dominated by the rise of information technology. Since the late 1980s, criticisms of the school have begun to mount, not only from its traditional critics such as humanistic psychologists and behaviourists, but from a variety of social constructionists, phenomenologists and philosophers (see Costall and Still, 1987, for a sample). Even if its career has peaked, cognitivism is no more likely to disappear than any other school of Psychological thought – it is far too congenial a doctrine for too large a contemporary psychological constituency to permit this to happen.

BIBLIOGRAPHY

Further reading

Costall, A. and A. Still (eds) (1987) *Cognitive Psychology in Question*, Brighton: Harvester. An influential collection of critical papers, invaluable for anyone seeking an introduction to current theoretical controversies regarding the nature, status and claims of Cognitive Psychology.

Gardner, H. (1987) *The Mind's New Science: A History of the Cognitive Revolution*, New York: Basic Books. The best general history of the school.

Hirst, W. (ed.) (1988) *The Making of Cognitive Science: Essays in Honour of G.A. Miller*, Cambridge: Cambridge University Press. Worth dipping into, though variable.

Johnson-Laird, P.N. (1988) *The Computer and the Mind*, London: Fontana.

Miller, G.A., E. Galanter and K.H. Pribram (1960) *Plans and the Structure of Behavior*, n.p.: Holt, Rinehart & Winston.

Posner, M.I. and G.L. Shulman (1979) 'Cognitive Science', in E. Hearst (ed.) *The First Century of Experimental Psychology*, New York: Erlbaum. For me this gets off on the wrong foot by saying that history is boring and dull, but it provides some good factual information and an interesting insiders' view of the story.

Some early cognitivist texts

Ashby, W. Ross (1952) *Design for a Brain*, New York: Wiley. Early exposition of how computing and information theory could be used to simulate mental processes.

Attneave, F. (1959) *Applications of Information Theory to Psychology: A Summary of Basic Concepts, Methods, and Results*, New York: Holt, Rinehart & Winston. Short summary of information technology and its applications to psychophysics. Introduced many psychologists to the field.

Broadbent, D.E. (1958) *Perception and Communication*, London: Pergamon.

Bruner, J., J. Goodnow and G. Austin (1956, reprint 1962) *A Study of Thinking*, New York: Science Editions.

Chomsky, N. (1957) *Syntactic Structures*, The Hague and Paris: Mouton. Classic exposition of his linguistic theories (in their first version).

McCulloch, W. and W. Pitts (1943) 'A Logical Calculus of the Ideas Immanent in Nervous Activity', *Bulletin of Mathematical Biophysics* 5:115–33. Exploration of the nervous system–calculating device analogy, routinely cited as a founding text.

Miller, G.A. (1956) 'The Magical Number Seven, Plus or Minus Two: Some Limits on our Capacity for Processing Information', *Psychological Review* 63:81–97.

Newell, A., J.C. Shaw and H.A. Simon (1958) 'Elements of a Theory of Human Problem Solving', *Psychological Review* 65(3):151–66.

Osgood, C.E., G.C. Suci and P.H. Tannenbaum (1957) *The Measurement of Meaning*, Urbana, Ill.: University of Illinois Press.

Shannon, C.E. and W. Weaver (1949) *The Mathematical Theory of Communication*, Urbana, Ill.: University of Illinois Press. Full theoretical statement of information technology.

von Neumann, J. (1958) *The Computer and the Brain*, New Haven: Yale University Press. He also introduced 'games theory', undiscussed in my main text, which had its own distinct influence on Cognitive Psychology and cognitively pitched Social Psychology.

Wason, P.C. and P.N. Johnson-Laird (1972) *The Psychology of Reasoning: Structure in Content*, Cambridge, Mass.: Harvard University Press.

The most extreme advocates of cognitive science now appear to be the Churchlands. See the following:

Churchland, Patricia S. (1986) *Neurophilosophy Toward a Unified Science of the Mind/Brain*, Cambridge, Mass. and London: MIT Press.

Churchland, Paul M. (1988, rev. edn) *Matter and Consciousness*, Cambridge, Mass.: MIT Press.

For the state of play at the height of Cognitive Psychology's influence, just prior to the schismatic tendencies of the last decade, see:

Anderson, J.R. (1980) *Cognitive Psychology and Its Implications*, San Francisco: Freeman.

Precursors besides Piaget and Gestalt Psychology

For a representative selection of historical readings:

Bartlett, F. (1932) *Remembering*, Cambridge: Cambridge University Press. Anticipated cognitivist studies of memory. Hailed in the 1970s as a neglected pioneering text, although its social constructionist dimension was discreetly ignored.

76 *Cognitive Psychology*

Binet, Alfred (1886) *La Psychologie du raisonnement*, Paris: Alcan.

Binet, Alfred (1903, reprint 1922) *L'Etude expérimentale de l'intelligence*, Paris: Schleicher Frères, A. Costes. Also, papers on calculators and chess players (1894) and, as well as the first intelligence test (with T. Simon), a study of the development of children's intelligence (1905).

Boole, George (1854) *An Investigation into the Laws of Thought*, London: Macmillan. Embodies the view that the laws of logic are the laws of thought and introduced the idea of binary logic.

Jardine, Robert (1874) *Elements of the Psychology of Cognition*, London: Macmillan. Completely forgotten but historically interesting as half-way between traditional philosophical concerns and psychological ones.

McCosh, James (1886, rev. edn 1892) *The Cognitive Powers*, New York: Scribner.

Mandler, J.M. and G. (1964) *Thinking from Association to Gestalt*, New York: Wiley.

Spearman, C. (1923) *The Nature of 'Intelligence' and the Principles of Cognition*, London: Macmillan.

Spearman, C. (1930) *The Creative Mind*, Cambridge: Cambridge University Press.

Spencer, Herbert (1855) *The Principles of Psychology*, London: Longman, Brown, Green & Longmans. Has, in retrospect, a distinct, if largely unacknowledged, cognitive air.

Vinacke, W. Edward (1952) *The Psychology of Thinking*, New York: McGraw-Hill. Possibly the last overall review prior to the rise of cognitive Psychology, summarising the state of play on the eve of the 'cognitive revolution'.

Events

- 1948: Hixon Symposium at California Institute of Technology on 'Cerebral Mechanisms in Behavior' (see L.A. Jeffress (ed.) (1951) *Cerebral Mechanisms of Behavior: The Hixon Symposium*, New York: Wiley). Crucial founding event. Subsequent symposia at Harvard, MIT and elsewhere promoted and consolidated cognitivism's status.

- 1958: In the United Kingdom – National Physical Laboratory Symposium on 'Mechanisation of Thought Processes' (published by HMSO, 2 vols, 1959). Not mentioned by Gardner. The list of participants is very illuminating.

- 1960: Bruner and Miller founded Harvard Center for Cognitive Studies.

8   Psychology and the meanings of madness

The images of psychologist, psychotherapist and psychiatrist have always been fused. Though annoying to psychologists, this is not entirely unfounded since Psychology has long been intimately involved with psychopathology. Many of its concepts, theories and tests (especially those relating to personality) originated in this area, while psychological theories have frequently been applied in therapeutic contexts. In this chapter I will first consider some of the questions raised by historical studies and the nature of Psychology's involvements with psychopathology, and then turn specifically to psychoanalysis.

Broadly speaking, Psychology's involvements may be identified as follows:

- Ideas about the nature of psychological processes often have their roots in clinical practice.
- Management of psychopathology presents psychologists with an important 'market' for their expertise (e.g. developing diagnostic techniques).
- The clinic often provides a testing ground for the application of psychological theories and models (e.g. behaviour therapy derived from learning theory).
- Psychopathology often supplies psychologists with ideas regarding normal psychological processes (e.g. aphasia in relation to language).
- Classifications of psychopathology may serve as a basis for theories of 'normal' personality differences (e.g. Eysenck's extraversion/neuroticism/psychoticism dimensions).

There are, none the less, some deeper aspects of the history of madness with which we must start. (Michel Foucault, 1967, marked the beginning of post-progressivist studies in this field.) The heart of the matter is the fact that a society's concept of madness is necessarily also a statement of its concept of normality (although each eludes neat formulation). The boundary defines both sides and, to be meaningful, sanity needs a counter-concept of madness. This renders the history of madness both interesting and difficult.

First, it places a question mark above the notion of 'illness' as an objective reality when dealing with much of the behaviour that is or has been considered 'mad'. Nobody would quibble about whether smallpox is an illness, but even a cursory glance reveals great variation across time and place regarding which behaviours are considered mad. Conduct labelled as symptomatic of 'hysteria' or 'mania' in one epoch could result in canonisation or burning at another. Sometimes behaviour once thought 'mad' has since turned out to be an organic, not a psychological or spiritual, illness (e.g. epilepsy). At a more mundane level the acceptability of, say, talking to oneself, cross-dressing or praying aloud in public, is subject to wide variation as is the 'normality' of much sexual behaviour. Thus cultures vary widely in where they set the boundaries of the 'normal'.

Second, the cultural meaning of madness is itself quite flexible. One of the things that Foucault first noted was the contrast between the late Renaissance (the 1500s–*c*.1640) and the eighteenth century. During the Renaissance madness was something to which people related as an ever-present possibility – we find it particularly in painting (e.g. Hieronymus Bosch and the elder Breughel) and literature (most obviously in Shakespeare's play's where madness is fully integrated as part of the human condition – especially in *King Lear, Macbeth, Hamlet* and *Othello*, and at a lighter level in *A Midsummer Night's Dream*). One condition exerting great fascination at this time was 'melancholy', the topic of one of the greatest early 'Psychological' texts, Robert Burton's *Anatomy of Melancholy* (1621).

In the 1700s the picture changes dramatically, the mad become qualitatively different from the sane, objects of amusement, less than human for having lost the Enlightenment's most valued human attribute – 'reason'. Rather than a universal part of the human condition, madness signifies exile from it. 'Melancholy', once resonant with profundity as the frequent stigma of artists and philosophers, is medicalised into 'melancholia'. It becomes a more or less physical condition, nicknamed 'the Black Dog', arising from the state of one's nerves, bad diet or the east wind. Meanings of psychopathology can therefore change for a number of reasons, including broad cultural factors. More specifically they relate in a complex way to explanations of madness, which have included astrology (bad aspects to Saturn or the Moon – hence lunacy), demonic or divine possession, trauma, witchcraft (especially for male impotence), bad living habits, divine punishment for sins and hereditary degeneration. In the present century new psychological and physical factors have been invoked, from 'double-binding' to vitamin D deficiency (in relation to 'possession' phenomena). Implicitly (and sometimes explicitly) each carries its distinct meaning, determining how the behaviour in question is perceived, evaluated, treated and located within the culture. Such causes vary along several dimensions: psychological vs. physical, optimistic vs. pessimistic, internal vs. external, ethically loaded vs. ethically neutral, empathic vs. objectifying. Although aetiologies of physical illness have been similarly subject to change, they have generally been seen as physical and ethically neutral (or divinely punitive in a fairly simple way). By contrast, their studies of the meaning of madness have increasingly led historians into such issues as the power relationship between doctor and patient, gender relations and interactions between treatment policy and wider cultural concerns.

Third, then, Foucault and his numerous successors were led to dismiss the traditional progressivist story of a rise from ignorance to medical enlightenment. This drove the first wedge into the 'progressivist' approach generally, unsurprisingly because it was perhaps the easiest area in which to demonstrate progressivism's inadequacies.

We can now look in more detail at just some aspects of the topic: (a) changing attitudes to treatment, (b) input from psychopathology into the study of personality, and (c) the 'anti-psychiatry' movement of the 1960s and early 1970s.

CHANGING ATTITUDES TOWARDS TREATMENT

First, see Table 8.1 for some quantitative data.

Table 8.1 Results of psychiatric hospital treatment

Hospital	Date	N	% R/I*	
Bethlem	1784–94	1,664	35	UK
Salpetrière	1803–7	1,002	47	France
The Retreat	1796–1811	149	48	UK
Salpetrière	1804–14	2,005	61	France
Dr Burrows	1820	242	92	USA
Hartford, CT	1827	23	91	USA
Bethlem	1830s	562	70	UK**
Bloomingdale	1821–44	1,841	59	USA
Worcester, MA	1839–43	922	49	USA
US Asylums	1844	2,092	41	USA
US Asylums	1859	4,473	57	USA
Worcester, MA	1880–4	1,319	20	USA
NY State	1912	7,238	22	USA

Source: Tourney (1967), *American Journal of Psychiatry* 124(6).
* Recovered or improved.
** Additional data from A. Morison (1838), *Physiognomy of Mental Disease.*

Although this is undoubtedly a crude sample and one must be wary of reading too much into it, these figures at least demonstrate that reported 'recovered or improved' (R&I) rates declined during the latter nineteenth century and that, for whatever reasons, New York State asylums in 1912 were doing worse than the main French asylum a century previously. Hardly a tale of medical advance!

To what can we ascribe this shifting pattern? First, the high early nineteenth-century figures reflect a retreat from the typical eighteenth-century attitude to madness towards a more positive view, associated with the rise of Romanticism. The gap between sane and insane narrows, reflecting Romanticism's emphasis on the emotional and irrational and the times' more egalitarian temper. Madness was reincorporated into the 'human condition'. A more psychologically oriented 'moral therapy' arose, challenging the Enlightenment's physical methods which had yielded little by way of therapeutic success (indicated in the first line of figures). The famed Dr Willis, who treated

George III, was a leading exemplar of this new approach, while the best-known British asylum adopting it was Samuel Tuke's 'The Retreat' at York. In France reform was initiated by Pinel and his successor Esquirol at the Bicêtre and Salpetrière asylums in Paris. This more humanitarian approach and greater optimism about the possibilities of cure, together with therapeutic innovations, boosted R&I rates for several decades. The very high US figures need to be viewed sceptically since Burrows' patients, for example, were highly selected. Two developments, then, reduce the R&I rates: (a) the building of much larger asylums in which the moral therapists' idealistic blueprints are watered down as the medical profession reasserts professional authority; (b) after *c*.1840, an increasing belief that insanity is hereditary and, later, a sign of degeneracy. The latter both reduces prognostic optimism (hereditary conditions resisting easy 'cure') and encourages a policy of confinement to protect the quality of the human stock by curbing degenerate procreation.

A further factor is that the kinds of thing earning the label 'mad' early in the century included numerous behaviours offensive to bourgeois society, such as chronic gambling, alcoholism and sexual promiscuity, which later cease to figure. Since 'curing' these was a matter of inculcating some kind of moral reform, 're-educating' or 'brainwashing' the deviant into accepting respectable social values, the possibility of R&I was clearly fairly high. There are some quite complex aspects to the 'moral therapy' movement as an expression of a contemporary urge to inculcate new middle-class values of 'self-control'. Foucault in particular recast Pinel's traditional heroic role more darkly, depicting him as the agent of a new bourgeois culture, using psychiatry as a channel for exercising social power.

During the latter nineteenth century, large institutions, therapeutic pessimism and eugenic fears of degeneration thus mutually reinforced each other to impoverish the lot of the 'insane'. This in turn heightened the stigma of insanity, hence middle-class neuroses (as we would now call them), especially among women, were dealt with in the asylum less frequently. It was in relation to these that twentieth-century psychotherapies exerted much of their early appeal. In the present century madness becomes an arena in which psychologists, heretical psychiatrists and orthodox medicine have constantly struggled for dominance, a struggle still unresolved – a point to which I return when considering the anti-psychiatry movement.

To return to our figures: the short answer to why they change as they do is that neither the meanings of madness nor cure (R&I) remain constant, and neither do the roles and functions of incarceration in an 'asylum'.

INPUT FROM PSYCHOPATHOLOGY INTO PERSONALITY THEORY

The task of classifying mental 'illnesses' has been a fertile source of ideas regarding personality. In the early nineteenth century, numerous models of personality and its dynamics (mostly now forgotten) were produced, especially by German psychiatrists (see H.F. Ellenberger, 1970; K. Doerner, 1969). (One should note here that the psychiatrist's or 'alienist's' relative independence, and, until the present century, isolation, facilitated a high degree of intellectual autonomy, which continues in some areas of psychotherapy. Being funded by one's clients means being economically beholden to no single source, a situation obviously congenial to theoretical originality.) Different personality types come to be identified as especially prone to different kinds of insanity. While earlier psychiatrists often drew on folk-psychological typologies as a starting point, in the present century the traffic has been in the reverse direction. Psychiatrists and clinicians such as Freud, Kraepelin, Kretschmer and Jung, and psychologists working in clinical settings such as H.J. Eysenck, have provided the major input into personality theory. Varieties of psycho-pathology are taken to represent the extremes of normal personality types or dimensions, as in Eysenck's model where schizophrenia and hysteria constitute extreme introvert and extravert modes of high neuroticism. Earlier Kretsch-mer devised a threefold typology (linked to body build): 'cyclothymes' (tendency towards manic depression), 'schizothymes' (prone to schizophrenia) and 'collodethymes' (calm, unexcitable, but displaying explosive bursts of irascibility), identifying three sub-types for each of the first two.

Many of the 'personality tests' with which we are familiar originated as clinical diagnostic instruments: the Minnesota Multiphasic Personality Inventory, Eysenck's EPI, the Blacky test for aggression, and the Rorschach inkblot test (now largely discredited) to cite but four. Even IQ tests are not unlinked with this since Binet first devised them for identifying genuinely 'sub-normal' children (though not now classed as insanity, 'imbecility' was classified as such until *c*.1900 and its history follows a similar course). The 'projective' thematic apperception tests (TATs) introduced by Henry Murray in the 1930s were based on the psychoanalytic notion that people uncon-sciously project their inner dynamics onto ambiguous stimulus material, an assumption underlying projective tests in general. (See Chapter 11 for further discussion of these.) George Kelly's personal construct theory also arose from his clinical experience and was most vigorously developed in the United Kingdom by Bannister and Fransella in the clinical setting. Indeed, it is hard to identify any area of personality theory or research that did not either originate in the clinic or owe its subsequent success to its clinical usage; Cattell's 'sixteen personality factor' theory perhaps comes closest. Input from this source is thus not confined to psychoanalysis and related schools, but extends to mainstream medical psychiatrists such as Kretschmer and to much psychometrics as well.

THE ANTI-PSYCHIATRY MOVEMENT

In recent times the problematic nature of madness is best illustrated by the 'anti-psychiatry' movement of the 1960s and early 1970s, associated with figures such as R.D. Laing, David Cooper, Thomas Szasz and Joe Berke. The roots of this reaction against mainstream medical psychiatry in Britain lay in the increasingly physiological orientation being adopted; many new psycho-active drugs had entered the psychiatrist's pharmacopoeia along with more or less intrusive physical techniques such as electroconvulsive therapy (ECT) and lobotomisation. One component of the intense cultural reaction against post-Second World War conformism, beginning in the mid-1950s, was hostility towards what many saw as the dehumanising nature of this physicalistic psychiatry, perceived as an agency for punishing deviance. Behaviours judged as socially unacceptable were, it was claimed, being medically objectified as mental illnesses. The US situation seems to have differed somewhat – in Britain this period coincided with a fairly sharp decline in the status of psychoanalysis, while in the United States it was at the peak of its popularity. Physicalistic approaches were also making headway in the United States, but with more competition from psychotherapy than in Britain.

In short, psychiatry still served the 'bourgeois' social control functions which Foucault had brought to the notice of discontented intellectuals as being its task around 1800. In the background was the primarily French philo-sophical movement of existentialism which greatly influenced Laing and had already forged links with psychiatry in mainland Europe (e.g. Ludwig Binswanger and Viktor Frankl). The result was a radical attack on mainstream practice, Laing's *The Divided Self* (1959) being the key text, in which it was claimed that all mental illness (especially 'schizophrenia', Laing's principal interest) was psychological in origin. Furthermore, such conditions possessed their own curative dynamic with which physical treatments interfered. A different approach was needed: provision of supportive environments within which the sufferer's 'self-cure' could be managed. Few such alternative institutions were created, but there were several short-lived attempts. For Laing 'schizophrenia' was the normal developmental outcome of being at the focus of confusing messages about one's identity, especially from parents. Special importance was given to 'double-binding' – similar to what is popularly called a 'Catch 22' situation. An example would be a parent verbally insisting on the importance of the child being independent but not actually permitting it to be so. If the child is dependent it is criticised as clinging and lacking initiative; if it is independent it is accused of causing worry and anxiety. It cannot win. (See also Chapter 13). The 'schizogenic mother' thus became a topic of considerable interest, and family dynamics in general were explored by Laing and his colleagues. For Cooper the family was the enemy of all self-fulfilment and he happily prophesied its end. 'Mental illnesses' reflected the problematic nature of the sufferer's 'being', thereby becoming almost philosophical, rather than medical, in character. Such arguments were bolstered by the American Thomas Szasz's provocatively titled *The Myth of Mental Illness* (1962). Szasz's thesis was that so-called 'mental illnesses' were really 'problems in living', not illnesses at all. The very act of labelling them 'illnesses' casts sufferers into a passive patient role, directly contrary to what is required if they are to regain control over their lives.

These developments occurred at a time when recreational drug use in the 'alternative culture' was widely happening for the first time in Britain, but this alternative culture was also an ideological and political movement. Drug experiences, notably LSD 'trips', were readily seen as yielding insights into 'schizophrenia' (thus Laing's approach was construed as enabling the patient to complete their 'trip'). But for those involved in the alternative culture the boundary between 'normal' and 'abnormal' was in any case becoming problematic. The 'sane' world's patent insanities at the time of the Cuban missile crisis and Vietnam War led many to happily reverse the whole evaluation – the 'mad' were sane martyrs, victims of trying to live honestly in an insane and evil world. For a while the 'schizophrenic' virtually became a hero figure. It is important to recognise that the era of 'flower power', hippies and 'permissiveness' was no mere eruption of youthful *joie de vivre* but a quite desperate expression of the first post-war generation's deep fears, confusion and frustration. It was the period, after all, when 'paranoia' entered the popular vocabulary. Allen Ginsberg, leading poet of the immediately preceding 'beat' movement, began his most famous poem *Howl* with the line 'I saw the best minds of my generation destroyed by madness'. In the 1960s the best defence seemed to be to destroy madness itself by totally subverting the sanity–insanity boundary.

This could not last. For one thing it was unrealistic – most psychiatric patients are not engaged in heroic existential quests. For another, to categorically deny a physiological dimension to 'schizophrenia' or any other condition was to be a hostage to fortune, and by the mid-1970s neurochemical factors were beginning to be implicated. The meanings of these were (and remain) debatable but, confronted with ever more sophisticated pharmaceutical methods, little headway was to be made in pushing for expensive 'self-cure' procedures. Things had nevertheless changed irrevocably.

First, the stage was set for the host of 'growth movement' therapies which took off from around 1970 (e.g. Gestalt therapy, primal therapy, encounter groups, psychodrama, transactional analysis and psychosynthesis). These mostly derived from different schools of psychotherapy created during the first half of the century but had a different, more positive, agenda. They began surfacing in the United States in the late 1940s, although their founders were frequently immigrants (e.g. Gestalt therapy's Fritz Perls). The sane/insane boundary had been permanently breached, *there was now a market for psychotherapy for normal people* – surely a development of huge, if as yet unappreciated, cultural significance. The aim was no longer 'cure' but personal growth, while everybody had some degree of psychopathology or psychological damage. It is from this that counselling and other current developments stem. The genuine insights of the anti-psychiatry movement, into family dynamics for example, were not lost either. The idea that therapy might need to move beyond a single 'sick' individual and consider the complex social dynamics of their life became well established.

For Psychology this has meant that since *c*.1970 clinical Psychology has expanded from being almost entirely an auxiliary for psychiatrists (providing diagnostic tests and what psychiatrists – if not practitioners – saw as mere morale-boosting activities like occupational and art therapy), to a sub-discipline therapeutically engaged in dealing with what are seen as psychogenic problems. The central core of 'mad' syndromes – psychoticism and what is problematically known as 'schizophrenia' (see Boyle, 1990) – nevertheless remain in the psychiatric realm, as do conditions with a clear physical basis (although psychologists may be involved with these in research contexts).

To pull all this together: 'madness' is not a fixed entity. Definitions, meanings and treatment have been in constant flux in Western culture since the Renaissance. While ostensibly a medical matter, medicine's boundaries cannot contain it. The thrust of psychiatry (a medical specialism only established in the United Kingdom around 1840 and generally a nineteenth-century innovation) has always been to explain insanity in physical terms, either, as in the late 1800s, as due to inherited neurological degeneration or, more recently, brain damage, neuropathology or some biochemical imbalance. The cultural role of madness as a definer of sanity has, however, always meant that it eludes this kind of neat objectification. Society as a whole, not just doctors, decides on what should count as 'normal' behaviour. And society is forever changing its mind.

For most of its modern history Psychology has been closely involved with the treatment, diagnosis and interpretation of psychopathology. This is evident in the dependence of personality theory on the clinical or 'abnormal' arena, the way in which psychologists have serviced psychiatric diagnosis and assessment, and finally, post-1970, in the way that the discipline has established itself as an appropriate professional authority in dealing with a wide assortment of behavioural and psychological problems, no longer considered in stigmatising fashion as madness, but as genuine problems of living requiring some kind of professional involvement for their solution. The aspiration is to render the seeking of Psychological help for such problems no odder than seeking medical help for physical ones, although differentiating these is difficult and raises a host of other issues (hence the rise of holistic approaches).

PSYCHOANALYSIS AND ASSOCIATED SCHOOLS

Culturally the single most influential point of connection between Psychology and madness has been psychoanalysis and associated schools of psycho-dynamic thought. Everyday language incorporates concepts and expressions invented or promoted by Freud and his associates to an extraordinary extent: having an inferiority or mother complex, projecting one's anger, regressing, doing something unconsciously, suffering from neurotic anxiety, being repressed or fixated, having a fragile persona or inflated ego, and free associating are but some of them. For academic Psychology, psychoanalytic thought has always presented a problem. While an enormously fecund source of concepts and hypotheses, psychoanalysis notoriously resists experimental evaluation. And while their influence on how we think about ourselves is a psychological fact in its own right, as 'scientific theories' the Freudian and allied systems patently failed to meet the criteria of 'good science' being proposed by philosophers of science. As the late Karl Popper claimed, they are simply unfalsifiable. Engagement with psychoanalytic thought was nevertheless unavoidable, since it seemed to illuminate a vast array of topics beyond psychopathology, ranging from child development to personality structure, from dreams to race prejudice, from subliminal perception to art and religion.

And behind all this lay the charismatic and enigmatic figure of Freud himself, which rapidly became modernist culture's iconic image of the bearer of Psychological expertise, the reader of our innermost thoughts. Say 'psychologist' and for most people it is Freud who springs to mind. Freud's personality still remains strangely elusive, he curiously maintains his professional role as target of our transferences and successive waves of historical and biographical attention seem only to have reinforced rather than dispelled his mystique.

Rather than again recount the basic tenets of psychoanalytic theory – available in a thousand books – it will be more useful here to step back a little and consider such questions as the following. Why, as a matter of psychological interest in its own right, *did* psychoanalysis have such an impact? Why do numerous schools of thought ultimately stemming from psychoanalysis continue to flourish? What does the phenomenon of psychoanalysis tell us about Psychology's place in our culture?. These are now more promising issues than the hoary debates about whether psychoanalysis is scientific or the validity of specific Freudian doctrines.

The impact of psychoanalysis

Three main reasons, I suggest, may be given for the cultural and psychological success of psychoanalysis. First and most obvious, although perhaps in the long run least important, it was about sex. The notion that before Freud discussion of sex was taboo has long been dispelled. Numerous late-Victorian psychiatrists and doctors (like Krafft Ebing) penned mighty tomes on the subject, while a flood of popular publications railed against the evils of masturbation and sexual licence. Late nineteenth-century culture was, in its way, as obsessed with the topic as ours. What was distinctive was that sexual discourse (other than the frankly pornographic) was seemingly impossible unless infused with official morality or packaged as something else. Writings on sex adopted one of two stances (to oversimplify somewhat). They could espouse an attitude of great squeamishness, as if dealing with inherently unpleasant and embarrassing matters, striving to eliminate the slightest hint of 'prurience'. This was common in popular 'advice' genres aimed at adolescents which posed as imparting necessary but delicate knowledge best kept from the immature and irresponsible. Alternatively there were books ostensibly for medical or scientific male professionals, seemingly scientific treatises on anthropology or sexual deviance containing detailed engravings of sexual organs, accounts of 'savage' sexual customs and medical cases, often with the more explicit passages in Latin. The border-line between genuine medical works and pornography posing as medicine or anthropology was in fact rather blurred (see also Chapter 15).

The Freudian move was unique not in openly discussing sex but in identifying it as the motivational force underlying all human behaviour from infancy onwards. In effect it sought to enable people to admit and confront their sexuality, identifying the primary aetiological factor in psychopathology as failure to do this. The centrality of sex, and the apparently reductionist implications of this, undoubtedly fuelled the initial *succès de scandale* which psychoanalysis enjoyed.

The second factor is that the theory incorporated numerous central ideas of turn-of-the-century science, notably the evolutionary perspective (with its stress on instincts) and the energy concept being developed in physics. Coupled with Freud's own brilliance at deploying expositional metaphors, often drawn from contemporary science, this amounted to the first thoroughly *modern* image of human nature. The times were ripe for this. All other areas of scientific knowledge had been revolutionised and now at last this revolution had reached human nature itself. A surprising number of Freud's ideas can be traced to various predecessors, but in integrating them as he did, Freud constructed a radically new and modern vision, transcending its clinical origins. It coincided with cultural revolutions on a much wider front in painting, literature and music, of which the turn from 'reason' to emotion and the 'primitive' was a common feature. Freud's scientific self-dethronement of reason by reason was the arch scientific example of this (although Einstein's theory of relativity contributed to the prevailing mood by overthrowing common-sense notions of space and time).

Again, however, since other psychologists were being equally, and more respectably, 'scientific', one may wonder why this image was not soon replaced by even more scientifically advanced ones. The key, I think, lies precisely in its central clinical character. The third factor I would suggest is that Freudian theory was immediately applicable by all who acquainted themselves with it. Adopt this framework and you discover an exciting, enlarged, inner world of primal dramas, significant dreams and secret motives. It promised lay aficionados and professional therapists alike a route for liberation from the stultifying effects of long-forgotten traumas and for re-evaluating themselves from a fresh standpoint. It was not just a theory *about* human nature, it offered an ostensibly 'modern' and 'scientific' procedure for self-exploration.

The endurance of psychoanalytically rooted theories

Insofar as Freud succeeded in establishing (although he did not create) the new role of 'psychotherapist', he may be said to have originated virtually every contemporary school of psychotherapeutic thought. And while non-Freudian approaches are now widespread, an extremely high proportion are theoretically descended from psychoanalysis. Controversy and disagreement are not necessarily indices of failure; on the contrary, they often signify where the action is. Discord is exciting. And so it was with psychoanalysis. A succession of followers found cause to break with Freud and develop their own variants, most famously Carl Jung and Alfred Adler. Even within the Freudian camp, by the 1930s there were increasing tensions regarding the future direction of psychoanalysis. In Britain, Melanie Klein and Anna Freud were at loggerheads. In the United States a new school of 'ego psychologists' were formulating a more optimistic version of the theory, and figures like Erik Erikson, Erich Fromm and Karen Horney soon extended, complemented and diverged from the original to varying extents. More radically, French psychoanalytic thought assumed an even more distinct form under Lacan, while in the United States Henri Marcuse sought to integrate it with Marxism. After 1970 a number of feminists began modifying and reformulating Freudian doctrines in order to expunge their inherent male-centredness (see Chapter 15).

Ironically it is partly because psychoanalysis does *not* conform to the canons of hard scientific theorising that it has been able to take so many different directions. Each generation and culture encountering it can rearrange, reinterpret and modify its conceptual repertoire to meet its own needs.

Now this begins to suggest something very important about the nature of psychoanalytic thought as a whole, at which we have already hinted. It is obviously *not* an orthodox scientific theory, but something both more and less than this, a framework for providing behaviour and experience with *meanings*. But unlike traditional religious or philosophical frameworks, its scientific *style* rendered it consistent with modernist culture. Any such framework or structure by which we bestow meaning on the psychological is in itself a psychological phenomenon, which leads us to the final question.

What psychoanalysis tells us about the place of Psychology

Understanding the extraordinary success of psychoanalysis can, I believe, help to clarify the place that Psychology occupied in modernist culture, and as yet continues to occupy in more post-modernist times. To be provocative, all Psychology to date aspires to the condition of psychoanalysis in the sense of aiming to eventually offer a complete scientific account of the psychological by which people will live more satisfactory lives. True, psychoanalysis never entirely succeeded in this, yet for a while it came impressively close. But the lesson of psychoanalysis is actually that this is a vain aspiration since the reason for its success lay, paradoxically, precisely in its fundamentally unscientific (in the hard positivist sense) nature. What psychoanalysis did was *bring about* a psychological change by, as we have said, providing a new system of psychological ideas within which people could construe their lives. It is the scale on which it did so, not the fact itself, that is so remarkable, for we can now begin to see that to a lesser degree this is what Psychology, when successful, always does. Psychology succeeds to the extent that people find it worth their while adopting its ideas in making sense of their lives – which means psychologically *changing* them. This requires that the new ideas must be felt to be an improvement on those that they already use. Clearly those suffering some form of mental distress will be especially receptive. This is, however, a disturbing perspective for it again raises the question of Psychology's scientific status. If *this* is how Psychology's theories and concepts are ultimately evaluated, if the populace at large is the final court of appeal and arbiter of their value as evidenced by how far 'folk psychology' assimilates them, what price the scientific virtues of rigour, consistency and amenability to empirical testing? Further discussion of this is best postponed until the final chapter.

CONCLUSION

I began by pointing out the universal need to differentiate between sanity and madness. Mad behaviour is, by definition, that to which we can give no meaning (although we may ascribe causes); it is irrational, crazy, deluded. But the situation just sketched is one in which Psychology serves to provide meanings. In relation to madness it seeks, in the case of psychoanalysis quite directly, to ascribe meaning to that which previously lacked it. Sometimes the meanings given may turn out to be physical ones – there has been brain damage or some neurochemical pathology – and 'madness' is clearly bracketed as an effect of physical pathology. When this is not so, we seek, as it were, to find routes by which the sufferer can be brought back across the boundary. (And a boundary can only be crossed and recrossed so often before it disappears.) These 'frameworks of meaning' which Psychology supplies are thus, when they pertain to psychopathology, part and parcel of the cultural process by which the boundary is continually revised and the meaning of madness itself constantly reformulated.

BIBLIOGRAPHY

Further reading

Alexander, F.G. and S.T. Selesnick (1966) *A History of Psychiatry*, New York: Harper & Row. Progressivist with Freudian bias, useful for reference.

Ellenberger, Henri F. (1970) *The Discovery of the Unconscious: The History and Evolution of Dynamic Psychiatry*, London: Allen Lane. Monumental and scholarly account of the pre-history and emergence of psychoanalytic schools.

Foucault, Michel (1967) *Madness and Civilization: A History of Insanity*, London: Tavistock. Additional chapter now translated: (1989) 'Experiences of Madness', *History of Human Sciences* 4(1):1–25. Key text, although less than half was translated into English.

Other references

The following are among the more important or useful texts in a vast literature:

Boyle, Mary (1990) *Schizophrenia: A Scientific Delusion*, London: Routledge. 'Schizophrenia' is an unacceptable category. Nobody now suffers from the original symptoms, which were indistinguishable from those of post-traumatic encephalitis (of which there had just been an epidemic).

Burton, Robert (1621, reprint 1896) *The Anatomy of Melancholy*, London: Bell. Under the guise of reviewing its causes, ends up as a polymathic discussion of everything under the sun from the perspective of a chronic sufferer.

Bynum, William F., Roy Porter and Michael Shepherd (1985, 2 vols) *The Anatomy of Madness: Essays in the History of Psychiatry*, London: Tavistock.

Castel, R. (1988) *The Regulation of Madness: The Origins of Incarceration in France*, Berkeley, Calif.: University of California Press. Disputes Foucault's account.

Cooper, David (1971) *The Death of the Family*, Harmondsworth: Penguin.

Doerner, Klaus (1969, English edn 1981) *Madmen and the Bourgeoisie: A Social History of Insanity and Psychiatry*, Oxford: Blackwell.

Drinka, G.F. (1984) *The Birth of Neurosis: Myth, Malady and the Victorians*, New York: Simon & Schuster. For the American scene and 'neurasthenia'.

Goldstein, J. (1987) *Console and Classify: The French Psychiatric Profession in the Nineteenth Century*, Cambridge: Cambridge University Press.

Hunter, R. and I. MacAlpine (1963) *Three Hundred Years of Psychiatry 1535–1866*, Oxford: Oxford University Press. Extracts tracking the 'progress' of psychiatric thought.

Jackson, S.W. (1986) *Melancholia & Depression from Hippocratic Times to Modern Times*, New Haven: Yale University Press.

Kretschmer, Ernst (1925) *Physique and Character*, London: Kegan Paul, Trench & Trübner.

Kretschmer, Ernst (English edn 1934, 2nd edn 1952) *A Text-Book of Medical Psychology*, London: Hogarth Press.

Laing, R.D. (1959) *The Divided Self*, London: Tavistock. This effectively launched British anti-psychiatry. He followed up with *The Self and Others, Knots*, etc.

Lyons, B.G. (1971) *Voices of Melancholy: Studies of Literary Treatments of Melancholy in Renaissance England*, London: Routledge & Kegan Paul.

MacDonald, Michael (1981) *Mystical Bedlam: Madness, Anxiety and Healing in Seventeenth Century England*, Cambridge: Cambridge University Press. Study of a seventeenth-century doctor's notebooks, acclaimed by historians for its new material and methodological innovations.

Micale, M.S. (1989) 'Hysteria and its Historiography: A Review of Past and Present Writings I', *History of Science* xxviii:223–51.

Micale, M.S. (1989) 'Hysteria and its Historiography: The Future Perspective', *History of Psychiatry* 1:33–124. Disputes accounts such as I. Veith's (below).

Porter, Roy (1988) *Mind Forg'd Manacles: A History of Madness from the Restoration to the Regency*, Harvard: Harvard University Press.

Scull, Andrew (1979, reprint 1982) *Museums of Madness: The Social Organization of Insanity in Nineteenth-Century England*, London: Allen Lane (reprint Penguin).

Skultans, Vieda (1975) *Madness and Morals: Ideas on Insanity in the Nineteenth Century*, London: Routledge & Kegan Paul.

Skultans, Vieda (1979) *English Madness: Ideas on Insanity 1580–1890*, London: Routledge & Kegan Paul.

Szasz, Thomas (1962) *The Myth of Mental Illness*, London: Secker & Warburg.

Szasz, Thomas (1971) *The Manufacture of Madness: A Comparative Study of the Inquisition and the Mental Health Movement*, London: Routledge & Kegan Paul.

Szasz's later works suggest that he is more a right-wing libertarian than a spiritual soul-mate of Laing and Co.

Veith, I. (1965) *Hysteria: The History of a Disease*, Chicago: University of Chicago Press.

Wolpert, Edward A. (1977) *Manic-Depressive Illness: History of a Syndrome*, New York: International Libraries Press. Only major monograph on the topic.

Zilboorg, Gregory (1941) *A History of Medical Psychology*, New York: Norton. A classic history of the area and good information resource.

9   Psychology and the brain

Psychology has always been shadowed by the question of brain functioning.
From the late 1600s the brain was understood as the major physical location of
psychological phenomena, although the site of the emotions in particular
remained debatable. With Franz Joseph Gall's craniology (later called
phrenology) in the 1790s the brain, along with the senses, became the principal
meeting-point between physiology and Psychology. Studying the brain
presented unique difficulties. The physical functions of most organs are
reflected in their morphology – e.g. how the heart pumps and the lungs
transfer oxygen from the air to the blood. Brain morphology, by contrast, is
unrevealing, presenting a gelatinous mass within which only the grossest
structural elements are easily discernible – the hemispheres, the major 'lobes'
and the cerebellum, for example. Only around 1800 did Gall and other
physiologists begin to find order in the chaotic folds of the cortex. Thus while
the brain was understood to be the focal point of the nervous system, and
accepted as the seat of consciousness, the manner of its operation remained
totally obscure. The phrenological account looks now to be simply a crude
allocation of faculties to different parts of the cortex, with no genuine theory
about how the brain worked; however, it highlighted, as R.M. Young has
explained in depth, a central theoretical problem, namely that of *empirically*
identifying the various psychological functions themselves.

  The problem arose because the traditional faculties – typically, as we saw,
reason, will, emotion, sensation (memory and imagination were sometimes
added) – tended to have an a priori status as self-evident givens; they had not
been 'discovered' by empirical enquiry. Associationist thinkers from Locke
onwards denied the reality of faculties altogether, seeing everything as rooted in
sensation. The choice was thus between the traditional catalogue and associationist reductionism. The Scottish 'common-sense' school, rejecting both
accounts, produced a more extended catalogue of the psychological 'powers'
deployed in our transactions with the world. Gall more self-consciously
stressed the need to identify these empirically, seeing them as modes of
adaptation serving the organism's survival needs. This 'functionalist' analysis
was radically different from the previously dominant approaches. Gall's
faculties turned out to closely resemble Reid and Stewart's 'powers' and, not

surprisingly, phrenology caught on very quickly in Scotland. Young argues that
the central theoretical issue of empirically identifying the units of functional
analysis relevant for studying brain anatomy was never adequately resolved.
When Gall's faculties were rejected, brain physiologists first simply fell back on
the traditional list, and then recouched the reductionist associationist model in
new terms by replacing 'association of sensations and ideas' with 'stimulus–
response' connections. Although this move retained a 'functionalist' character
by focusing on the organism–environment relationship, it left no place in brain
physiology for the kinds of psychological faculty category that Gall and his
successors elaborated. The brain was simply conceived as a neurological
storage and clearing house where sensory inputs and motor responses were
matched up.

Physiologically, the main difficulty with phrenology was that experimental
demonstration of localisation of brain functioning was extremely difficult, and
ablation experiments by the French anatomist Flourens in the 1840s were
widely believed to disprove localisation altogether – only general behavioural
deficits ensued from removing parts of an animal's brain, not specific losses. By
the 1860s, however, a counter-shift was initiated following the discovery of the
speech area ('Broca's area'), and in 1870, Fritsch and Hitzig reported highly
localised motor regions of the cortex, discovered using new electro-stimulation
techniques. These findings left the theoretical issue of functional units
unresolved since the phenomena that these areas governed were defined purely
in terms of physical movement such as 'opening of mouth and retraction of
tongue' or 'turning of eyes downward and to opposite side'. The speech area
was interpreted in terms of muscular control of speech organs. By the end of
the nineteenth century a new generation of neurologists like David Ferrier and
H.C. Bastian were espousing what they termed a 'new phrenology' – we could
indeed identify the cortical regions controlling certain behavioural movements
– but these were conceptualised as categories of behavioural response which
could be connected to stimuli, no longer as *psychological* functions.

In the 1920s and 1930s Karl Lashley swung the pendulum back against
localisation. His research on rats apparently demonstrated the 'equipotentiality' of different areas of the brain; in other words, destruction of cortical
areas was followed, with a few exceptions, as in Flourens' findings, by a general
performance deficit, not a specific one. Furthermore it appeared that functions
served by destroyed areas could in time be taken over by the remaining brain.

In the 1940s and 1950s Wilder Penfield and various associates again
reversed the picture, their work on the stimulation of human brains exposed
during surgery disclosing very fine-grained localisation – specific memories
would be evoked, or highly distinct smells. Taken in conjunction with the
growing data from brain-damage cases, this was initially greeted as a route for
finally unravelling the functional structure of the brain, but the interpretation
of such findings proved problematic. Basically there is a general problem of
inferring the function of a component of a complex system from the
consequences of removing or manipulating it. Break a button on your

sound-system and you will be unable to control the volume – but volume is not 'localised' in that button. A car engine with a flat battery will not fire, but firing is not 'localised' in the battery; lack of fuel or spark-plugs has the same result. In the absence of some understanding of how the system works as a whole we are merely floundering in the dark. Only rarely, as perhaps in the case of hemispheric differences, can purely empirical data give us relatively unambiguous information regarding structural organisation.

Next question, then – how does the brain work? The history of the study of the brain from this perspective has really been the record of the application of technological and scientific metaphors, particularly those related in some way to the recording, processing and transmission of information (as we saw in the case of Cognitive Psychology). Somehow, it is argued, the formal organisation of the brain resembles that of the technological phenomenon in question. Thus we move from 'telephone exchange' models, common around 1900, through Gestalt's 'field theories' to computing models of progressively greater complexity and chaos theory, not forgetting Karl Pribram's hologram theory of memory. Physiology meanwhile provides increasingly detailed information on the brain's cell structure and neurochemistry. The current task for researchers in this area is primarily to try to integrate the physiological data with models of the formal organisation of the brain's information processing (parallel processing, connectionism and the like). We seem to be reaching a point where expert familiarity with information systems might facilitate recognition of the kind of 'machinery' present in the brain – just as familiarity with pumps and lenses enabled seventeenth-century physiologists to recognise similar machinery in the heart and eyes.

Since the mid-1980s writers such as Roland Penrose have raised the possibility that brain functioning cannot be understood without taking account of the principles of quantum physics. There seem to be fairly good empirical grounds for taking this seriously, and in one sense it marks a return, at a more sophisticated level, to Gestalt Psychology's attempt at incorporating the latest ideas from physics. Reviewing these latest developments is beyond our present scope, but one should note that they entail an interesting shift in our image of the universe which has not been widely recognised. We are now used to the idea that beneath the everyday world of objects lies an arcane realm of atomic and subatomic particles and waves only comprehensible by mathematicians and physicists. We have dealt with this, as the term 'beneath' indicates, by adopting a 'layer-cake' model in which we can ignore the nature of micro-level processes in understanding more macro-level ones. But if Penrose and Edelman (1992) are right, this is too simplistic, at least as far as organic phenomena are concerned, in that such micro-level processes continue to play a pervasive role even in determining the most large-scale phenomena (and you cannot get much bigger than consciousness itself – in which, as St Augustine said long ago, are 'the sky, the earth, the sea, ready at my summons'!). If the 'layer-cake' image is being eroded, then so, in a sense, is the reductionist aspiration itself, to which this image is absolutely central – involving as it does the notion of a hierarchy of 'higher' and 'lower' explanatory 'levels'.

And yet the original conceptual problem of defining what the brain actually *does*, psychologically speaking, what its *psychological* functions are, remains as elusive as ever. Implicit in much of the work on brain functioning is the assumption that since *all* psychological phenomena are ultimately located in the brain, a complete understanding of the brain would be equivalent to a complete understanding of psychology. This leads Paul Churchland, for example, to argue that we will eventually replace what he sees as our crude unscientific folk-psychological vocabulary with an objectively correct vocabulary referring to the physiological events in our brain (which we will somehow learn to perceive introspectively with complete accuracy). Psychology would thus be completely reduced to brain physiology. Probably few would accept quite such an extreme position, but the difficulty is endemic to the field. Obviously the brain *is* ubiquitously involved in all psychological phenomena, but does this mean that all psychological functions and phenomena are, in the final analysis, exclusively physiological? Is it not possible that this conclusion is an error similar to that identified previously – of localising phenomena in single components of a larger system? People do not exist in isolation, and many, possibly most, psychological phenomena pertain to our interactions with others and our environment. A purely *individual* psychological system is actually inconceivable, which suggests that many psychological phenomena are not localised completely in individual brains but emerge within a larger system of interacting brains.

This raises the issue of 'meaning', which warrants a somewhat more extended discussion related to the earlier remarks on language (Chapter 1). Crucially, and highly damaging for reductionism, the two levels of psychological and physiological meaning cannot be fused. While it is common to use physiological expressions to communicate psychological meanings, this only renders them ambiguous. 'This is giving me a headache', for example, may refer to one's physical condition, but may also, psychologically, mean 'this problem is proving very difficult to solve'. As understanding of brain physiology spreads, expressions drawn from this body of knowledge will no doubt be adopted for psychological purposes – people already say things like 'she's a very right-hemisphere person', meaning she's artistic, intuitive rather than rational, and so forth. And I sometimes say 'there's a neurone not firing' to refer to a tip-of-the-tongue experience. (This has already happened with computer terminology. We might say 'I can't access it' rather than 'I can't remember it'.) To put it technically, the truth conditions of the proposition 'she's a very right-hemisphere person' differ according to whether it is understood as a physiological proposition (evaluated by testing her hemispheric dominance physiologically) or a psychological one (observing whether she really is artistic, intuitive, etc., in her overt behaviour and social relations). Whether or not a physiological expression is adopted in this way depends not on its scientific accuracy but on whether it adds a new expressive nuance or has become trendy because it has attracted popular attention, etc. It is not at all clear why one should abandon 'you're making me very angry' and *universally* substitute 'the stimulus configuration you're presenting is stimulating my limbic system' – although there may be particular interpersonal situations in which a speaker might feel that this best captures or expresses what she feels. But this would probably be because something about her attitude to the listener could be communicated, *not* because it was 'scientifically correct'.

In short, there would appear to be large areas of psychological concern where knowledge of brain functioning as such is simply irrelevant even though brain events are indisputably occurring. To claim the converse would be to claim, in effect, that all psychological problems, all hopes, fears, plans, virtues and vices, could, in principle, be cured, enhanced, altered and controlled by some form of surgical or pharmacological intervention. The problem with this claim is not so much that it is false (in some senses it is probably, in the era of Prozac, in fact true) but that it is tantamount to denying the meaningfulness of the psychological level in the first place. Hopes, fears, plans, vices and virtues become mere side-effects of physiological processes which (given the requisite technology) we can hedonistically alter. Rather than change our circumstances or our behaviour, by tinkering with neurones and biochemistry we simply change how we experience the world. But even so, the object of the exercise is to bring about a *psychological*, not a physiological, result. This blurs an absolutely vital distinction between those instances in which the brain *is* genuinely implicated (primarily when something is going *wrong* physically) from those when it is not. Memory loss problems may symptomatize incipient Alzheimer's disease, but they may also arise from a life-style that places too many demands on the memory system.

Although comprised of them, psychology is not just brain processes, and the old problem of the status of psychological concepts and categories persists. We know a vast amount about the neurophysiology of visual perception, but we can say very little about the neurophysiology of 'beliefs' – indeed some writers like Steven Stitch consider 'belief' to be a folk-psychological concept of no scientific value. The fact is, as just argued, that psychological concepts are often simply not *about* physiology or brain processes in the first place, but about, for example, construing and managing interpersonal relations. 'I sorely miss you, my dear, and anxiously await your return' is not a primitive 'folk-psychological' substitute for a 'more accurate' account of brain events. The psychologist's tack in considering such a self-report should surely not be to seek brain processes associated with 'sorely missing' and 'anxiously awaiting' and the state of feeling that someone is 'dear', but to inquire more deeply into the nature of the relationship being signified by this utterance – which could obviously be produced in a variety of situations (and in many tones of voice too). But even more technical Psychological concepts such as intelligence, prejudice, learned helplessness, territoriality and motivated forgetting are not just provisional terms awaiting a 'scientific' physiological synonym. Thus the problem remains of how to relate brain processes *per se* – consisting of neurone firings and neurochemical reactions – to the psychological phenomena that they 'subserve' (as William James put it).

The role of brain research within Psychology is thus rather complex. The role of Psychology in brain research is perhaps more straightforward. Certainly much Psychological theorising is constrained within the terms of current understanding of the brain. It is a necessary condition for plausibility that theories, models and hypotheses be *consistent* with such understanding. It is even more a point in their favour if they heuristically suggest novel ideas for brain-functioning research itself (as much cognitivist work has done). No one would dispute that we now know an enormous amount about brain function-ing, nor that such knowledge is of relevance to Psychology. On the other hand there are, as we have seen, some aspects of the situation that remain problematical. A further conceptual difficulty should also be noted.

Knowledge about the brain influences the psychological categories we use to construe our psychological experience of ourselves and others. Most common in recent years has been the aforementioned notion of hemispheric division of function. Whereas in the nineteenth century the split was between the civilised and bestial halves of our nature, represented by our cortex and more central regions of the brain respectively, we now also see it as between left- and right-hemisphere modes of operating. This is a highly reflexive situation since, quite literally, what is going on is brains construing their own modes of operation in terms of what they believe they have discovered about these modes of operation. If the 'constructs', to use Kelly's term, that we use to construe ourselves are themselves somehow physically embodied in the brain, when they are also derived from our studies *of* the brain it is hard to avoid the conclusion that brains are somehow altering their own operation to fit with how they believe they operate!

Another conceptual problem is locating the source of events. What, physiologically speaking, is volition or 'the will'? Earlier brain researchers progressively pushed this issue ever upwards, so to speak, as their under-standing of neurological functioning pushed higher and higher up the spine, medulla oblongata and cerebellum, finally leaving it aside altogether or getting bogged down in the minutiae of the differences between involuntary and voluntary movement. It is a variation, of course, on the mind–body problem – somewhere in the brain, it seems, is the active conscious person, the agency for whose benefit the whole thing exists. Interestingly some neurologists, such as Sir John Eccles, even today end up opting for dualism. At present this 'agency' question is a matter of intense debate among those interested in AI and the nature of consciousness.

The relations holding between Psychology and brain-function research have never, I think, been entirely happy. Brain research has often been felt to hold the promise of eventually providing definitive answers to questions worrying psychologists, while psychological phenomena have often helped to guide the brain-research agenda. Nor have either of these lacked success. In the end, though, I cannot help feeling that psychologists use contemporary accounts of the brain as metaphors or models for the psychological, or for human nature, which leads to the reflexive circularity noted earlier. Knowing what the brain looks like from the outside might well affect how we experience it from the inside, and vice versa, but neither standpoint can be fully substituted for the other.

Finally, we might ponder a curious fact which is rarely confronted. If the brain is the site of all psychological phenomena, then it must be able to analogue or represent *everything* of which we become aware. Insofar as our knowledge of the world (including brains) actually does resemble the world as it, unknowably, 'really is', it must be because the brain has the capacity to somehow be 'like' that world. Whatever aspects of the world the brain cannot 'be like', it can never know about. At this point we return to Kant and basic metaphysical conundrums. The immediate point, however, is only that this fact – virtually a tautology – must raise doubts about the adequacy of any models and theories drawn from a *sub-set* of our other fields of knowledge (physics, chemistry, computing, etc.) to provide a *complete* account of the brain. One could tangle things yet further, but it is perhaps more prudent for present purposes to call a halt here.

BIBLIOGRAPHY

Further reading

Edelman, G.M. (1992) *Bright Air, Brilliant Fire: or the Matter of the Mind*, London: Allen Lane.
Penrose, R. (1994) *Shadows of the Mind: Search for the Missing Science of Consciousness*, Oxford: Oxford University Press.
Young, R.M. (1970, reprint 1990) *Mind, Brain and Adaptation in the Nineteenth Century*, Oxford: Oxford University Press. Best account of the influence of phrenology via Herbert Spencer and the work of Broca, Fritsch and Hitzig, and Ferrier.

Chronological listing of some key texts

Willis, Thomas (1664 in Latin, 1681 in English, reprint 1965) *The Anatomy of the Brain*, ed. W. Feindel, Montreal: McGill University Press. The beginning of serious anatomical research on brain functioning.
Gall, F.J. (1809) *Recherches sur le système nerveux en général, et du cerveau en particulier*, Paris: Schoell. Full statement of Gall's phrenological theory.
Flourens, M.J.P. (1824) *Experimental Researches on the Properties and Functions of the Nervous System in the Vertebrate Animal*, Paris: Crevot (in French). First major 'anti-localisation' text.
Combe, G. (1836, 4th edn) *Elements of Phrenology*, Edinburgh and London: Maclachlan & Stewart, Longman & Co. Standard account of the developed phrenological model as popular in Britain.
Broca, P.P. (1861) 'Remarks on the Seat of the Faculty of Articulate Language followed by an Observation of Aphemia', trans. G. von Bonin (1960) in *Some Papers on the Cerebral Cortex*, Springfield, Mass.: Thomas. Discovery of 'Broca's area'.
Fritsch, G. and E. Hitzig (1870) 'On the Electrical Excitability of the Cerebrum', trans.

G. von Bonin (1960) in *Some Papers on the Cerebral Cortex*, Springfield, Mass.: Thomas.

Carpenter, W.B. (1874) *Principles of Mental Physiology*, London: Kegan Paul, Trench & Trübner. Abandons phrenological faculties in favour of traditional categories.

Ferrier, D. (1875) 'The Functions of the Brain', in *Manchester Science Lectures*, 7th and 8th series, Manchester: Heywood. The 'new phrenology' accepting localisation of function but abandoning holistic faculties. His books *The Functions of the Brain* (1876, 2nd edn 1886) and *The Croonian Lectures on Cerebral Localisation* (1890) provide the fullest accounts.

Calderwood, H. (1879) *The Relations of Brain and Mind*, London: Macmillan. Comprehensive review of the state of knowledge post-Ferrier, falls back on mind–body dualism with regard to highest faculties and ends on religious note.

Bastian, H.C. (1882) *The Brain as an Organ of Mind*, London: Kegan Paul, Trench & Trübner.

James, W. (1890) *The Principles of Psychology* (2 vols), New York: Henry Holt. See especially vol. 1, chs 2 and 3.

Lashley, K. (1929) 'Brain Mechanisms and Intelligence', in W. Dennis (ed.) (1948) *Readings in History of Psychology*, New York: Appleton-Century-Crofts. See also Lashley reference in Chapter 5.

Campion, G.G. and G. Elliot Smith (1934) *The Neural Basis of Thought*, London: Kegan Paul. Attempts to formulate an account of the relationship between neural activity and thought. Anticipates Hebb's more influential work.

Hebb, D.O. (1949) *Organization of Behavior*, London: Methuen. Incorporates new neurophysiological knowledge in integrating behaviourist and Gestalt orientations. Brain develops by build-up of 'reverberating cell assemblies'.

Penfield, W. and T. Rasmussen (1950) *The Cerebral Cortex of Man*, New York: Macmillan.

Ashby, W. Ross (1952) *Design for a Brain*, New York: Wiley. Applies cybernetic concepts to the problem of simulating brain activity, reports his invention of the 'homeostat' device.

Walter, W.G. (1953) *The Living Brain*, London: Duckworth. More popular, but influential review, with cybernetic/information theory emphasis.

Penfield, W. and L. Roberts (1959) *Speech and Brain Mechanisms*, Princeton: Princeton University Press. Highly important review of direct brain-stimulation findings showing very high degrees of localisation.

Dimond, S.J. and D.A. Blizard (eds) (1977) *Evolution and Lateralization of the Brain*, New York: New York Academy of Sciences. Numerous papers representing the state of play in hemispheric differences research.

Bradshaw, J.L. and N. Nettleton (1983) *Human Cerebral Asymmetry*, New York: Prentice-Hall. Later textbook reviewing the same area.

Jerison, H.J. and I. Jerison (eds) (1988) *Intelligence and Evolutionary Biology*, Berlin: Springer-Verlag. See Deacon's papers reviewing brain-evolution data; other papers set human brain functioning in evolutionary context.

Secondary sources

Danziger, K. (1982) 'Mid-Nineteenth-Century British Psycho-Physiology: A Neglected Chapter in the History of Psychology', in W.R. Woodward and M. Ash (eds) *The Problematic Science: Psychology in Nineteenth-Century Thought*, New York: Praeger.

Fearing, F. (1930) *Reflex Action: A Study in the History of Physiological Psychology*, Baltimore: Williams & Wilkins. Still useful.

Neuberger, M. (1897, reprint 1981) *The Historical Development of Experimental Brain and Spinal Cord Physiology before Flourens*, ed. E. Clarke, Baltimore and London:

Johns Hopkins University Press. The most exhaustive and detailed study of the early period, Clarke's annotations and comments fully incorporate findings of later historical research.

Richards, G. (1992) *Mental Machinery: The Origins and Consequences of Psychological Ideas, Part One 1600–1850*, London: Athlone Press. See chs 4 and 6.

10 Looking at perception

Visual perception has received the attention of scientists and 'natural philosophers' for longer than any other psychological topic. The 'moon illusion' (the moon's, and in fact sun's, larger appearance when near the horizon) was known in ancient times and discussed in the *Philosophical Transactions of the Royal Society* in the late seventeenth century. With the advent of lenses, and optical instruments incorporating them, much attention was paid to optics, the lens character of the cornea being recognised from early on. How far perception was learned or innate was discussed by Locke and his Ulster associate Molyneux, whether a congenitally blind person suddenly given sight would be able to identify shapes becoming known as 'Molyneux's question'. A little later the philosopher Berkeley (1709) addressed the function of binocularity.

During the eighteenth century philosophers argued about whether visual perception was direct or representational, i.e. whether we see what is really before us or only a representation of it in the brain. The latter position can lead to an infinite regress – we have to postulate some internal equivalent of the eye to 'see' the representation and another to see that 'eye's' representation of the representation and so on *ad infinitum*. The 'direct' perception position (strongly advocated by Reid) is also fraught with difficulties since it was appreciated from early on that nothing in the eye itself directly constituted a 'picture' of the outside world, while perception is obviously prone to errors. A more sophisticated version of this controversy continues, as we shall see, to be a major axis of debate.

Not surprisingly it is in the study of perception that we find the first stirrings of experimental Psychology in the early 1800s, primarily in Germany. This was partly because experimental physiology had naturally turned its attention to such phenomena and partly because the validity of sensory perception was becoming an issue of concern to scientists in general. It is in this form that science's data presented themselves, so for the scientist to report data accurately and 'objectively' it is necessary to know what perceptual errors and distortions might enter into the situation. It is no coincidence that colour blindness was discovered by the chemist Dalton, who suffered from it. Historians of experimental Psychology have often not recognised how intimately the early growth of German experimental Psychology was bound up with the rise of the modern scientific laboratory itself and the problems of instrumentation and reliability of data reports to which this was giving rise. The oft-told tale of how reaction-time studies originated in astronomy needs to be understood in this context. A false impression is given that the 'scientific laboratory' was a fully developed pre-existing institution which Psychology simply copied.

The study of perception has never been monopolised by Psychology, and during the latter nineteenth century psychologists such as Wundt, Christine Ladd-Franklin and Carl Stumpf worked in association with physiologists, ophthalmologists and physicists. Subsequently the approaches and interests of these disciplines parted, and by the 1920s perception research had become highly fragmented, but between the late 1850s and *c*.1900 it constituted a fairly unified project. This was due to two main factors: first, it was geographically located almost exclusively in German-speaking countries (an exception being Donders in Holland), and second, it was dominated by a far-reaching and complex theoretical battle between the doyen of German scientists, Herman Helmholtz, and his rival Ewald Hering which served as the focus for everyone in the field whatever their disciplinary allegiances. The Helmholtz and Hering camps were well defined. Those identifying with neither sought a mediating role, but their publications were invariably read as tending to support one side or the other. German experimental Psychology did not therefore begin as an entirely autonomous venture, but as a particular approach to psychophysical phenomena also being studied by physiologists and physicists, the methodologies of all three disciplines developing jointly.

But what was the dispute about? At heart it was about the 'nativism vs. empiricism' issue, and to some extent it created this perennial controversy in its modern form (although Galton too was instrumental in this). Helmholtz espoused a highly empiricist position in which perception was largely the product of learning and experience; Hering, on the other hand, was cast as a 'nativist' (although he disputed the validity of the dichotomy). It centred on two main topics: space perception and, increasingly, colour vision. In essence Helmholtz, drawing on an earlier theory of the English 'natural philosopher' Thomas Young, further developed in the 1840s by Clerk Maxwell, argued for three primary colour sensations, red, green and blue (or violet), while Hering argued for three basic processes, one determining blue–yellow perception, one red–green, and the third black–white (brightness). Each of these was conceived as reciprocally inhibiting, thus we cannot experience mixtures of red and green or blue and yellow, although we can experience bluish greens and reddish yellows, etc. The nativism vs. empiricism issue entered in the following way. Hering was insistent that the task of perceptual theories was to explain phenomenological or subjective experience, which he believed could only be done by relating this experience to physiological processes – the 'psychophysical interface'. From this perspective our colour perceptions were essentially built-in. The Helmholtz view was that the task was to account for the fidelity of perceptual experience to the objectively existing physical world. This left the door open for a greater role to be played by higher-level processing and learned adaptation, as well as a leaning towards a more reductionist, physics-based, theoretical orientation. Thus the absence, in the Young–Helmholtz theory, of yellow as a primary sensation did not matter, as this could be explained as due to higher-level processing. As far as the physics of the eye was concerned, the tri-colour theory sufficed. This oversimplifies a highly complex issue of course, but highlights how an apparently clear-cut scientific question – how do we perceive colours? – can be formulated, and theoretically framed, in radically incompatible terms.

As far as the innate vs. learned controversy is concerned, Turner (1994) argues that even now the controversy has not been entirely resolved, although current understanding of colour perception incorporates both Helmholtzian 'tri-chromaticity' (at the retinal level) and Hering's 'opponent-process' account (at the lateral geniculate nucleus level). In many respects it was irresolvable because the underlying theoretical positions and the language used to refer to phenomena were incommensurable. As historians of science have it, the dispute resisted 'closure'. (Turner, incidentally, suggests that the very nature of their research resulted in the Helmholtz and Hering camps actually seeing the world differently in some crucial respects.) By the 1930s it looked as if Helmholtz's approach had won the day; however, post-Second World War developments have swung the pendulum back to positions bearing a closer resemblance to Hering's account. But even if it ultimately evolved from it, the present situation cannot be easily mapped onto this earlier controversy.

A further, contextual point is worth noting. One reason that colour vision became so important in the 1880s was a Swedish train crash. This, it was believed, happened because a colour-blind railway employee misread a signal. Suddenly the question of railway safety (an intense Europe-wide anxiety during this period) pushed the issue of colour vision to the top of the perception-research agenda.

Until about 1905 research (of various kinds) on the senses dominated laboratory-based experimental Psychology. Subsequently, if no longer so overwhelming, it has remained at the heart of Psychology's experimental enquiries. It constantly impinges on other topics: the involvements of motivation, learning and personality with perceptual performance have been studied from a multitude of directions including the psychodynamic and social. Perceptual processing has been studied in the context of cognitive and information-processing theories, and as bearing on quite fundamental theoretical issues (as in the 'direct' vs. 'indirect' debate). It encompasses psychophysiology at one extreme and extra-sensory perception (ESP) at the other.

From the present angle of interest an obvious question arises – can we find evidence of social and contextual factors operating even in relation to research on such an apparently basic and universal function as perception? The answer is 'yes', but a reflexive point is necessary in order to clarify why. The traditional

'Martian' might ask, 'How does the human species' perceptual system work?' In answering this the alien would first, presumably, study our biological sensory apparatus. But when it comes to the subsidiary question, 'How do humans deal with perceptual problems and difficulties?', part of the answer at least is that they have now evolved a collective strategy which they call 'doing Psychological research on perception'. (Another strategy has been technological expansion of perceptual capacities using instruments such as telescopes, microscopes, radar and thermal imagers – the invention and distribution of which are again collective in nature.) In other words, research on perception is itself part of our species' current perceptual system, coming into play primarily when perception is proving problematic. This ranges from the colour-blindness case just mentioned to the problems faced by Second World War fighter pilots (studied by Kenneth Craik, for example) and the physiology of perceptual processing in a medical (or quasi-medical) context (as studied by, for example, Colin Blakemore). One might also recall that Wertheimer's research on apparent movement, which initiated the immensely influential Gestalt approach to perception, coincided with the advent of moving film. This is not, I stress, a denial that 'basic' or 'pure' research on perception is in some sense possible, or has been and is being undertaken. It is only to draw attention to the enveloping, almost tautological sense in which research on perception is framed within current concerns regarding perceptual phenomena and performance. These *include* current scientific concerns emanating from sources such as broader cognitive theorising, AI and physiology. More obscurely perhaps, they also include current philosophical assumptions about the very nature of the relationship between the world as perceived and the world as it really is (an issue underlying the Helmholtz–Hering controversy). From this perspective 'the Psychology of perception' itself serves a psychological function as a collective aspect of the very process it studies.

There is a risk, however, of casting the Psychology of perception in too sombre a light. Of all Psychology's topics it is probably the most ludic in nature. Like everyone else, psychologists revel in playing games with visual images, exploiting the effects of toying with our perceptual mechanisms and playing tricks on our eyes – a realm that Richard Gregory, for one, has made his own.

We cannot offer here anything approaching a comprehensive review of current research on perception, only sketch the major theoretical issues being tackled. Two approaches now dominate the field. First, the 'ecological' approach initiated by the late J.J. Gibson, which found its fullest expression in Gibson (1979). This is generally held to represent a 'direct' perception position. The visual system has evolved over millions of years to enable us to extract 'invariants' from the information-rich dynamic flow of light in which our eyes are constantly bathed. These pertain to those features of our environment most relevant to survival in our ecological niche. He adopts the term 'affordances' to refer to these, claiming that we see objects directly in terms of what they enable us to do – grasp them, stand on them, eat them, etc. Ultimately this invariant information is about the properties of light-reflective surfaces. This aspect of perception was, Gibsonians argue, ignored in earlier research because it concentrated on unrealistically simple laboratory tasks lacking 'ecological validity'. While this achievement obviously involves complex physiological processes, Gibsonians claim that there is little need to postulate internal representational systems of a cognitive kind – the perceptual system directly ascertains or experiences the real properties of external objects insofar as they are relevant to the ecological needs of the organism in question.

This ran directly counter to the more orthodox tradition of empirical research as typified by Richard Gregory, for example. Those in this camp argue that the vast range of visual illusions and effects signifies that perceptual experience is the output of a highly sophisticated and complicated set of constructive processes whereby the organism creates an image representing the external world from a fairly chaotic barrage of incoming light sensations located at the retina. Progress made in unravelling the neurophysiology of perception since the Nobel Prize-winning research of Hubel and Wiesel (1962) is interpreted as supporting this. The most influential opposition to Gibson, however, has, since the late 1970s, come from those in the cognitivist AI school, in particular those developing an approach initiated by David Marr, who died (aged 35) in 1980 and whose posthumously published *Vision* (1982) is widely considered the most important single text on perception since Hubel and Wiesel's work. Those seeking a full account of his theory should consult one of the numerous current perception textbooks (e.g. Gordon, 1989; Bruce and Green, 1990; Sekuler and Blake, 1994). Marr's model comprises four stages: first, the 'image' on the retina consisting purely of a range of light intensities; second, the 'primal sketch' in which the distribution of changes in light intensity is analysed to yield information about likely surfaces; third, the now famous (or notorious!) '2½ -D sketch' in which surfaces are represented from the immediate standpoint of the observer; and fourth, the full 3-D representation of the world as containing persisting stable objects. Stated thus baldly, it may be difficult to understand all the fuss, but it entailed an insightful analysis of the kinds of question involved in researching perception and, when elaborated, it facilitated the incorporation and integration of a large range of research findings.

To simplify somewhat, we are faced with two broad camps: the Gibsonians, and the cognitivists exploring Marr's ideas and models such as parallel distributed processing (e.g. Rumelhart and McClelland, 1986). Gibsonians may be seen as continuing a tradition of interactionist thought (going back to Dewey) in which the stress is on the inter-relatedness of organism and environment, or even on challenging the objectivity of this very distinction. In Britain a number of psychologists such as A. Costall, J. Good and A. Still are attempting to use Gibson's work as a basis for developing what they call a 'mutualist' theoretical position of a general kind (the anthropologist T. Ingold also has affinities with this camp). This is, in some respects, an attempt at moving beyond simple social constructionism. In perception theory, however, it is widely felt that Gibson was unable to deal satisfactorily with those higher levels of meaningful perception involving knowledge and experience of the world. None the less, even his opponents acknowledge the value of Gibson's demands for ecological validity and his insistence that perception is but one aspect of the total ensemble of our active engagements with the world. The cognitivist approaches for their part are a facet of the wider cognitivist neuropsychology movement, closely linked to AI. While Marr was certainly not guilty of this, the risk here is an unjustifiably reductionist account which, ironically, given the generally positivist aspirations of those involved, ends up espousing a secular parody of Berkeley's idealism – everything is in the brain.

Where does this leave the two perennial issues of innate vs. learned and direct vs. indirect views of perception? There are few now who would see the first as a fundamental question. Most accept that perceptual phenomena range from the 'hard-wired' to those that are almost completely products of learning, training and culture. Some of the hard-wired aspects of perception also appear to require certain environmental conditions to be met if they are to mature, especially during the early months of life. Reading is a perceptual activity *par excellence*, but you have to know the language of the text to be able to do it. On the other hand, there are numerous visual illusions (like the 'moon illusion') that resist all efforts at 'unlearning'. The real task facing psychologists is to gain some purchase on the spectrum from simple physical object or property perception (this is round, or blue) to those capacities for perceptual discrimination requiring expertise and knowledge, but no less immediate for those capable of them (e.g. bird spotters, art connoisseurs, ice-skating contest judges and field geologists). This can be a collective as well as individual achievement – we wonder how on earth anyone was fooled by Victorian fake photographs of mediums exuding 'ectoplasm' or those of the Cottingly fairies, as they now quite simply *look* like fakes. Presumably the stars were seen as seven miles up to our medieval forebears, while to us they look awesomely distant. Gordon (1989) raises the question: 'How is it that so many things from a particular era seem to have something in common: the period style? The cars, buildings, dresses and factories of the 1920s all seem to cohere in a subtle but unmistakable manner' (p. 249). One might add that this extends to 1920s music as well, making it even more puzzling. It has been suggested that we should differentiate between our perceptions of the natural world in which we evolved (to which the Gibsonian account might well apply) and the human-made world, but it is hard to believe that things are quite as dichotomous as that. The real lesson is perhaps that perception (in any modality) cannot be studied in isolation from other psychological processes except with regard to a relatively constrained (though vital) set of questions about its neurological implementation. The innate vs. learned issue ceases to be a matter of fundamental principle and dissolves into a mass of micro-level questions regarding specific phenomena.

The direct vs. indirect issue appears to be of a somewhat different conceptual order. Some of its continuing heat perhaps arises from the lingering persistence of obsolete philosophical connotations which, on closer inspection, do not clearly relate to the specific points now at issue. We tend initially to understand the controversy in terms of analogies drawn from everyday experience. We think of 'indirect' perception by analogy with, say, watching a shopping mall through a CCTV monitor or navigating by radar, 'direct' perception being unmediated looking at the shopping mall or flight route with our eyes. The 'indirect' position is thus thought of as claiming that the 'picture' that we see of the world is like that generated by some kind of in-built TV system. This clearly will not do. Gibsonians have, rightly I think, seen this thinking as a legacy of philosophical dualism in which the mind 'sees' a picture in the head 'representing' the external world. However, few modern psychologists in either camp would espouse mind–body dualism of this kind. So how do 'indirect' theorists conceptualise the 'direct' perception which they are denying? What, in their terms, would count as 'direct perception'? And, conversely, how do 'direct' theorists conceptualise the 'indirect perception' which *they* are denying? What would *they* consider as counting as 'indirect perception'? I would suggest that this is a pragmatic issue of definition. In one sense *all* perception must be indirect since it occurs in the brain, involves complex neurological processes, etc. – but what could 'direct perception' mean in this context? Alternatively these mediating processes might constitute the method *by which* direct perception is achieved. On this basis even CCTV monitors and radar screens could, in McLuhanish fashion, be construed as extensions of our nervous systems and *all* perception be said to be direct. One is bound to wonder whether this amounts to anything more than a dispute about how to deploy theoretically the metaphors 'direct' and 'indirect' – which is not an empirical question at all but a matter of convention.

It then transpires that what Gibsonians and the Marr or Gregory schools are arguing about has little to do with the older philosophical debate. It is a more technical debate about how the 'extraction of invariants' in the optical array presented to the retina is accomplished, and how it should be described, not about how far perception 'really' resembles the objectively existing external world or whether what we see is 'really there'. The latter is generally understood to be a false question, since we cannot know what the objectively existing external world is 'really' like except via our perceptual processes. (We can of course play tricks with visual cues, but these are only remarkable because they *do* contrast with normal, presumably error-free, perception, this presumption itself being a *necessary* one. One should also be alert to the danger of equating *incomplete* perception, e.g. colour blindness, with *erroneous* perception, e.g. in the Ames Room set-up.) In some respects the schools are at cross-purposes. Gibsonians are relatively uninterested in the neurological details of invariant extraction, and more concerned with the holistic level of organism–environment transactions. It thus makes sense to argue that since any species' very survival depends on these transactions, its perception of that environment will evolve in the direction of ever greater accuracy. However 'invariants' are actually extracted, they pertain directly to real features of the perceptual world. The Marr camp is, by contrast, more concerned with understanding the 'how' of the situation as a problem challenging information-processing theory. From this perspective the output of the system must, almost by definition, be some kind of 'symbolic representation'. But again we risk being misled by a metaphor: 'representation'. Literally this means to present again, to re-present – which assumes an initial 'presentation'. A scene 'presents itself' to me and I 're-present' it by drawing a picture or map (the status of photographs is oddly ambiguous here). Taken too literally, therefore, this position seems to be suggesting that there are *no* presentations – only *re*-presentations.

This situation has certain features reminiscent of the ancestral Helmholtz– Hering controversy in that the controversy hinges not on 'facts' but on deeper, almost philosophical, differences. The two parties are asking different kinds of question in the contexts of differing assumptions about what they are trying to explain or understand. The Gibsonians apparently see perception as a central issue in the elaboration of a broader vision of human nature as a whole, as dynamically and actively engaged in, and part of, the world. There are no hard and fast divisions between organism and environment, the innate and the learned, stimulus and response. For cognitivists, by contrast, perception is the most challenging, complex and subtle of information-processing accomplishments. It is managed by a neurological system which possesses properties demonstrably similar to those implementable in electric circuits. The challenge is to understand the architecture of this system – an achievement promising direct pay-offs in the fields of, say, engineering and medicine. The most salient property of the output of this system, however, is the phenomenological or conscious experience itself. At this point the study of perception connects up with ongoing debates in philosophy and AI circles about the nature of consciousness.

Both approaches may, finally, be seen as responses to contemporary challenges to the human perceptual system. In Gibson's case, one need was to relate Psychological work on perception to the real perceptual worlds in which people lived, worlds being rapidly changed by technology (his research began in the context of military research on the spatial perception of pilots). As these technologies required actively engaging the world in novel ways, and on ever greater scales, the dynamic nature of perception came to the forefront. Driving a car at 60 mph raises the role of the flux in the optical array to consciousness in a way that lumbering along in a cart at 5 mph does not. But he was also able to incorporate an evolutionary and 'ecological' dimension into his thinking coincidentally with the rise of ethology and post-behaviourist interest in evolutionary theory. In the case of cognitivist approaches, the challenges range from the medical to extending the capabilities of AI systems. But I will end with a rather different observation: perception has been our species' primary epistemological tool – we gain knowledge by looking and by changing, enhancing and playing with ways of looking. Science has, since the Renaissance, proceeded in tandem with artistic developments of visual media – from the discovery of perspective to time-lapse photography. In studying perception itself we are again engaged in a tightly reflexive enterprise. The perception of objects and the perception of meanings have proved impossible to separate, as have the meanings of objects and how we perceive them. What, then, is going on when we treat perception itself as an object, and whence arise the meanings of what we see when we do so?

NOTE

Although this discussion is restricted to visual perception, which has dominated the field, most of the conceptual points raised apply to other modes. I have also only considered the core area of theories of the visual system although, as indicated, most psychological topics have a perception dimension to them, from attitude studies to Developmental Psychology, from personality (e.g. the Lüscher colour test) to psycholinguistics and non-verbal communication. What I have tried to do here is indicate how even a psychological topic as apparently scientifically 'hard' as perception is not immune to constructionist and reflexive binds. I must again stress, particularly since I suspect that colleagues in the perception field will be inclined to read this chapter as an attack, that, crimes against the primate cortex aside, I have no desire to subvert research in this fascinating area. On the contrary, I am, if anything, trying to suggest how some conceptual difficulties, like the direct–indirect perception controversy, may be overcome.

BIBLIOGRAPHY

Further reading

Boring, E.G. (1942) *Sensation and Perception in the History of Experimental Psychology*, New York: Appleton-Century-Crofts. The most exhaustive historical account available.
Bruce, V. and P.R. Green (1990, 2nd edn) *Visual Perception: Physiology, Psychology and Ecology*, Hove and London: Lawrence Erlbaum. An excellent textbook.
Gordon, I.E. (1989) *Theories of Visual Perception*, Chichester: Wiley. A highly accessible critical overview of the major theoretical positions. A good starting point for anyone new to the topic.
Hamlyn, D.W. (1957) *The Psychology of Perception: A Philosophical Examination of Gestalt Theory and Derivative Theories of Perception*, London: Routledge & Kegan Paul. An interesting, if rather neglected, conceptual analysis of what we mean by 'perception' itself, and how this has been ignored by psychologists.
Koffka, K. (1935) *Principles of Gestalt Psychology*, New York: Harcourt Brace.
Sekuler, R. and R. Blake (1994, 3rd edn) *Perception*, New York: McGraw-Hill.

Additional references

Berkeley, G. (1709, reprint 1957) 'An Essay Towards a New Theory of Vision', in *Berkeley: Essay, Principles, Dialogues with Selections from Other Writings*, ed. M.W. Calkins, New York: Charles Scribner.
Blake, R.E. and G.V. Ramsey (eds) (1951) *Perception: An Approach to Personality*, New York: Ronald Press. This remains an interesting compendium including papers by a number of eminent figures.
Costall, A. and A. Still (eds) (1987) *Cognitive Psychology in Question*, Brighton: Harvester.

Craik, K. (1966) *The Nature of Psychology: A Selection of Papers, Essays and Other Writings*, ed. Stephen L. Sherwood, Cambridge: Cambridge University Press. See the bibliography by Mrs S.J. Macpherson for titles like 'A Note on Windscreen Design and Visibility from Fighter Aircraft' (1941).

Gibson, J.J. (1950) *The Perception of the Visual World*, Boston: Houghton-Mifflin. Gibson's first full-length book containing the initial exposition of his approach.

Gibson, J.J. (1979) *The Ecological Approach to Visual Perception*, Boston: Houghton-Mifflin. His final theoretical statement.

Gregory, R. (1970) *The Intelligent Eye*, New York: McGraw-Hill.

Hubel, D.H. and T.N. Wiesel (1962) 'Receptive Fields, Binocular Interaction and Functional Architecture in the Cat's Visual Cortex', *Journal of Physiology* 166:106–54.

Marr, D. (1982) *Vision*, San Francisco: W.H. Freeman.

Rumelhart, D.E. and J.L. McClelland (eds) (1986) *Parallel Distributed Processing*, Cambridge, Mass.: MIT Press.

Turner, R.S. (1994) *In the Eye's Mind: Vision and the Helmholtz–Hering Controversy*, Princeton: Princeton University Press. A brilliantly researched monograph, insightful at many levels.

11 Some problems with measurement

Measurement has always been central to experimental science and the data with which scientists are happiest are numbers produced by measuring instruments like rulers, voltmeters, thermometers and chronometers. For Psychology, quantifying the phenomena that it studies has been a perennial problem. For many thinkers, like Kant, it was the apparent impossibility of doing so that excluded Psychology from natural science. Furthermore, while, as the American psychologist Thorndike said, 'everything which exists must exist in some quantity and can therefore be measured', the converse is not necessarily true: everything that can be measured does not necessarily exist. This paradox will become clearer later. There is, moreover, the question of the relationship between the measurement as such and what is being measured. How do you measure something without changing it? This riddle arose first in physics (where the answer is an unambiguous 'you can't'), but we are coming to realise that it arises in Psychology too. It must be stressed, then, that the nature of measurement raises deep philosophical questions and present-day historians and philosophers of science have revealed it to be a less straightforward and logical matter than one might initially assume.

The task facing Psychology once it moves beyond simple phenomena like reaction times (RTs) has been identifying overt, publicly 'measurable' indices of the essentially inaccessible phenomena that it seeks to study – like memory, motivation, thinking, imagery, the structure of personality, and intelligence. We saw how the behaviourists tried to solve this by eschewing such topics altogether and concentrating on overt behaviour alone. Even they, however, excepting Skinner, were eventually driven to postulating sundry 'intervening variables'. If we wish to measure, say, intelligence, we have first to select a set of behaviours that we believe displays this. Initially we will be guided by 'common sense' – the notion of intelligence is already well established in 'folk psychology' and its meaningful use presents no great difficulty. Thus ability to do sums is part of its meaning while food preferences are usually not (although eating at certain popular fast food chains might well be!). The things that we select as relevant must have 'face validity' – they must bear some obvious relationship to this ordinary meaning.

But remaining content with this is to accept existing folk wisdom uncritically, abandoning the hope of finding out anything more – we will simply be elaborating on current beliefs, unpacking the 'folk meaning' of a term without challenging it. And what was discovered early in the history of intelligence testing was that some of the things that people assumed were good indices of intelligence barely correlated with others. Given the cultural salience of IQ testing, the history of this topic is a particularly instructive case and warrants examination in a little more depth.

MEASURING INTELLIGENCE

Although a few anticipations have been spotted, the history of psychometrics really began with Galton's use of Cambridge tripos examination results to measure ability but it was obviously necessary to devise other procedures if the project was to progress any further. One major challenge facing him was to devise some way of measuring the variations between people in psychological characteristics in the wake of Darwin's theory of evolution (see Chapter 3). The mathematical basis of this had been laid by Quetelet in the early years of the nineteenth century and was developed further by Galton and Pearson to provide the now familiar parametric techniques for calculating standard deviations and correlation (see Chapter 3). This approach assumed that variations were distributed on a normal distribution curve, thus it became possible to generate scales in terms of either 'decans' or, later, 'standard deviations', the problem now presenting itself being what to measure and how to measure it. Using the techniques for measuring RTs and similar psychophysical phenomena developed in Germany, Galton assembled a sizeable battery of measures which he administered to a large sample of visitors to the Natural History Museum in South Kensington in the 1880s – who paid a penny for the honour. These data provided a basic index of population norms over a number of psychophysical and physical measures.

In the United States Cattell, sharing Galton's assumptions that intelligence and higher-level functions would correlate with such lower-level phenomena as RTs and memory span, embarked on a programme at Columbia University in which all freshmen were measured. Their final degree results were eagerly awaited. When, four years later, they alas proved to correlate poorly with the measures obtained, Cattell's hopes of devising a diagnostic or selection instrument on the basis of such data were dashed. Meanwhile in France, against a background of growing eugenic concern, the Paris educational authorities commissioned Alfred Binet, already renowned for his proto-cognitive work, to devise a way of identifying sub-normal and backward children. With an associate, Simon, he produced the first intelligence test in 1905, comprising a series of tasks of increasing difficulty through which the child had to work its way. The average level attained at each age was identified and on this basis a child could be graded according to its mental age (i.e. the age for which the score that it had obtained was the average). A mental age:chronological age ratio was thus obtainable – later multiplied by 100 (by the German Wilhelm Stern) to provide the now familiar IQ score in which 100 is the average (i.e. MA = CA). The Binet–Simon scale was rapidly adopted by Terman at Stanford University in the United States (who produced the Stanford–Binet test) and Cyril Burt in the United Kingdom. Meanwhile another British psychologist, C. Spearman, was doing similar investigations into children's intellectual abilities and devising statistical techniques for analysing them, resulting in the first version of factor analysis. From his research he concluded that there was a general factor of intelligence *g* plus a number of specific abilities; *g* nevertheless correlated with these and accounted for much of their variance.

At this point IQ measuring was still based on the MA:CA ratio and used almost exclusively on children, who were assessed individually. During the First World War, in 1917, the US Army was faced with the task of evaluating thousands of conscripts and several leading psychologists (headed by R.M. Yerkes) rapidly responded, producing Army Tests Alpha and Beta (for illiterates), 'group tests' designed for mass administration. The MA:CA ratio was, it was realised, meaningless for adults since about the highest achievable MA was 18. IQ was now calculated in terms of deviation from the mean adult score (still scored 100). From then on the devising of tests of mental abilities, both general and specific, took off in a big way, although even by 1914–15 it took Whipple two volumes to review all the Psychological tests available. This burgeoning of the assessment industry was related to America's socio-economic needs, providing techniques for large-scale assessment and evalua-tion of people in relation to occupational choice, educational level and, in the United States, the quality of European immigrants (see Chapter 16). Galton's eugenic concerns indeed underlay the whole movement and anglophone psychometricians espoused strong hereditarian positions (not entirely shared by Binet). A theoretical controversy over the nature of intelligence then erupted, pitting Thurstone and T.L. Kelley – two leading US experts – against Spearman and Terman: namely whether it was multi-factor (Thurstone and Kelley) or 'two-factor' (*g* + specific, as Spearman and Terman claimed). The grounds for this were a mixture of statistical theory and interpretation of experimental findings on transfer of learning, which Thurstone argued showed abilities to be highly specific – even learning poetry off by heart in one language left the ability to do so in another unimproved. Statistically, the controversy hinged around theoretical points relating to extraction of factors using factor analysis. In the intelligence-measuring psychometric tradition nobody, for a while, seemed to be studying intelligence any more, only wrangling about statistics! In a sense the methodology became the theory. The work by Piaget on child cognitive development, Gestalt studies of thinking and the later rise of Cognitive Psychology yielded numerous new theoretical models of intelligence but these were long ignored by the single-factor IQ testers whose only interest was in the data yielded by IQ tests consisting of batteries of items chosen in a more or less atheoretical, intuitive fashion. Although the controversy has never been fully resolved, the single-factor view is undoubtedly theoretically weaker, but the sheer simplicity and appeal of a single number has largely overridden conceptual objections. In the 1930s a new, rigorously standardised intelligence test was introduced, the Wechsler–Bellevue, which came in two versions (plus retest ones): the Wechsler Adult Intelligence Scale (WAIS) and the Wechsler Intelligence Scale for Children (WISC). These soon established themselves as the most widely used IQ tests, the scaling being in terms of standard deviations (each SD = 15 IQ points).

From Galton onwards the psychological meaning of 'intelligence' was continually redefined and rethought, a process marked by considerable controversy. Notably, as we have just seen, was there such a general factor as intelligence at all? Or only specific abilities not necessarily related to one another? If so, how many? More profoundly, is the psychometric approach really the most appropriate method for tackling the issue? And how justified are the hereditarian assumptions of the single-factor school?

One odd consequence of this was that Psychology ended up with two different research areas: cognition or thinking on the one hand, and intelligence on the other. More detailed study of the history of this area would, I believe, yield numerous insights into how, in Psychology, method-ology and theory can get inextricably entangled. There is a risk that the very existence of a measuring technique will mislead us into ascribing an unwarrantedly concrete or objective status to the thing being measured (an error sometimes called 'reification'). This is very evident in Social Psychology's efforts at attitude measurement, which overlaps with the study of personality. Again a look at the history of this area is rewarding.

MEASURING ATTITUDES

In the 1920s social psychologists and personality theorists began exploring ways of measuring attitudes and personality. For Social Psychology, in which attitude measurement was a leading theme (see Chapter 12), questionnaire design assumed great prominence, with Likert and Thurstone introducing their eponymous scaling techniques. A primitive rating scale was used by some phrenologists in the 1840s, and questionnaires are known from even earlier, but major technical issues remained to be tackled if questionnaires were to serve as measuring instruments. The outcome has been a plethora of questionnaire designs ranging from forced choice to seven-point scale and open-ended, as well as statistical procedures for item selection and standard-isation. Designing questionnaires is, of course, not simply a matter of thinking up twenty ostensibly relevant questions and counting up the 'yeses'. I have no immediate quarrel with these procedures. What is of more concern is the status of the things that they purport to measure.

Consider the concept of 'authoritarianism' developed immediately after the Second World War as part of a widespread effort, involving many different kinds of psychologists, to understand Nazi anti-semitism. Some of these came to believe that a particular syndrome or combination of traits was implicated, known as the 'authoritarian personality': authoritarians were rigid and closed minded, intolerant of ambiguity, happiest in hierarchical organisations, held obedience to authority in high esteem, disliked modern art and so forth. One curious point, which immediately alerts us to the problem of how 'objective' such labelling is, was that in the 1930s a Nazi psychologist, Jaensch, arrived at a very similar notion, but his version had the evaluative loading in the reverse direction – his 'authoritarian', the 'J' type, was strong willed, disciplined, had clear unmuddled ideas, etc., whereas the opposite 'S' type – or *Gegentypus* ('anti-type', the good 'democratic' type according to authoritarianism theorists) – was undisciplined, dreamy, changeable, unwilling to respect authority, etc.

But is authoritarianism really a permanent feature of the human condition? Will some people always display this pattern of traits? And how would we find out? This last question brings us back to measurement. We would have to continue administering authoritarianism questionnaires to successive generations over a long period of time, analysing responses to individual items to see whether they continued to correlate. But how would we select the items? The problem is that, of all psychological phenomena, the accepted indices of such attitudes are perhaps the most obviously historically and culturally embedded.

Here are some items selected from the original 1950 'F (for 'fascism') scale' of authoritarianism (all scoring positive):

1 After the war, we may expect a crime wave; the control of gangsters and ruffians will become a major social problem.
2 Reports of atrocities in Europe have been greatly exaggerated for propaganda purposes.
3 Homosexuality is a particularly rotten form of delinquency and ought to be severely punished.
4 Although many people may scoff, it may yet be shown that astrology can explain a lot of things.

Here are some others from Eysenck's 1957 'social attitude inventory' scale (in which he differentiated radicalism–conservatism from tough–tender-mindedness in order to incorporate the existence of left-wing authoritarianism – 'tough-minded and radical' – now required by the Cold War):

1 Divorce laws should be altered to make divorce easier.
2 Birth control, except when recommended by a doctor, should be made illegal.
3 European refugees should be left to fend for themselves.
4 It would be best to keep coloured people in their own districts and schools, in order to prevent too much contact with whites.

A number of difficulties are immediately apparent: some items have changed their connotations (e.g. belief in astrology) or their context (e.g. 'easier divorce laws' – divorce laws *have* since become easier so the very meaning of the item has changed); some are simply obsolete ('after the war');

some, though perhaps still relevant in principle, are couched in obsolete terms (the anti-homosexual item); others have largely faded from public concern (e.g. the birth-control issue). The 'coloured people' item assumes that all respondents are white – in fact none of these 1950s questionnaires could be used to measure either non-white or (somewhat curiously in fact) Jewish authoritarianism. Obviously, if you were starting from scratch in the 1990s you would also include topics absent from the original scales (green issues, privatisation, feminism and drugs, for example). But then comes the crunch – *if you have changed the items, how can you be said to be measuring the same thing?* And with a little historical imagination we can envisage that the typical middle-class Victorian Englishman would probably appear to us as highly authoritarian – even if he was a liberal or socialist. Returning to the seventeenth century, the notions of authoritarianism and radical/conservative would be highly suspect. A seventeenth-century Eysenck would much more likely have devised a 'popery' or 'heresy' scale, depending on his religious allegiance.

Now I am not saying that the authoritarianism concept has no validity – at least at present – nor am I denying that these scales in a sense measured it in the 1950s. What I am suggesting is (a) that the permanent existence of this syndrome is by no means guaranteed, and (b) that keeping our questionnaires up to date would actually reflect a drift in meaning of the concept itself. Moreover, as Jaensch's case demonstrates, in this area it is impossible to eliminate the evaluative connotations of the factor and deal with it in a 'neutral and objective' manner. We all 'know' that authoritarianism is supposed to be bad and being 'democratic' good. And curiously, soon after the Korean War, during which there was an upsurge of concern about alleged Chinese 'brainwashing' of American POWs, psychologists came up with another dimension: 'resistant to persuasion' vs. 'easily persuasible'. While it was, implicitly, good to be 'open-minded', it was also implicitly bad to be 'easily persuaded' (and vice versa for dogmatic vs. resistant to persuasion). In effect the same dimension was available in two versions, depending on which end you wanted to approve!

MEASURING WHAT DOES NOT EXIST

Let us return to a point made at the start – not everything that can be measured necessarily exists. This may sound puzzling, but is actually not so self-contradictory as it seems. The argument is best made using a hypothetical example: were we living in the Middle Ages, we might be very concerned about how devout people were. To measure this, we devise a questionnaire containing such items as 'I prefer reading a holy book to attending a tournament', 'A strange feeling of grace sometimes descends upon me', 'I enjoy attending High Mass', or to counterbalance the direction, 'I often find sermons boring' ('I have never been tempted by lust' could serve as a lie item). It is surely feasible that at the end of the day our 'sanctity scale' would appear to provide a handy way of measuring how holy people were. But no psychologist proposes that there is a measurable 'sanctity' dimension to personality, and not even the most devout psychologists have attempted to devise such a measure. Nor is this as far fetched as you might imagine: among the earliest pioneers of scientific measurement were the fourteenth-century French scholars Jean Buridan and Nicolas D'Oresme whose efforts were spurred by the desire to quantify the amount of grace in communion wafers.

MEASURING PERSONALITY

In personality measurement one major pioneer in the 1930s was Henry Murray whose intensive research programme at Harvard generated the projective thematic apperception test (TAT). More statistically oriented psychologists also turned to personality, believing that factor analytic techniques could unravel the dimensions of personality variation; thus the actual devising of such tests became a research method in its own right. Eysenck had opted for the two-factor extraversion/neuroticism model by the end of the 1940s, producing a forced-choice questionnaire, the EPI (later MPI – Maudsley Personality Inventory), to measure these dimensions. A little later R.B. Cattell, using a different factor analysis (FA) technique, identified sixteen personality factors (to which more have been added) measurable by his '16PF' questionnaire. Another popular US test produced in the 1940s was the Minnesota Multiphasic Personality Inventory (MMPI) which became a standard clinical diagnostic instrument. Freudian ideas inspired such instruments as the Blacky aggression test, relying on the notion of 'projection' (see Chapter 8). The famous Rorschach inkblot test dates as far back as 1911, but rater reliability of its interpretation has proved notoriously low. The Draw-a-Man test was devised by Florence Goodenough (1926) for use with children, first as an alternative way of measuring intelligence, but this too came to be seen as having some of the properties of a projective test and thus usable for personality assessment. While psychologists have continued to identify new personality traits such as level of aspiration, field dependency and locus of control, the underlying conceptual difficulties already mentioned persist: how 'real' are they? How far are they an artefact of the procedures used to 'discover' them? How far are they permeated by culturally contingent evaluative connotations? In personality research one manifestation of this is the long-standing controversy between 'trait' and 'type' theorists. Psychometrically oriented theorists such as Eysenck and R.B. Cattell have favoured 'traits': relatively independent dimensions along which individuals can vary, identifiable empirically from correlations between discrete behavioural units. Others, such as those influenced by Freud or G.A. Kelly, favour more holistic categorisations of people into 'types', emerging from their broader theoretical models.

MORE GENERAL ISSUES

From the start, the overriding task of psychometrics has been to develop techniques for measuring psychological processes by identifying reliable operational expressions of these. This has, however, proved difficult, in spite of its superficial simplicity because part of Psychology's aim is to discover what these psychological processes are in the first place. It is easy to devise procedures yielding numbers which can be treated as scores and submitted to elaborate statistical procedures from which a pattern of some sort emerges – say, a set of factors – of which we have to make sense. The temptation, as we saw, is to treat this as representing some objectively existing reality. It is commonly recognised that behaviours that everyday language identifies by a single classification (intelligent, aggressive, etc.) may not in fact be manifestations of single psychological processes, but may variously lump together more than one such process or be only partial. The task of identifying the underlying processes has gone hand in hand with the project of measuring them, and in FA in particular it was, as earlier indicated, felt that psychometrics was concerned with discovery as well as measurement. The problem with this is its circularity, especially when tackling personality, since there is a difficulty in giving the resultant factors or dimensions a meaning at all unless they can be translated back into everyday psychological language; thus they are either not new or incomprehensible.

It is hard to see how psychometrics alone can actually generate new psychological concepts. However, when we have a non-psychometrically based theory the situation is different, for these may propose genuinely novel psychological concepts or hypotheses which can be psychometrically tested. We should, for example, be able to derive from psychoanalytic theory a series of statements identifying behavioural traits typifying 'oral aggression' and then see if they do in fact correlate. If we succeed, we then pride ourselves on having measured oral aggressivity or our ability to identify 'oral aggressive types'. Similarly, a theory of cognitive development like Piaget's may provide the basis for an intelligence test of more profundity than a purely statistically derived test, measuring specific 'operations' theoretically identified as significant indices of intellectual attainment. *Even so, those with different theoretical preferences, different 'frameworks of meaning', will reject the concepts of 'oral aggression' and 'operations' as mythical in the first place and, if the scores prove technically robust and reliable, will strive to substitute quite different labels.* Again – because you have measured oral aggressivity that does not mean it exists.

Attempts at substituting psychometrics for theory construction have, I feel, not been too successful, notwithstanding the eminence of some of those involved; they, at best, have a practical function enabling the rapid classification of the respondent. Psychodynamics also tend to elude such models. The semantic differential of Osgood, Suci and Tannenbaum (1957) is an interesting case, since it apparently identified three dimensions of meaning that had not been teased out before: evaluative, potency and activity. Yet close examination of this, particularly the 'evaluative' dimension, suggests that some linguistic illusion might underlie the results. The key evaluative term 'good', for example, is highly polysemic, and its apparent dominance does not signify that a single 'meaning' is pervasive ('good' can mean ethically good, functionally good, unbroken or sound, matching a criterion, etc.), only that it can sensibly be applied to almost anything in one sense or another, while other adjectives have less range. Where psychometrics has been successful is in (a) measuring specific abilities where the face validity of equating the ability to everyday classifications is unproblematic, and (b) in theory-related contexts, such as many of the personality and cognitive-style measures developed from the 1950s to the 1970s, although, as already indicated, the reification problem remains.

The final point to be noted is the close intimacy between measurement and technology. The availability of new instruments immediately stimulates us to think of ways of exploiting them. But instruments are not theoretically neutral for they encourage those using them to theorise about their subject matter in the way most consistent with it being amenable to investigation by such instruments. Thus using mazes encourages 'trial and error' theories of learning. Prominent in pre-1914 Psychology textbooks is the 'kymograph' or 'ergograph' (as A. Mosso called his version) – ancestor of the modern recording drum. A role of lampblacked graph paper is wrapped round a cylinder and a pointer scores a line as the cylinder rotates. Psychologists of the day were quite carried away, using this to investigate such things as fatigue, amplitude of finger movements, muscular reactions and the like. At the end of the day they could see that this behaviour translated into a nice wobbly line. Such research yielded many interesting findings, and the data were 'objective', readily quantifiable and so on. Similar techniques are still in our repertoire. But at the same time the ergograph's availability led researchers to prioritise those topics most amenable to it, and to try to think of ways of rendering them so. I recently encountered a saying applicable here: 'When the only tool you have is a hammer everything begins to look like a nail'.

However, the most insidious effect of this kind is that of statistics itself. The use of statistics requires that you design your experiments to fit the particular statistical procedure that you will be employing. But these procedures themselves contain numerous assumptions about the properties of the data to which they are being applied. To some degree they shape the experiments, the kinds of hypothesis that can be tested and the kinds of theory or model that the researcher produces. This is too complex an issue to cover at length here, but recent work by Gerd Gigerenzer has started to unmask some curious problems: in particular – and most tellingly – he shows how the use of statistical methods, which is centrally about calculating probabilities, led psychologists to produce theories that viewed psychological processes themselves as involving quasi-statistical calculations of probabilities. Since their method led *them* to think in this way, they began to believe that *all* thinking was essentially similar.

The growth of psychometrics has, of course, not occurred in a vacuum but may be interpreted in contextual as well as internalist terms. Much of the impetus for devising tests between the wars lay in the needs of US culture generally, and the role of eugenics in the promotion of IQ testing is well known. For psychologists the production of testing instruments was a way of acquiring some expert input into industrial society with its attendant needs for personnel evaluation, certification of expertise, etc. In the United Kingdom, meanwhile, the National Institute of Industrial Psychology was flourishing under C.S. Myers and psychologists were being employed by numerous companies to study factors ranging from fatigue to training, devising many tests on an *ad hoc* basis for particular studies. The market research area has, however, been the greatest commercial beneficiary of psychometrics, exploiting expertise in questionnaire design and administration to produce highly focused evaluations of new products. This may provide us with our closing observations. While market research superficially appears to be about measuring attitudes to consumer products, it more covertly serves to *create* such attitudes where they previously did not exist, thereby producing a cultural climate in which 'consumers' (all of us) become psychologically adjusted to the requirements of the economic system itself. We tend to assume that the questions that we are asked are sensible. Asked whether we prefer jellies to be round or angular, we usually produce an answer – the very question conjures the attitude into existence. More sinisterly, however, it helps to create a population for whom issues such as jelly shape are psychologically important. The act of psychological measuring has changed that which is being measured, 'psychology'.

BIBLIOGRAPHY

Further reading

Gigerenzer, Gerd, Z. Swijtink, T. Porter, L. Daston, J. Beatty and L. Krüger (1989) *The Empire of Chance: How Probability Changed Science and Everyday Life*, Cambridge: Cambridge University Press. See ch. 6 on statistical methods becoming theories.

Hornstein, G.A. (1989) 'Quantifying Psychological Phenomena: Debates, Dilemmas, and Implications', in J.G. Morawski (ed.) *The Rise of Experimentation in American Psychology*, New Haven: Yale University Press, pp. 1–34.

Sokal, M.M. (1987) *Psychological Testing and American Society 1890–1930*, New Brunswick: Rutgers University Press. Explores the cultural dimension of psychological testing and has good coverage of the First World War US Army tests.

Sternberg, R. (1990) *Metaphors of Mind: Conceptions of the Nature of Intelligence*, Cambridge: Cambridge University Press. Excellent overview of concepts of intelligence.

Additional references

For English and American versions of the Binet–Simon test, see the following:

Burt, C. (1921) *London County Council Mental and Scholastic Tests*, London: P.S. King.

Terman, L.M. (1919) *The Measurement of Intelligence: An Explanation of and*

Complete Guide for the Use of the Stanford Revision and Extension of the Binet–Simon Intelligence Scale, London: Harrap.

On the Spearman vs. Thurstone debate and a proposed resolution invoking 'group factors', see:

Vernon, P.E. (1961, 2nd edn) *The Structure of Human Abilities*, London: Methuen.

The 'Likert scale' method of attitude measurement uses a statement with a five-point scale from 'strongly agree' to 'strongly disagree':

Likert, R. (1932) 'A Technique for the Measurement of Attitudes', *Archive of Psychology* 140.

The 'Thurstone scale' offers the alternatives agree/disagree:

Thurstone, L.L. and E.J. Chave (1929) *The Measurement of Attitudes*, Chicago: University of Chicago Press.

Both of these preceded the fully developed factor analytic methods used by R.B. Cattell and H.J. Eysenck.

Adorno, T.W., E. Frenkel-Brunswik, D.J. Levinson and R.N. Sanford (1950) *The Authoritarian Personality* (2 vols), New York: Science Editions. Includes the authoritarianism scales.

Cattell, R.B. (1965) *The Scientific Understanding of Personality*, Harmondsworth: Pelican. Includes his 16PF inventory.

Eysenck, H.J. (1957) *Sense and Nonsense in Psychology*, Harmondsworth: Pelican. Includes his social attitude inventory.

Oppenheim, A.N. (1966) *Questionnaire Design and Attitude Measurement*, London: Heinemann. A useful introduction to the issues as understood up to *c*.1970.

Osgood, C.E., G.C. Suci and P.H. Tannenbaum (1957) *The Measurement of Meaning*, Urbana: University of Illinois Press.

For the 'ergograph', see the following:

Mosso, A. (1906, 2nd edn) *Fatigue*, London: Swan Sonnenschein.

Schulze, R. (1912) *Experimental Psychology and Pedagogy*, London: George Allen.

For a critique of the whole IQ business see:

Gould, S.J. (1984) *The Mismeasure of Man*, London: Penguin.

12 Social Psychology

Of all Psychology's sub-disciplines, Social Psychology is that in which involvement with socio-cultural context is most intense. The priorities, problems and concerns of the societies in which social psychologists live largely determine the matters with which they deal. Their personal social positions, including gender, social class and ethnic group, will, moreover, play a part in determining *how* they deal with them, while, as members of society, they have ideological and political beliefs which may figure prominently in deciding the goals of their Psychological work. Let us consider the nature of Social Psychology at three times and places in this light: France at the turn of the century, the United States between the two World Wars and both Britain and the United States since *c*.1950.

TURN-OF-THE-CENTURY FRANCE

Although Social Psychology's origins date from the late 1700s and earlier nineteenth-century German *Völkerpsychologie* it is widely held that in its modern form it begins with Gustav Le Bon's *The Crowd* (1896). Le Bon, a popular science writer, became an eminent pundit on political and social issues on close terms with leading psychologists, politicians, philosophers and military figures – whose friendships he cultivated at sumptuous gourmet dinners. He was a passionate patriot, loathing socialism and communism and desperate to renew French culture, and this ideological agenda pervaded his Psychology. His concern with the crowd stemmed from several factors. First, ever since the French Revolution (1789) crowds had played a prominent part in French political life – uprisings in 1830 and 1848, and the Paris Commune (1871) being the most notable events. Riots were, however, endemic and the latter nineteenth century was constantly punctuated by violent strikes and left-wing demonstrations. In short, the crowd was playing a peculiarly prominent role in French history, creating a permanent sense of insecurity in its rulers, exacerbated by defeat in the Franco-Prussian War (1870), which had severely wounded patriotic morale.

Second, French Psychological thought as represented in works like Tarde (1890) and wide clinical concern with hypnotism and kindred phenomena, combined with the evolutionary perspective, promised Le Bon seemingly profound insights into crowd behaviour. Graumann (1988) notes the additional impact of the 'contagion' metaphor drawn from the medical discoveries of Pasteur and Koch, which provided Le Bon with his notion of 'mental contagion'. Third, and centrally, he believed that understanding the 'laws' of crowd behaviour would enable national leaders to cultivate patriotic pride and self-confidence. *The Crowd* is thus offered as a resource for enabling France's rulers to maintain and exercise social power in fighting to preserve French civilisation from perfidious socialism. (For Le Bon democracy is only the least worst option, while there is also a racial dimension to his thought – see Chapter 16.)

Le Bon's crowd is a seething, irrational mass governed by 'mental contagion' via the powers of 'suggestion'. Regressing to an earlier evolutionary stage, it can be manipulated by orators skilled in instilling the right suggestions, in a similar fashion to the hypnotist's control of hypnotic subjects. Individual identity disappears, buried within the superordinate, but more primitive, 'crowd mind'. Crowd behaviour is pathological and comprehensible in terms of the new scientific understanding of suggestion and hypnotism. Le Bon seeks to teach society's 'natural rulers' how to use and harness these laws to co-opt and direct the instinctive energies ever threatening to break loose. Civilised white (especially French!) male reason teeters on top of a fermenting unrest. Ruthless mass manipulation and discipline are required to create the new 'race ideal' without which French civilisation must perish.

Le Bon's target audience was receptive, and his views played a major role in determining French military tactics in the First World War (during which he wrote morale-boosting propaganda) – war was a battle of wills, armaments less important than will-power, morale and the blindly loyal obedience of the troops. Mainstream French psychologists like Binet, Tarde, Ribot and Dumas endorsed his analysis. He was a friend of both Raymond Poincaré (later President) and the philosopher Henri Bergson. *The Crowd*, in retrospect, emerges as one of the most sinister modern texts, second only to Hitler's *Mein Kampf*, for we now know that Hitler, Stalin and Mussolini avidly assimilated its message. Mussolini's heavily annotated copy still exists. It *is* nevertheless primarily a Psychology text – offering a theory of crowd behaviour in what were understood as scientifically respectable terms. Thus Le Bon's ideological position can be seen by contemporaries as the scientifically objective and 'true' standpoint.

For several decades European psychologists such as, in Britain, William McDougall (1920) and Morris Ginsburg (1921) tended to follow in Le Bon's wake, seeing their task as understanding the 'group mind' and tracing the psychological roots of the rise and decline of nations and 'peoples'. The idea that the leader–follower relationship resembled that between hypnotist and subject was further developed by Freud (1922), while a tendency to equate social structure with individual psychological structure – the 'masses' representing the unconscious – was endemic among psychodynamic thinkers. C.G. Jung's 'collective unconscious' also had affinities with this concept.

THE UNITED STATES IN THE 1920s AND 1930s

Across the Atlantic, however, things were taking a different turn. Prior to the Second World War at least thirty-five books appeared in the United States with the phrase 'Social Psychology' in their titles, the earliest by Ellwood (1901). Previously the sociologist Lester Ward had published *Psychic Factors in Civilization* (1892), while the first US Social Psychology experiment was published by Triplett in 1898. The most eminent 1920s pioneers were Floyd Allport and Emory Bogardus. Particularly interesting for us, however, is James M. Williams' *Principles of Social Psychology* (1922). For Williams, Social Psychology is 'the science of the motives of people living in social relations' (p. 2). Motives are based on instincts which are moulded by learning and habit into 'dispositions'. Once established, these tend to be conservative although modern developments like immigration and greater information are weakening this. The mechanism underlying social relations is how conflicts of interest are negotiated. This, in brief, is his core psychological model – a picture of behaviour as instinctively rooted but extremely flexible, with social relations being determined by the management of differences in interests. Nothing here about suggestibility or atavistic regression to earlier states, and very little interest in the crowd at all. Two-thirds of the chapters are organised under six broader headings of the form 'The Conflict of Interests in ... Economic Relations/Political Relations/Professional Relations/Family Relations/Cultural Relations/Educational Relations'. He ends with 'The Social Reactions of Suppressed Impulses' – all social organisation requiring some 'suppression of impulses'. Even this, however, is not tackled psychodynamically, being devoted to the effects of slavery, class control and military suppression.

Unlike Le Bon's world, Williams' is that of the professional businessman, teacher and American family life. No deep-seated military caste is present as in France, or mystical fantasising about national souls and 'race ideals'. Le Bon is not even referenced. Williams' interests are more immediately practical – 'Labor Relations', education, medical ethics and such, covering virtually every facet of social life including art and religion. Like much work during this period it hovers between sociology and Psychology, but his central explanatory level is, as we saw, the Psychological one. The major difference between this and the Social Psychology that began to appear later in the decade is that Williams does not see it as an experimental discipline. Rather, it requires immersion in specialist information from disciplines like economics, sociology and history. His bibliography is actually quite extraordinary – a book on artificial-flower makers, others on coal-mine workers and tramps, these jostling with Thorndike and Titchener, Theodore Roosevelt's autobiography, a biography of Brahms and reports from the US Supreme Court.

America's geographical isolation perhaps made the 'national character' issue, so dominant in Europe, relatively unimportant – but in any case it was a society self-consciously building a new culture, not having to maintain long-standing sets of values, customs and social class interests (although in reality the defence of established WASP economic interests against black and South European immigrant aspirations was quite passionate).

By 1930 US Social Psychology's methodology is rapidly changing. Thorndike and Likert have introduced their methods of questionnaire design and attitude scaling, while much pioneer empirical research dates from this period, such as LaPiere's famous 1934 experiment on prejudice involving ringing up a restaurant to book a table for a party including Chinese guests. The often cited Hartshorne and May experiments on honesty in children were reported 1929–30 and Sherif (1936) published experimental studies of group effects on perception. Monographs appear on such topics as the psychological effects of unemployment, mass media, public opinion formation, race prejudice, delinquency, industrial conflict and language. G.H. Mead's extensive study of the social processes by which the 'self' is formed also appears, but this remained somewhat marginalised until the 1960s and yielded no immediate body of empirical experimental research. The influence of anthropological work on child-rearing and gender roles by Margaret Mead and others must also be noted as a factor affecting accounts of the family and child development (as well as the 'race' issue) at this time.

Overall, what we are seeing during the inter-war period in the United States is the creation of an experimental Social Psychology to provide both commentary on, and insight into, numerous social phenomena and problems – from 'race' to radio, industrial relations to crime. In doing so it largely abandons the European tradition, becoming resolutely individualist, a tendency culminating, it has been claimed, in Murchison (1935). It is overridingly pragmatic and practical in orientation, though somewhat influenced by the general behaviourist climate. If there was an ideological agenda it tended, in the 1930s, to be a 'New Deal' Rooseveltian liberal one. Dunlap (1934), for example, is hostile to 'racial psychology', wary of the 'civilised' vs. 'primitive' polarity, is very sympathetic to women, and views eugenics with scepticism. At this time too, however, Social Psychology splits into Psychology-oriented and sociology-oriented camps (a division in the offing since the previous century). Space constraints preclude further discussion of this here.

It is pertinent at this point to consider a central feature of US culture: the ubiquitous demands, arising from its distinct political and economic character, for feedback regarding the effects of behaviour. Politics requires constant information about reactions to political decisions and the state of public opinion. Effects of campaigning and lobbying demand rapid assessment. If true to some extent of all Western democracies, this operates in the United States at a unique pitch – far more civil posts are elected than in Britain, and in some states changes in the law can be achieved by putting 'propositions' on the ballot. Similarly, from an earlier date than elsewhere, the US market economy hinged around market research and assessing the effectiveness of advertising and brand-image promotion. To a degree unknown in Britain, Americans are voting from their first school-days onwards – from whether to permit gum-chewing in the playground to the classmate most likely to succeed. In this climate attitude assessment assumes great importance. – and it was around this, above all, that US experimental Social Psychology crystallised in the 1930s. The specifically American context provided both setting and rationale for the exploration of attitudes and all that comprises – measurement, how to change them, their motivational roots and structure. This is, in principle, ideologically neutral – anyone can use knowledge of attitude change techniques. Few shared French worries about the security of existing political institutions, national morale, and unruly mobs regressing to primitive bestiality and threatening civilisation. Rioting may happen of course – indeed it does – but it is no longer construed in a degenerationist framework (I have identified only one pre-1940 US book on the crowd, by Everett D. Martin, 1920, which barely mentions Le Bon). For a Le Bon measuring people's attitudes would have seemed unimportant – using 'crowd psychology' effectively, rulers can instil whatever attitudes they want. Even if covertly, there is then an implicit ideological assumption in US Social Psychology's concern with attitudes – a belief in collective democratic procedures of decision-making as against, say, belief in a class of natural leaders, obedience to whom is the natural order of things.

BRITAIN AND THE UNITED STATES IN THE 1960s

British Social Psychology only emerged as a distinct sub-discipline after the Second World War. While this largely reflected the importation of US methods and concerns, there were some distinctive features of British Social Psychology at this time. First, British social psychologists (such as Basil Bernstein in his work on language, 1971) took social class far more seriously than their American counterparts. Like British sociologists, they treated social class as a cultural as well as economic variable. While this may actually also be true of the United States, cultural differences between British social classes were far more evident, being both longer established and sustained by lower levels of social mobility. While British social psychologists tended, ideologically, to be on the left in an oppositional role, in the United States they tended to support a prevailing egalitarian ideology in which the admission of fundamental social class differences was heretical. Second, the British did not initially always take that easily to the questionnaire-based research methodologies developed across the Atlantic. Some, like Michael Argyle, much preferred a more discreet observational style (although US psychologists also deployed observational techniques). This lent itself to the study of topics like interpersonal distance and non-verbal communication. Third, the long-standing nativist strand in British Psychological thought made some in the field more receptive to ideas from ethology than their US colleagues. As discussed in Chapter 14, this work had considerable impact during the 1960s. By and large, however, these factors did not entirely differentiate the British and US traditions, the former really representing a regional variant on the latter.

Post-war US Social Psychology revolved around a number of key themes: the complex of issues related to authoritarianism, conformity and prejudice; small group dynamics and the nature of 'leadership'; the broader area of attitudes; communication and media; and, on the sociology border-line, the area known as 'role theory'. Only a few can be sketched here.

As discussed in Chapter 11, following the Holocaust psychologists were naturally preoccupied with trying to understand how Nazism arose and operated. Thereafter a substantial sector of US Social Psychology became even more closely engaged with contemporary events. While Adorno et al.'s *Authoritarian Personality* (1950) dealt primarily with anti-semitism and identifying a distinct authoritarian personality type, priorities rapidly shifted as the civil rights movement grew and the Afro-American's plight took centre stage. In this context Social Psychology effectively became part of the intellectual wing of the civil rights movement. Since the 1930s Social Psychologists had come to view 'prejudice' as a form of psychopathology and proposed linkages between prejudice and other negative personality attributes. In doing so they were really adopting a tactic akin to Le Bon's – if from a diametrically opposite direction. Opponents of civil rights were not simply espousing a different opinion, they were people who we could 'objectively' and 'scientifically' demonstrate had something wrong with them. This is not a criticism: the lesson is that issues like 'prejudice' simply *cannot* be addressed from a neutral position – your very language will be loaded with evaluative meanings, while almost certainly your underlying motivation will be, to some degree, ideological. A tendency to objectify or naturalise ideological positions or values is endemic to 'social science'.

Among the attitude theorists, one of the most stimulating was Leon Festinger whose 'cognitive dissonance theory' in effect married Cognitive Psychology to Freudian notions of 'rationalisation'. This had the appeal of coming to occasionally counter-intuitive conclusions – e.g. people read advertisements more *after* purchasing the product than before. He identified numerous 'dissonance reducing strategies' used to resolve cognitive dissonance – a situation arising when one cognitive element (e.g. I am a good mountaineer) implies the opposite of another (e.g. I just fell from a 3-foot ladder). This yielded an exhaustive elaboration of the rationalisations that we use in such situations. As a scientific theory in the orthodox sense it was flawed perhaps in that it could account for any outcome (although Festinger and his associates undertook much empirical research). One of the best-known studies was of a sect that believed that the end of the world was due on a certain date (Festinger, Riecken and Schachter, 1956). Taking advantage of this, the sect's career was traced up to, including and following the fateful day. The dissonance involved – 'I believed that the end of the world was coming yesterday' and 'It didn't' – could hardly be greater. It was found that sect members unable to be with the others on the day in question quickly defected, whereas the rest became more evangelical and outgoing (having previously been an inward-looking group) in the aftermath of the failed prophecy. Their faith had been tested and not found wanting, thereby averting God's apocalyptic wrath.

The study of language expanded rapidly in the post-war years, stimulated by the rise of Cognitive Psychology. Roger Brown, Jerome Bruner and Charles Osgood published numerous works on its social psychological aspects: Brown (1958), Bruner, Olver, Greenfield et al. (1966) and Osgood, Suci and Tannenbaum (1957) being among the most important. Studies of primate language acquisition were one strand in this. This American work was rather different from Bernstein's research on social class differences in language, concentrating on its developmental aspects and the nature of 'meaning'.

Another research area which briefly flourished between 1953 and 1961 was 'achievement motivation', or 'n.Ach.' ('need for Achievement'), a concept initially introduced by the personality theorist Henry Murray. David McClelland and his associates attempted to develop this into a major social psychological variable, believing that achievement motivation levels in different cultures and societies could be measured and compared. Again, the economic circumstances and Cold War climate of the 1950s obviously provided a favourable background. This was even truer of the large body of group dynamics and leadership research, primarily funded by either the US Office of Naval Research or the US Air Force, as well as the Rockefeller Foundation and Carnegie Corporation. Much of this was brought together in D. Cartwright and A. Zander (1953), which remains invaluable in providing a picture of the state of play in this field in the mid-1950s.

As the Vietnam War took its toll during the 1960s, US Social Psychology became deeply embroiled – many in the discipline opposed the war, while others joined the US military's 'psy ops' (psychological warfare) programme. Anti-war activists eagerly applied Psychological concepts and theories to government policies – authoritarianism, scapegoating, inappropriate cognitive dissonance reduction strategies, displaced aggression, etc., could all be unmasked. Together with continued involvement in the intensifying civil rights struggle, by the end of the 1960s this was pushing sections of US Social Psychology into a more oppositional role *vis-à-vis* official policies on both foreign and domestic issues. Precisely because social psychologists had raised so many irrational social processes to conscious awareness, collusion with their continued operation in public life became more difficult.

In the early 1970s, however, Social Psychology entered a period of crisis. Two decades of increasingly sophisticated and reflective thinking about social behaviour finally yielded a growing suspicion that an objective, scientific, 'neutral' view of social psychological phenomena was unattainable. At this point, with growing pressure from feminists, blacks and gays, Kenneth Gergen (1973) began to argue for a more up-front social constructionist position, acknowledging the historical nature of the subject. By the mid-1970s much of the classic attitude literature was looking quite inadequate as more complex approaches – such as attribution theory – began to make headway.

The reasons that post-war US Social Psychology expanded and developed as rapidly – and in the directions – it did, did not lay in its socio-political setting alone. It had also attracted eminent exiled European psychologists, often unable to find positions in the discipline's more central areas (e.g. the Gestalt psychologists mentioned in Chapter 6). In some respects therefore it was a sub-discipline of a perhaps unusually high intellectual calibre. Submitting the issues vexing their host society to an outsider's gaze, they adopted an increasingly critical stance. In Britain in the meantime, with a closer exposure to contemporary developments in European thought, the move towards a constructionist position was possibly more easily achieved, aided by the more sociologically conscious character of British social psychological thought. On the other hand, European (including British) Social Psychology never achieved the cultural prominence that it enjoyed in the United States between 1950 and 1970.

Because Social Psychology is especially closely embedded in the concerns and priorities of its host societies, this does not mean that insights are not transferable – although sometimes they may not be. It does mean that, being aware of this embeddedness, social psychologists now find themselves in a rather uncomfortable position, half inside, half 'objective observers' of, the contemporary social world which they study. Few now would be as happy as Le Bon to ally themselves uninhibitedly with established agencies of social power. On the other hand, few desire permanent outsidership. In practice, one suspects, many contemporary social psychologists prefer focusing on specific micro-level problems (e.g. public perception of disabilities), where they can effectively work for change, to open ideological confrontation and grand theorising. Others, meanwhile, are further developing the constructionist approach by looking at some of the traditional topics of experimental Psychology, like memory, and how far they have a transpersonal social dimension which must be addressed (Middleton and Edwards, 1990; Parker and Shotter, 1990).

BIBLIOGRAPHY

Further reading

Allport, G.W. (1954) 'The Historical Background of Modern Social Psychology', in G. Lindzey (ed.) *Handbook of Social Psychology, Vol. 1: Theory and Method*, Reading, Mass. and London: Addison-Wesley. This rather orthodox account remains useful but has since been criticised by writers such as C.F.Graumann.

Graumann, C.F. (1988, reprint 1989) 'Introduction to a History of Social Psychology', in M. Hewstone, W. Stroebe, J.-P. Codol and G.M. Stephenson (eds) *Introduction to Social Psychology: A European Perspective*, Oxford: Basil Blackwell, ch. 1.

Karpf, F.B. (1932, reprint 1972) *American Social Psychology: Its Origins, Development, and European Background*, New York: Russell & Russell. A comprehensive study of the earlier phase.

Primary sources

Adorno, T.W., E. Frenkel-Brunswik, D.J. Levinson and R.N. Sanford (1950) *The Authoritarian Personality* (2 vols), New York: Science Editions.

Argyle, M. (1967) *The Psychology of Interpersonal Behaviour*, Harmondsworth: Pelican.

Atkinson, J.W. (ed.) (1958) *Motives in Fantasy, Action, and Society*, Princeton, N.J.: Van Nostrand.

Bernstein, B. (1971) *Class, Codes and Control*, London: Paladin.

Brown, R. (1958) *Words and Things*, New York: Free Press.

Bruner, J., R.H. Olver, P.M. Greenfield et al. (1966) *Studies in Cognitive Growth*, New York: Wiley.

Cartwright, D. and A. Zander (eds) (1953) *Group Dynamics: Research and Theory*, Evanston, Ill.: Row, Peterson; London (1954): Tavistock.

Dunlap, K. (1934) *Civilized Life: The Principles and Applications of Social Psychology*, Baltimore: Williams & Wilkins.

Ellwood, C. (1901) *Some Prolegomena to Social Psychology*, Chicago: Chicago University Press.

Festinger, L. (1957) *A Theory of Cognitive Dissonance*, New York: Row, Peterson.

Festinger, L., H.W. Riecken, Jr. and S. Schachter (1956) *When Prophecy Fails*, Minneapolis: University of Minnesota Press.

Freud, S. (1922) *Group Psychology and the Analysis of the Ego*, London: Hogarth Press.

Gergen, K.J. (1973) 'Social Psychology as History', *Journal of Personality and Social Psychology* 26:309–20.

Ginsburg, M. (1921) *The Psychology of Society*, London: Methuen.

Hartshorne, H. and M.A. May (1929–30) *Studies in the Nature of Character*, New York: Macmillan.

LaPiere, R.T. (1934) 'Attitudes and Actions', *Social Forces* 13:230–7.

Le Bon, Gustav (1896) *The Crowd*, London: Fisher Unwin.

McClelland, D.C. (ed.) (1955) *Studies in Motivation*, New York: Appleton-Century-Crofts.

McClelland, D.C. (1961) *The Achieving Society*, Princeton: Van Nostrand.

McClelland, D.C., J.W. Atkinson, R.A. Clark and E.L. Lowell (1953) *The Achievement Motive*, New York: Appleton-Century-Crofts.

McDougall, W. (1920) *The Group Mind*, New York and London: Putnam.

Martin, E.D. (1920) *The Behavior of Crowds: A Psychological Study*, New York: Harper.

Mead, G.H. (1934) *Mind, Self, and Society: From the Standpoint of a Social Behaviorist*, Chicago: Chicago University Press.

Mead, M. (1928) *Coming of Age in Samoa*, New York: Morrow.

Mead, M. (1930) *Growing Up in New Guinea*, New York: Morrow.

Middleton, D. and D. Edwards (1990) *Collective Remembering*, London: Sage.

Murchison, C.A. (ed.) (1935) *Handbook of Social Psychology*, Worcester, Mass.: Clark University Press.

Murray, H.A. (1938) *Explorations in Personality*, New York: Oxford University Press.

Osgood, C.E., G.C. Suci and P.H. Tannenbaum (1957) *The Measurement of Meaning*, Urbana, Ill.: University of Illinois Press.

Parker, I. and J. Shotter (eds) (1990) *Deconstructing Social Psychology*, London: Routledge.

Sherif, M. (1936) *The Psychology of Social Norms*, New York: Harper.

Tarde, G. (1890, Eng. trans. 1903) *The Laws of Imitation*, New York: Holt.

Triplett, N. (1898) 'The Dynamogenic Factors in Pacemaking and Competition', *American Journal of Psychology* 9:507–33.

Ward, Lester (1892) *Psychic Factors in Civilization*, Boston: Ginn & Co.
Williams, J.M. (1922) *Principles of Social Psychology*, New York: Knopf.

Secondary sources

Brown, R. (1965) *Social Psychology*, New York: Free Press. One of the best 1960s textbooks, providing an excellent picture of contemporary concerns.
Graumann, C.F. and S. Moscovici (eds) (1986) *Changing Conceptions of Crowd Mind and Behavior*, New York: Springer-Verlag.
LaPiere, R.T. and P.R. Farnsworth (1949, 3rd edn) *Social Psychology*, New York: McGraw-Hill. Has an enormous bibliography.
Nye, R.A. (1975) *The Origins of Crowd Psychology: Gustav Le Bon and the Crisis of Mass Democracy in the Third Republic*, London and Beverly Hills: Sage.

13 Psychology and the child

Since ancient times children have been scrutinised by savants, philosophers and (later) scientists, and became one of Psychology's most important subject groups. Books on education and child-rearing began appearing in the sixteenth century and a modern 'Psychological' approach is discernible in John Locke's *Some Thoughts Concerning Education* (1693). During the latter 1700s a plethora of educational works appeared inspired by Rousseau's *Emile, ou de l'éducation* (1762). In Britain Richard and Maria Edgeworth, Thomas Day, Elizabeth Hamilton, Erasmus Darwin, Joseph Priestley and Hannah More were among the most important writers, while in mainland Europe Pestalozzi and Herbart further developed Rousseau's ideas. In the 1820s Friedrich Froebel, inventor of the 'kindergarten', developed an advanced system of primary education. By the mid-1800s 'sub-normal' children were receiving attention from the French educationist Séguin, the Swiss Güggenbühl and the American Gridley Howe. This topic may be dated to Itard's efforts at educating Victor (see Chapter 2). Later in the century, as explained in Chapter 3, child study acquired a new significance in the light of the evolutionary idea of 'recapitulation'.

In this chapter I will explore the 'images' of the child that have underlain Developmental Psychology. All cultures produce such images to guide and justify child-rearing and educational practices, and in European cultures some have served, often covertly, to underpin Psychological work. It is, I suggest, the presence of such underlying meanings of childhood that accounts in part for the diversity of approaches that Developmental Psychology has taken.

To bring some order to this we can identify the following images:

1 Empiricist (originating with Locke).
2 Romantic (originating with Rousseau).
3 Evolutionary (originating with Darwin and Haeckel).
4 Behaviourist (developed most notably by J.B.Watson).
5 'Christian' (the child as innately sinful, which affected nineteenth-century popular attitudes towards child-rearing).
6 Psychodynamic (primarily from Freud, but with several variants).
7 Ethological (later version of the evolutionary image).

8 Social constructionist (e.g. Vygotsky and social constructionist approaches to gender identity formation).
9 Existentialist (e.g. in Laing's account of the origins of schizophrenia).
10 Cognitive (e.g. Jerome Bruner).

Two important dimensions of variation underlie these. The most obvious is how far innate factors are invoked as opposed to learning and experience – the 'nature–nurture' question. The second may be termed 'optimism vs. pessimism' – optimistic images include both the romantic and behaviourist, pessimistic ones both the Freudian and existentialist (though not in all versions). There is no clear-cut correlation between these two dimensions. Individual psychologists may well, of course, incorporate elements of more than one image into their thinking.

Of all these, the most deeply influential has been the romantic image. Its central feature as formulated by Rousseau, Pestalozzi and Froebel is the notion that the child contains the innate potential for a more or less unique fulfilment – an explicit metaphor is frequently that of the seed and the flower with the educator cast as gardener. Given a sufficiently nurturing and insightful developmental regime, the essentially good child fulfils this potential, maturing into an integrated and happy adult. The educator must attend to the child's individual needs, identifying its strengths and helping it to overcome weaknesses. This notion of the flowering of an individually unique potential has been a persistent theme in European developmental thought.

The precise terms in which writers developed the romantic image were affected by their broader philosophical and religious allegiances, thus Froebel's system is structured around a triad of faculties: feeling, doing (the will) and thinking constituting a 'tri-unity' which must be developed in balance with each other. This is fairly typical of contemporary German *Naturphilosophie*, but Froebel gives it a more pious spin by equating these with love, life and light respectively, which in turn signify humanity, nature and God. Notwithstanding its very devout character, Froebel's system was based on intense study of children and implemented in his own pioneering educational practice. He stressed how the three faculties must all be kept involved and placed great emphasis on mother–child interactions. He even identified a very early 'sucking-in' phase, adumbrating Freud's 'oral' stage. Herbart, for his part, more sternly stressed the need to help the child to develop a strong will to rein in its unruly instincts.

While the evolutionary image somewhat darkened the picture, the romantic image of childhood was readily incorporated by evolutionary writers like James Sully – for whom infancy remains a golden age, a state of enchanted consciousness with which we have great difficulty in regaining contact. Clearly the doctrines of recapitulation and 'unfolding inner potential' bear some resemblance to one another, detectable in the ongoing predilection of European psychologists for stage theories of development. Nor has the view that childhood provides a route for gaining access to earlier stages of human evolution entirely disappeared. Although no longer pursued in recapitulationist terms, human evolution research has rediscovered a place for the child in comparative studies of child and primate development.

While one could not strictly call Piaget a romantic, his image of a natural dynamic unfolding process of cognitive and moral development clearly descended from the romantic tradition; he also taught in Geneva at the Institut Rousseau – the choice of name being no coincidence. (Jung's concept of individuation, along with that of archetypes, as well as his tendency to quote Goethe at the drop of a hat, clearly place him in this lineage too, although he did not deal extensively with child development.) The German Wilhelm Stern (1924), while attempting to reconcile empiricist and nativist approaches, again stressed the holistic and active nature of development and reiterated the 'gardening' analogy. The Gestalt psychologist Koffka (1928) was far less romantic in tenor, but once more expounded a holistic model of the developmental process.

In general, while the recapitulationism of such pioneer child psychologists as Preyer, G.S. Hall, Claparède, Groos, Stern and Sully is theoretically distinct from Romanticism, the enthusiasm with which European writers adopted this approach owed much to its perceived continuity with the traditional romantic 'unfolding' concept of the child. Only perhaps in Freud was this romantic connotation explicitly dismissed. Romantic optimism resurfaced dramatically after the Second World War in US humanistic Psychology and post-Freudianism. Once more the goals of 'self-realisation' and 'individualisation' are held up as 'natural' outcomes of truly healthy development. One should also mention the Adlerian variant of psychodynamic theory with its focus on the striving, power-seeking nature of development (it was Adler who coined the term 'inferiority complex'). Such approaches in turn affected American popular views on child-rearing, notably the rise of 'permissive' approaches (famously associated with Dr Spock) calculated to avoid creating neuroses and other debilitating hang-ups in the child.

The Psychological legacy of this image may be identified therefore in the following: (a) belief in a realisable innate potential, (b) a holistic concept of development, (c) tendency towards stage theories and models, (d) a view of the child as actively participating in its development (although emphasis on this varies), and (e) belief in a qualitative difference between child and adult modes of consciousness.

The opposite 'Lockean' camp has also always had powerful advocates, except during the heyday of recapitulationism. For them development is essentially a process of learning, and adult character a product of developmental experience. Instincts are downplayed, or even ignored. Up until the early 1800s this was most popular in Britain, but in modern Psychology it has taken three major forms, North American behaviourism and two more socially oriented, often ideologically left-wing, European versions. For Watson the child was almost entirely malleable by applying learning-theory principles. His project was to create scientific child-rearing methods that would eliminate the deleterious consequences of irresponsible parenting and excessive 'love-conditioning' (especially by mothers), which rendered children emotional, dependent, undisciplined and unhappy. Watson (1928) is a rich source of material, stating this in terms that now sound quite extraordinary.

> There is a sensible way of treating children. Treat them as though they were young adults. Dress them and bathe them with care and circumspection. Let your behavior always be objective and kindly firm. Never hug and kiss them, never let them sit in your lap. If you must, kiss them once on the forehead when they say good-night.
>
> (pp. 81–2)

There is much more in this vein. Watson was extreme even by US standards. His contemporary Arnold Gesell embarked on a large-scale empirical investigation of child development norms guided by a more orthodox biological–evolutionary orientation. Nevertheless the underlying rationale for this was also to provide firm scientific data to inform child guidance clinics and child-rearing advice manuals.

The factors behind the emergence of this unromantic view of child-rearing are complex but two may be singled out here: first, the absence of elaborate indigenous folk wisdoms regarding child-rearing, such as there were originating in the old self-reliant pioneering rural culture, a culture often infused with fairly extreme Protestant attitudes. Second, there was the future-oriented nature of US society with its belief in scientific and technological solutions to social problems. The thesis of an entertainingly polemical feminist analysis by Ehrenreich and English (1979) is that child-rearing practices are determined by economic needs and interests, the behaviourist phase being promoted by fund-giving agencies to produce the kind of workforce required by contemporary US capitalism. Although somewhat overstated, their argument contains a number of important insights, but cannot be easily applied to the European context.

Equally environmentalist or 'nurturist', but quite different in tenor, was the Marxist-influenced approach developed in Europe by people like Karl and Charlotte Bühler and Lev Vygotsky in which the social nature of child development was emphasised (in the United States G.H. Mead's social behaviourism has some affinities with this, as does the rise of comparative anthropological work by people like Margaret Mead and Wayne Dennis). This holds that consciousness is a product of social relations and child development is socially managed in a pervasive fashion. The child's concept of its 'self' is learned via its social relationships, as are the meanings that it gives to its experiences. The Marxist view would be that psychological structure is an internalisation of social structure, hence psychological conflicts and pathologies are created by, and reflect, social conflicts and pathologies.

For social constructionists the very meaning of childhood is socially produced, historical and cross-cultural studies disclosing wide differences in how far children are viewed as autonomous/dependent, good/sinful, adult/infantile, responsible/irresponsible, or sexual/asexual. The central issue of gender identity is similarly seen as culturally determined: what behaviours are considered typically male or female, at what age gender differences become significant, attitudes towards homosexuality, and the appropriate age for sexual activity to begin, are all matters of cultural, not biological, meaning.

The second European version of environmentalism stems from existentialism. This ultimately places responsibility back on the individual – we all have to choose what we are to be, there is no 'human nature' analogous to the species natures of other animals. 'Existence precedes essence', as Sartre somewhat enigmatically put it. The implications of this for child development were explored primarily in the psychiatric field. In Britain R.D. Laing in particular traced schizophrenia and other psychopathologies to the social dynamics of the family during childhood (see Chapter 8). According to this thesis, children create their identities from the messages received from those around them; if these are contradictory or confused they are driven to increasingly bizarre lengths in trying to understand what is going on. In addition to the 'double-bind' phenomenon (see Chapter 8) there may also be mystifications about parenthood (e.g. the child is told that its grandmother is its mother when in fact it is the child of an older 'sister'), or straightforward denial of the child's experience (e.g. the parent insists that the child has always liked school when the child denies it, the parent then says it is lying). From these all kinds of 'knots' (as Laing called them) are created, and the meanings of love/hate, dependence/independence, etc., can become distorted. This image of the child is of someone constantly facing the task of self-creation on the basis of available evidence – the child, like everyone else, has to choose what to be in the absence of a clear-cut genetically given identity.

While behaviourism is, in its own terms, optimistic, European versions of environmentalism are less so. The existentialist view in particular has a basically pessimistic air about it. And while behaviourism guarantees its results by applying the scientific laws of learning, the existentialist child is active, rather than passive: experience remains the raw material, but it makes its own choices, interpretations and decisions. Unlike the optimistic neo-Romanticism of US growth movement approaches (which sometimes co-opted existentialist ideas) there is no guarantee of ever finding your 'true self' – indeed you probably cannot – life does not stand still and you are forever faced with new existential choices, earlier 'true selves' appearing in retrospect more or less 'inauthentic'.

The most radically new Psychological image of the child was undoubtedly Freud's, the roots of which are especially tangled. He was certainly working within an evolutionary framework (though not a crude recapitulationist), but the formal structure of his theory (particularly the super-ego/ego/id division) was foreshadowed several times in earlier nineteenth-century German psychiatric thought. The primacy of the irrational and unconscious harks back to Romanticism, but the entirely negative character that Freud ascribes to it clearly conforms to late nineteenth-century positivist thinking. And then there was the theoretical centrality of sex which, if not unprecedented, had never before been spelled out so explicitly. In terms of nature vs. nurture, psychoanalysis was ambiguous – the stages of psychosexual development, the primacy of the sexual instinct, the structure of the psyche, were all biological givens. On the other hand, the interaction of these with the demands of the child's domestic world was crucial in determining each adult's unique constellation of fixations, sublimations and repressions. As a therapeutic procedure it might be thought that it was optimistic – after all, therapy seeks to cure and assumes this as a viable possibility. In fact it became rather pessimistic – cures were never complete, and some degree of psychopathology was the price universally paid for our 'civilised' life-style. In the United States the 1940s generation of psychoanalysts rejected much of this pessimism, introducing such notions as ego autonomy, and reverting to a more romantic vision. (See also Chapter 8.)

In the 1950s a revised 'ethological' version of the evolutionary image emerged, adopting a number of concepts initially developed by ethologists studying animal behaviour, notably 'attachment', 'imprinting' and 'innate releasing mechanisms'. From this angle child behaviour appeared to share some typically mammalian features: the mother–child linkage was not due to a simple conditioned association between food and mother in learning-theory fashion (this was experimentally refuted by the Harlows – see Chapter 14) but represented a complex, innately governed system which had evolved to ensure successful child-rearing. The child 'imprinted' onto the mother and formed specific 'attachments' to particular adults. Both infant and parent behaviour had evolved to maintain the communicative links between them (hence the notion of maternal 'bonding'). Some Freudians, notably Bowlby, assimilated much of this, thereby de-emphasising the primacy of essentially 'sexual' instincts. 'Attachment' remains a major focus of developmental research. Among other things, this perspective brought about a radical rethinking of the psychological character of separation and loss in children.

At present there is a risk of the wood and the trees becoming indiscriminable. While research on everything from effects of adverse life events to neonate perception, from cognitive development to origins of gender differences flourishes we should be wary of losing sight of the persisting influence of implicit underlying views of the child. Psychologists have no more reached agreement than anyone else on such fundamental questions as how far children should be controlled, how far they can be trusted (e.g. current controversies over reliability of child witnesses), and how far their personalities are 'learned' or 'innate' (and is this a sensible question?). Even the simple question of how much attention should be paid to them has not really been satisfactorily answered. Children are perfect projective material – adults fantasise about them endlessly – and perhaps it is these fantasies that, for better or worse, children end up realising. And our adult fantasies about children are also fantasies about our own childhoods. What I am suggesting here is that we continue to have a variety of such fantasies about the child: as original sinner, as innocent embodiment of spiritual potential, as primitive adult, as raw material for producing a good citizen, as existential victim of conscious existence, as mirror of society, as an amoral seeker of instinctual gratification, as an amusing and charming example of wildlife, and more recently (though not discussed here) as a self-programming information processor. This plurality generates a constant tension between the ideas of psychologists and those of others like politicians and religious leaders whose own images may diverge from those currently prevailing in Psychology. At this more sceptical end of the twentieth century, unlike certain previous periods, no image is culturally dominant; each has its advocates. Developmental Psychology is less able than it has occasionally been in the past to promote its latest theories authoritatively under the banner of 'scientific knowledge'.

Even so, Psychology has clearly acquired a role as the site where society's concerns and anxieties regarding children and child-rearing are most systematically and authoritatively debated. In this sense Developmental Psychology constitutes the institutionalisation of a universal social practice – discussing how children should be treated and raised.

My own position, for what it is worth, is an unsatisfactory fusion of romantic and social constructionist. The sheer range of individual differences in temperament, ability and personality from even earliest infancy seems too great to be completely explained in even the subtlest social constructionist terms; I am romantic enough to believe that general rules of good child-rearing are probably an illusion except for that which says that you should focus on the specific individual needs of each child. But it is, nevertheless, in the social and cultural arena that values and meanings originate, where the child has to find the content that can give its existence meaning. And it is certainly in this arena where Developmental Psychology itself does so.

BIBLIOGRAPHY

Further reading

Aries, P. (1962) *Centuries of Childhood*, London: Cape. Classic French social historical study.

Cleverley, J. and D. Phillips (1988) *Visions of Childhood: Influential Models from Locke to Spock*, London: Allen & Unwin. Very useful, fairly short survey with an orientation similar to that adopted here.

Ehrenreich, B. and D. English (1979) *For Her Own Good: A Hundred and Fifty Years of the Experts' Advice to Mothers*, New York: Pluto Press.

Morss, J.R. (1990) *The Biologising of Childhood: Developmental Psychology and the Darwinian Myth*, London: Erlbaum. Critique of Developmental Psychology, identifying its adoption of a primarily biological orientation as the major flaw.

Richards, G. (1992) *Mental Machinery: The Origins and Consequences of Psychological Ideas, Part One: 1600–1850*, London: Athlone Press. See ch. 4 for the eighteenth century, and ch. 7 for Froebel.

Romantic image

Romanticism proper

Day, T. (1789–93) *Sandford & Merton*, London: A. Miller.
Edgeworth, M. and R.L. Edgeworth (1798) *Practical Education*, London: A. Johnson.
Froebel, F. (1826, English edn 1897) *The Education of Man*, New York and London:
    Appleton. As with Herbart, there was a later revival of interest. See: W.H. Herford
    (rev. edn D.B. and C.H. Herford, 1916) *The Student's Froebel*, London: Pitman;
    and E.R. Murray (1914) *Froebel as a Pioneer of Modern Psychology*, London:
    George Philip.
Herbart, J.F. (1835) *Outlines of Educational Doctrine*, New York and London:
    Macmillan. There is a large literature from *c.*1890 to 1910 due to a revival of
    interest among educationists. The best accounts are the following: H.B. Dunkel
    (1970) *Herbart and Herbartianism: An Educational Ghost Story*, Chicago: Chicago
    University Press; and F.H. Hayward (1903) *The Critics of Herbartianism*, London:
    Swan Sonnenschein. Also provides useful coverage of much German nineteenth-
    century educational thought.
Itard, J. (1799, trans. 1972) *The Wild Boy of Aveyron*, London: New Left Books.
Pestalozzi, J.H. (1803) *Buch der Mütter*, collected works 1819–26. English editions of
    his work seem scarce, but see K. Silber (1960) *Pestalozzi: The Man and His Work*,
    London: Routledge & Kegan Paul.
Rousseau, J.-J. (1762) *Emile, ou de l'éducation* (4 vols), Amsterdam: Néaulme.

Romantic influenced

Boden, M. (1979) *Piaget: Outline and Critique of his Theory*, Brighton: Harvester. The
    Piagetian literature, primary and secondary, is vast and easily accessible. This is a
    general introduction.
Koffka, K. (1928) *The Growth of the Mind*, London: Kegan Paul, Trench & Trübner.
Montessori, M. (1913) *Pedagogical Anthropology*, London: Heinemann. Prolific
    writer whose approach continues in Montessori Schools.
Montessori, M. (1936) *The Secret of Childhood*, London: Longmans Green.
Stern, W. (1924) *Psychology of Early Childhood up to the Sixth Year of Age*, London:
    Allen & Unwin. Based on an observational diary by his wife Clara.

Anti-romantic

More, Hannah (1799, 12th edn 1818) *Strictures on the Modern System of Female
    Education* (2 vols), London: Cadell. Also representative of a certain kind of
    Christian evangelical viewpoint.

Empiricist

Classic

Hamilton, E. (1801) *Letters on the Elementary Principles of Education* (2 vols),
    London: Robinson. She later became a follower of Pestalozzi.
Locke, J. (1693, reprint 1902) *Some Thoughts Concerning Education*, Cambridge:
    Cambridge University Press.
Spencer, H. (1861, 2nd edn 1929) *Education, Intellectual, Moral and Physical*, London:
    Watts. Spencer's evolutionary associationist perspective.

Behaviourist, etc.

Gesell, A. (1925) *The Mental Growth of the Pre-School Child*, New York: Macmillan. First in a series which continued up to the 1940s, e.g. see the following reference.

Gesell, A. and F.L. Ilg (1946) *The Child from Five to Ten*, London: Hamish Hamilton.

Watson, J.B. (1928) *Psychological Care of Infant and Child*, New York: Norton.

Evolutionary

See the references in Chapter 3 for evolution-influenced developmental titles.

Psychoanalytic and post-Freudian

Erikson, E. (1950, rev. edn 1965) *Childhood and Society*, Harmondsworth: Penguin.

Freud, Anna (1926, English edn 1959) *The Psycho-analytical Treatment of Children*, London: Imago.

Klein, M. (1932, rev. edn 1935) *The Psycho-Analysis of Children*, London: Hogarth Press.

Klein, M. (with Joan Riviere) (1937) *Love, Hate and Reparation*, London: Hogarth Press.

Rickman, J. (ed.) (1936) *On the Bringing Up of Children*, London: Kegan Paul. Collection of popular papers including one by Klein tying herself in knots trying not to say that without breastfeeding all is lost.

Winnicott, D.W. (1971) *Playing and Reality*, Harmondsworth: Penguin. Exponent of Kleinian object-relations theory.

For Freud see especially the following:

Freud, S. (1905, 1970) *Three Essays on the Theory of Sexuality*, London: Hogarth Press. 'One of the two most important books Freud ever wrote' (Ernest Jones).

Marxist and social constructionist

Bühler, C. (1935) *From Birth to Maturity*, London: Kegan Paul.

Bühler, K. (1930, reprint 1949) *The Mental Development of the Child*, London: Routledge & Kegan Paul.

There are few Marxist texts explicitly on childhood. For the general Marxist theory of consciousness see the following:

Sève, L. (1978) *Man in Marxist Theory and the Psychology of Personality*, Brighton: Harvester.

For L.S. Vygotsky, see the following:

Newman, F. and L. Holzman (1993) *Vygotsky: Revolutionary Scientist*, London: Routledge.

Vygotsky, L.S. (1978) *Mind in Society: The Development of Higher Psychological Processes*, Cambridge, Mass.: Harvard University Press. Most accessible English statement of his, hardly party-line Marxist, views.

Wertsch, J.W. (ed.) (1985) *Culture, Communication and Cognition: Vygotskian Perspectives*, Cambridge: Cambridge University Press. See especially Part III for discussion of Developmental Psychology.

See also the growing corpus of post-1970 work on gender roles.

Ethological

Bowlby, John (1969) *Attachment and Loss, Vol. 1: Attachment*, Harmondsworth: Penguin. Combined ethology and psychoanalysis.

There is a vast subsequent literature on attachment and related issues. On Bowlby see the following:

Holmes, J. (1993) *John Bowlby and Attachment Theory*, London: Routledge.

Existentialist

Laing, R.D. (1959) *The Divided Self*, London: Tavistock.
Laing, R.D. and A. Esterson (1964) *Sanity, Madness and the Family*, London: Tavistock.

Other

Dennis, W. (1940) *The Hopi Child*, New York: Appleton-Century.
Gregory, J. (1765, reprint 1798) *A Comparative View of the State and Faculties of Man with Those of Animals*, London: Cadell & Davies. Interesting Scottish Enlightenment work in which children are considered as driven by instincts rather than reason; a stage theory is suggested, and later 'eugenics' ideas on breeding foreshadowed.
Maccoby, E.E. (ed.) (1967) *The Development of Sex Differences*, London: Tavistock.
Mead, M. (1928, reprint 1943) *Coming of Age in Samoa*, Harmondsworth: Penguin.
Mead, M. (1930, reprint 1973) *Growing Up in New Guinea*, Harmondsworth: Penguin.
Mussen, P.H. (1963) *The Psychological Development of the Child*, Englewood Cliffs, N.J.: Prentice-Hall. Orthodox US mainstream approach of the post-Second World War period.

14 Psychological uses of animals

Animals have been central to human psychology at least since the first cave paintings 30,000 years ago. Their behaviour has been used to encode psychological insights certainly since Aesop's *Fables* and the biblical *Book of Proverbs* while folk-psychological language is rich with animal terms. Physiognomists like the Italian della Porta in the sixteenth century and Lavater in the eighteenth century drew heavily on similarities between human and animal forms as indicators of character. After Darwin the relationship became even closer, if different in kind, and Psychology continued the traditional practice of looking to animal behaviour to provide insight into our own. What I want to do here is consider some of the ways that Psychology has used this 'resource'. Although animal behaviour may be studied in its own right, it is invariably, perhaps inevitably, construed as having broader implications relating to human behaviour. There are, I think, four, infrequently spelled out, uses to which animal behaviour research has been put. Each has been particularly in vogue at different times and places, although none were ever entirely absent. One underlying message is that the use being made of animal behaviour evidence will determine the kind of theories being produced. That is to say, psychologists do not approach animal behaviour in a neutral fashion, but with prior assumptions about why they are doing so. (Before proceeding further I would draw attention to Donna Haraway, 1989: a provocative exploration of this line of thinking in regard to primate research.) The four kinds of use which I am provisionally identifying are as follows:

1 To trace the evolutionary roots of human behaviour.
2 As 'behavioural units' for studying something called 'behaviour'.
3 As sources of insight into behavioural dynamics, especially social dynamics.
4 To trace the border-line of what is distinctively human.

Each of these makes its own demands and has its own requirements. There is one common assumption of course, namely that animal behaviour is somehow *simpler* than ours, although how precisely this simplicity is conceptualised varies, and sometimes the aim is to show that it is less simple than hitherto assumed.

TRACING THE ROOTS OF HUMAN BEHAVIOUR

The evolutionary perception of a continuum between human and animal behaviour quickly generated an interest in identifying what we might call 'the animal in the human' – how far human behaviour retains pre-human ancestral features. Entailing the existence of in-built determinants of behaviour, this involved the elaboration of the concept of 'instinct'. Prior to Darwin this typically referred to ways of behaving built into the animal by God, but evolutionists radically changed this by replacing God with inheritance (although this meaning was not novel). Aside from a relatively quiescent period from *c*. 1915 to the late 1930s (roughly during the height of behaviourism), 'instinct' theories have maintained a strong presence in Psychology. The lineage runs from Darwin's own followers (such as Romanes) through Lloyd Morgan, McDougall and Drever to the ethologists Lorenz, Tinbergen and Eibl-Eibesfeldt down to contemporary socio-biologists. That hiatus was important nevertheless, because it ended with a further shift in the concept's meaning. Earlier theorists viewed instinct in terms of innate goals or drives of a general kind: sex, food, aggression, maternality, etc. Behaviour was construed as driven by such instincts, which might have specific energies allocated to them, and human behaviour was instinctive insofar as it was in the service of these. With behaviourist environmentalism the concept fell from favour, and rightly, since it amounted to little more than listing the necessary conditions for survival – but the fact that all organisms reproduce does not mean that they share a common 'sexual instinct'.

The ethologists gave the term a more specific meaning, no longer referring to broad goals but to behavioural patterns of a more or less fixed and unlearned kind, often highly species-specific. A new vocabulary of fixed action patterns (FAPs), innate releasing mechanisms (IRMs) and 'imprinting' was developed to deal with this. Far from hampering the application of their findings to humans, it became apparent that much human behaviour had close parallels in other species, suggesting that, for example, territorial marking, postural signalling and mother–child attachment had a high innate component because human behaviour of these kinds had a high *formal* resemblance to behaviour in some other species. Lorenz (1966) was a classic example of this logic. As the evidence came crowding in during the 1960s and early 1970s, some psychologists such as John Bowlby began incorporating it into their theories of child development (see Chapter 13). This evidence had a twofold effect. First, it had a salutary impact on how behaviour hitherto dignified by traditional political, moral and cultural values was perceived – military emphasis on epaulettes was upgraded bristling of shoulder hair as shown in angry gorillas, the courting male's presentation of food to the female was basically the same whether Black Magic chocolate or the bird's worm, while the boss's vast desk was pure social hierarchy signalling no different essentially from the top stag's behaviour during the mating season. Kneeling at prayer was a typical primate submission posture. The first effect, then, was a fairly direct psychological influence on those reading the literature, changing their way of looking at the world – advertisements became territorial markers, political speeches rival bellowings of would-be dominant walruses.

But there was a second effect, somewhat slower to manifest itself: a revival of the nineteenth-century doctrine known somewhat misleadingly as social Darwinism (social Spencerism would be more accurate). This held that human, like animal, behaviour was governed by the goal of maximising reproduction and competing for the resources enabling one (or one's closest kin) to do so. This was formulated using concepts emerging in evolutionary theory such as 'inclusive fitness'. From this stemmed 'sociobiology', effectively launched in E.O. Wilson's 1975 book of that title. The lesson of this is generally read as being that various aspects of human behaviour are so deeply rooted genetically that attempts at modification are totally misguided; sex differences in behaviour, certain features of social organisation and human conflict are irremovable. Altruism is but selfishness in disguise. Are these valid conclusions? The attempt to override or modify such 'instinctive' behaviours is also surely a fact of human behaviour. Nor does genetic mean unchangeable – after all, evolution is itself a process of genetic change. (In G. Richards, 1987, I provided a fuller critique of this controversial position.)

Such questions may be debated at great length. More to the point here – what are the features of this type 1 usage of animals? First, it is very wide ranging in the species that it studies. Although Tinbergen concentrated primarily on the herring gull and Lorenz on geese and dogs, field research now covers species from gorillas to bats, dingoes to elephants. One consequence of this which we ought to mention in passing is that whatever human behaviour you are dealing with, *somewhere* in the animal kingdom you will find a parallel. This perhaps weakens rather than strengthens the case for human behaviour being instinctive because really such behaviour should be of a species-specific stereotyped character. We ought, then, to expect human behaviour to resemble one particular lineage – but in fact it seems to resemble them all!

Second, stemming from this, the nature of the inference from animal to human is usually analogical. Except, arguably, when dealing with closely related primate species we are not really seeing the evolutionary roots of our own behaviour; at best we are seeing what is called 'convergent evolution' – in which unrelated species evolve similar solutions when faced with similar problems. Third, this evidence is basically of a field-study rather than laboratory-based kind, lending the findings themselves an ecological validity lacking in laboratory work. The wider effect, bolstered by heavy media coverage of wildlife and green concerns, has been to narrow the perceived gap between humans and animals by demonstrating our similarities with other species, however problematic the reasons for these resemblances. While sociobiology seemed to be taking things in a politically conservative direction in the 1980s, replaying nineteenth-century arguments that competition and national strife were somehow 'natural', the force of this now appears to have diminished. I must stress here that interpreting behaviour in ethological terms does not exclude alternative interpretations with different meanings. Saying that a particular behaviour is 'territorial', for example, does not actually exclude alternative meanings – like 'patriotic', 'projected patricidal wish' or 'result of cognitive calculations regarding reward expectancy'. We are free to choose the 'framework of meanings' that suits us – we cannot prove one 'true' and others 'false'.

ANIMALS AS BEHAVIOURAL UNITS

I will say relatively little about this here, having already covered this usage in discussing behaviourism (Chapter 5). From this point of view the animal is interesting not as a unique example of instinctive adaptation patterns but as a convenient learning or behaving machine, suitable for study because it shows learning (or some other) behaviour in a simpler form to that which it takes in humans, because it can be experimented on with fewer moral qualms, and because it can be easily reared and housed.

As we saw, research of this kind focused on a very small range of species: the Norwegian white rat, the domestic dog (in Pavlov's conditioning research) and the pigeon (in much of Skinner's work). I drew attention in the earlier chapter to the underlying circularity in all this as far as its support for environmentalist theories was concerned. By the 1950s and 1960s primates, particularly rhesus monkeys, were being added to the repertoire both because they had become available and for face-validity reasons – they were closer to humans and so more suited for the study of behaviours present in only rudimentary form in rats and dogs. This was construed in terms of their being more generally intelligent rather than in terms of differences in 'instinctive' make-up. Thus we find Brady's experiments on 'executive monkeys' and the massive programme of research on rhesus monkeys undertaken by Harry and Margaret Harlow. In neither case were the researchers interested in monkeys but in a general behaviour category: 'anxiety' in Brady's case and 'attachment behaviour' in the Harlows'.

This usage is not necessarily environmentalist in orientation – it can involve (as with the Harlows) experimental exploration of ideas originating from ethology. What we need to note is (a) the focus on a category of behaviour rather than on a species of animal, and (b) the assumption of generalisability from animal to human with due allowance for the greater complexity of human behaviour. In recent years the environmentalist assumptions common in such research have declined somewhat due to the discovery of apparently innate factors preparing or counter-preparing animals for certain kinds of learning task (see Chapter 5).

SOURCES OF INSIGHT INTO SOCIAL BEHAVIOURAL DYNAMICS

Associated, though not exclusively, with the ethological and sociobiological work, has been the use of animals to explore the effects of environmental factors on social behaviour. This varies from experimental work on rodent overcrowding to inferences from field studies regarding, for example, the differences between plain-dwelling South African baboons and rocky valley-dwelling North East African ones. This does not claim to be identifying the roots of human behaviour so much as identifying relationships between species' environments and their social organisation. The boundary between this and the first category may at times become blurred, but the basic distinction is that the behaviours studied are not so much 'innate' as logical consequences for a species of a particular type having to adapt to the environment in question. The assumption of a human–animal resemblance in salient respects is, of course, maintained.

Sociobiologists have, however, insisted that the basic explanatory level for even these social dynamics lies in the optimising of 'inclusive fitness' (enhancing the survival of one's genes by promoting the reproductive success either of oneself or one's closest kin, who in part share them). Thus infanticide among langurs, lesbianism among gulls and food-sharing among vampire bats can all be viewed as logical solutions to the inclusive fitness problem. Theoretically much of this work hinges around the notion of 'reciprocal altruism' introduced by Hamilton and Trivers. (In Richards, 1987, I tried to elucidate what I see as the logical incoherence of this position.)

Prior to the rise of sociobiology, the effect of this kind of work was similar to much of that in the first category, particularly the work on overcrowding in rats which resulted in increased violence, increased abortion, abnormal sexual behaviour, drop in grooming standards, 'forced mating' (i.e. rape), etc. – although they did not actually throw petrol bombs. Again the change in perception was to see human responses to overcrowding as 'natural' responses to extreme conditions and to narrow the human–animal gap.

TRACING THE HUMAN–ANIMAL BORDER-LINE

Consider first a preoccupation of many people around 1900: the presence of consciousness in animals (e.g. Margaret Washburn, 1908). This direction of concern is the reciprocal of the first of our categories: instead of tracing the animal in humans, we are here tracing the human in animals, especially, in recent decades, in higher primates. Best known are studies of the linguistic capacities of chimpanzees, gorillas and pygmy chimpanzees (bonobos). Similar research has been conducted with dolphins (Herman et al., 1984) and sea-lions (Schusterman and Krieger, 1984). The ethological work of primatologists such as Goodall (1971), Boesch and Boesch (1981) (both on chimps), the late Diana Fossey (1984), Schaller (1963) (both on gorillas) and

Altmann (on baboons) – to mention only some of the best-known research – derives much of its appeal from demonstrating the presence in other species of such supposedly human behaviours as grief, ornamentation, tool use, warfare, pathological jealousy and traditions of socially learned behaviour. This has been supplemented by experimental work comparing primates and humans, e.g. Vauclair (1984) on cognitive development and Suarez and Gallup (1981) on self-recognition. This remains a flourishing area, increasingly closely related to human evolution research (see Gibson and Ingold, 1993).

Although such work primarily focuses on higher primates and, to a lesser extent, cetaceans, the species studied may include any of the higher mammals felt to approach us in abilities of one kind or another. Here we are not concerned so much with the roots of human behaviour as with the very nature of human uniqueness, and the trend in recent years has been to continue that whittling away of neat criteria begun by Darwin (1871).

Thus we can utilise animals in various ways, and I must stress that within particular research programmes elements of more than one of these may occur. We can perhaps rearrange our original listing more neatly by identifying three underlying orientations:

1 Minimising animal–human differences by animalising humans.
2 Minimising animal–human differences by humanising animals.
3 Denying any essential, 'innate' character altogether, especially to humans but also as far as possible to animals.

A fourth angle, which by definition generates no animal research, is the following:

4 Maximising the animal–human difference by denying the applicability of animal behaviour research to humans.

Of these the first two are now most active, for the third has lost credibility in the light of findings within its own tradition, while the fourth is fighting a losing battle against the sheer intrinsic appeal of animal behaviour research. (I am here ignoring purely physiological studies, although they would most easily fit under the first point.)

I would like to end on a more distanced note – seeing this whole topic as an expression of the intrinsic psychological significance of animals for humans. Anthropologists have, since the eighteenth century, utilised the idea that all societies distinguish between culture and nature – the human and the natural worlds. Culture converts nature into new cultural forms, a process that Marxists ascribe to our supposedly unique 'labour'-based life-style. Humans identify themselves as somehow apart from nature, however intimate their involvements with it. The Psychological uses and meanings of animals are rooted in this cultural processing of animals, first into food, clothing and ornament, and then as a psychological resource – as models of how to behave, spiritual symbols, external templates for mapping human diversity of temperament and character, and moral emblems of virtues and vices. The complementary moves of putting the human into the animal and bringing the animal into the human have always, it seems, been present. And notwithstanding the hard strictures of Lloyd Morgan and others of his generation against the former, as unscientific 'anthropomorphism', the intertwining of the two subverts the apparent simplicity of such injunctions. The fact that modern Psychology is still involved in this game, at however sophisticated a level, further testifies to the inseparability of Psychology and psychology.

The preferred direction of movement – animalising humans, humanising animals, assertion of separation, denial of distinction – reflects contemporary cultural preoccupations. Although this cannot be explored in depth here, consider the shift from mid-Victorian 'anthropomorphic' humanising of animals to the Darwinian reversal of animalising humans. The former is a kind of psychological imperialism: animals embody all kinds of human virtues, their behaviour is laden with moral lessons for us, their meaning is as exemplars of divine wisdom designed for our edification in a creationist, divinely engineered universe. This image then moves into reverse – evil becomes transformed into the beast within (see Chapter 3), and the animalisation of European humans continues with Freud's demotion of the power of reason in favour of that of the sexual instinct, culminating in an orgy of mutual projection in the First World War. At this point the Americans opt for a denial of any essential difference between animal and human at all – there is only behaviour and behaving organisms, humans included. The Second World War in its turn brings a sense of difference from nature – all that humans have is consciousness, they define themselves, they are responsible for their own fate, the rest is denial of freedom and responsibility – optimists plump for Maslow and Rogers, pessimists for Sartre and existential angst. But what of those who cannot grasp the nature of this human freedom? Generals and businessmen, politicians and status-seekers – under the new ethological gaze they suffer a Circean metamorphosis, their behaviours mere unconscious enactments of animal rituals. Ethology thus returns animals to the role of moral emblems, turning the wheel full circle. Psychology participates in and reflects these shifting cultural moods and phases. One is driven to Lévi-Strauss's dictum – 'animals are good to think with'. Of all natural phenomena, animals are psychologically the most potent – a still unexhausted source of ways of thinking about ourselves. From animal-headed Egyptian gods to Greenpeace, our relations towards animals define who and what we think *we* are. But animal behaviour really exists in and of itself, it is not an argument for or against anything. So is it we who supply animal behaviour with its meanings – or is it animal behaviour that supplies the meanings for our own?

BIBLIOGRAPHY

Further reading

Boakes, B. (1984) *From Darwinism to Behaviourism*, Cambridge: Cambridge University Press.

Desmond, A. (1979) *The Ape's Reflexion*, London: Blond & Briggs. Meditation on the psychological relationship between humans and higher primates.

Haraway, D. (1989) *Primate Visions: Gender, Race, and Nature in the World of Modern Science*, London: Routledge. Controversial feminist critique of the entire topic.

Richards, G. (1989) *On Psychological Language and the Physiomorphic Basis of Human Nature*, London: Routledge. See especially chs 1 and 3 on 'anthropomorphism' and the natural world sources (including animals) of psychological concepts.

Other references

Boesch, C. and H. Boesch (1981) 'Sex Differences in the Use of Natural Hammers by Wild Chimpanzees: A Preliminary Report', *Behaviour* 83:585–93. They have produced numerous additional papers since.

Bowlby, John (1969) *Attachment and Loss, Vol. 1: Attachment*, Harmondsworth: Penguin.

Brady, J.V. (1958) 'Ulcers in "Executive Monkeys"', *Scientific American* 199:95–100.

Campbell, J. (1984) *The Way of the Animal: Powers Historical Atlas of World Mythology, Vol. I*, London: Times Books. Jungian-influenced work by a renowned authority on mythology. A resource for exploring the psychological significance of animals for humans.

Darwin, C. (1871) *The Descent of Man*, London: Murray.

DeVore, I. (ed.) (1965) *Primate Behavior: Field Studies of Monkeys and Apes*, New York: Holt, Rinehart & Winston. A collection of pioneering papers.

Drever, J. (1917) *Instinct in Man*, Cambridge: Cambridge University Press. Classic statement of then mainstream British 'instinctivist' position.

Fossey, D. (1984) *Gorillas in the Mist*, New York: Houghton-Mifflin.

Gibson, K.R. and T. Ingold (eds) (1993) *Tools, Language and Cognition in Human Evolution*, Cambridge: Cambridge University Press. Ingold's last two chapters especially valuable.

Goodall, J. (1971) *In the Shadow of Man*, London: Collins.

Harlow, H.F. and M.K. Harlow (1965) 'The Affectional Systems', in A.M. Schrier, H.F. Harlow and F. Stollnitz (eds) *Behavior of Non-human Primates*, New York: Academic Press.

Herman, L.M., D.G. Richards and J.P. Wolz (1984) 'Comprehension of Sentences by Bottle-nosed Dolphins', *Cognition* 16:129–219.

Klingender, F. (1971) *Animals in Art and Thought to the End of the Middle Ages*, London: Routledge & Kegan Paul.

Köhler, W. (1917, English edn 1925, reprint 1957) *The Mentality of Apes*, Harmondsworth: Penguin. The ethological aspects have been overshadowed by the learning experiments.

Lauder Lindsay, W. (1880) *Mind in the Lower Animals* (2 vols), London: Kegan Paul, Trench & Co. Full-blooded anthropomorphism – heroic horses, criminal magpies, canine suicide, etc.

Lorenz, K. (1966) *On Aggression*, London: Methuen.

Richards, G. (1987) *Human Evolution: An Introduction for the Behavioural Sciences*, London: Routledge & Kegan Paul. See especially ch. 5 on sociobiology and altruism issues.

Romanes, G. (1882) *Animal Intelligence*, London: Kegan Paul, Trench & Trübner.

Schaller, G.B. (1963) *The Mountain Gorilla*, Chicago: Chicago University Press.

Schusterman, R.J. and K. Krieger (1984) 'California Sea Lions are Capable of Semantic Comprehension', *Psychological Record* 34:3–23.

Suarez, S.D. and G.G. Gallup (1981) 'Self-recognition in Chimpanzees and Orangutans but Not in Gorillas', *Journal of Human Evolution* 10:175–88.

Tinbergen, N. (1953) *The Herring Gull's World*, London: Collins.

Trivers, R.L. (1985) *Social Evolution*, Menlo Park, Calif.: Benjamin/Cummings. Hard sociobiology position statement.

Vauclair, J. (1984) 'Phylogenetic Approach to Object Manipulation in Human and Ape Infants', *Human Development* 27:321–8.

Washburn, M.F. (1908) *Animal Mind*, New York: Macmillan.

Willis, R. (1974) *Man and Beast*, London: Hart-Davis. Interesting anthropological study comparing the cultural significance of specific animals for three African cultures. Illuminates how we use animals to define ourselves.

Wilson, E.O. (1975) *Sociobiology: The New Synthesis*, Harvard: Harvard University Press. The sociobiology 'manifesto'.

Yerkes, R.M. (1943) *Chimpanzees: A Laboratory Colony*, New Haven: Yale University Press. Yerkes' chimp colony was the major site of US primate research from the 1920s until the mid-1940s.

15 Psychology and gender

Few topics are currently more controversial than gender differences and the 'psychology of women'. It is a telling fact that until R.Miles (1991), the idea of a 'psychology of men' had never been seriously broached. I cannot do justice here to recent feminist scholarship, but hope, in focusing primarily on the earlier period, to provide a complementary historical perspective. Traditionally Psychology saw no need to differentiate between the sexes regarding basic processes such as perception, memory and learning (although the existence of sex differences in performance was always asserted); otherwise the white male was considered as the norm and primary focus of interest. With a few notable exceptions attitudes towards women found in mainstream Psychology between 1850 and 1950 are mostly little more than restatements of prevailing stereotypes and assumptions given an authoritative 'scientific' gloss. Terman and C.C. Miles's (1936) 'M–F' (masculinity–feminism) scale, for instance, still took stereotypical gender-trait linkages as unproblematic. Gender issues largely remained a side issue until the 1950s but expanded rapidly with the 1960s revival of feminism, also a period when larger numbers of women were entering the discipline. In 1969 the student ratio was about 60:40 in favour of males; today (1996) it is about 80:20 in favour of females. Thus the rise in concern reflects the cultural preoccupation with the position of women and their influx into the discipline – one aspect of their changing position and aspirations associated with that preoccupation.

It is sometimes difficult to isolate Psychological work from the wider body of texts published since the late 1960s. Was Germaine Greer's *The Female Eunuch* (1970) Psychology? Or Foucault's volumes on the history of sexuality? Or Kate Millett's *Sexual Politics* (1971) and Sheila Rowbotham's *Woman's Consciousness, Man's World* (1973)? It was in the very nature of their task that those critically rethinking the issue had to move beyond conventional Psychological genres to make their case. Not that there is an absence of readily classifiable 'Psychological' work, Mitchell (1974) being an early example, Morawski (1994) a recent one. The APA's Psychology of Women Division was established in 1973 and the journal *Psychology of Women Quarterly* followed in the late 1970s; the British Psychological Society (BPS)

Psychology of Women Section was founded in 1988, the British journal *Feminism and Psychology* being launched in 1991.

Although prior to the 1960s Psychology paid women relatively little explicit attention, psychoanalytic schools were a major exception, not least because women figured prominently as both practitioners and their clients. Neo-Freudian women analysts like Karen Horney also contributed to the beginnings of modern feminism in the late 1940s and early 1950s. Sabina Spielrein's role in Jung's intellectual development, his relationship with Freud and the dissemination of psychoanalytic thought in the post-revolutionary Soviet Union has only recently been recovered (Kerr, 1994).

One difficulty in focusing on 'Psychology and gender' as a specific topic is that discipline and subject-matter levels are fused even more than usual. Comprehensive treatment would involve venturing into the realms of social history and the numerous works of writers such as Foucault, Lawrence Stone (1977), P.-G. Boucé (1982), Pearsall (1969) and Marina Warner (1976) on the history of gender relations in European culture. Starting in the mid-nineteenth century is to enter a story that had been running for centuries and had seen many vicissitudes. We discover a situation in which the idealisation and infantilisation of women (particularly middle-class women) was at a singularly high pitch, and evolutionary thought soon provided new arguments to reinforce this. Compared to Victorian men, Victorian women were weaker, more emotional, less rational, more fickle, more dogmatic, more infantile, more aesthetically sensitive, more prone to hysteria, much less or far more sexual, more suggestible, superficially more spiritual and talked too much. Regarding a woman's place being in the home, here is Mrs Copley writing some time in the 1850s:

> Are married women never to go abroad? are they to be confined to the storeroom, and to the nursery, as to a nunnery or prison ? No: this is not required of them; though it will be found that the best and happiest wives and mothers are those who, without any irksome feeling of confinement, are so constantly, and agreeably, and usefully employed at home, that it requires a very clear and imperative call of duty to get them abroad, and a very strenuous effort on their parts to comply with it; and, even then, they can hardly take their hearts with them, but in the midst of society are 'stung with the thought of home'.
>
> (*c*.1860, p. 203)

When nineteenth-century Psychological writers mention women it is generally in passing – Galton, for example, somewhat at odds with prevailing notions of greater female sensitivity:

> I found as a rule that men have more delicate powers of discrimination than women, and ... business experience ... seems to confirm this view. The tuners of pianofortes are men, and so I understand are the tasters of tea and wine, the sorters of wool, and the like. These latter occupations are well

salaried, because it is of the first moment to the merchant that he should be rightly advised on the real value of what he is about to purchase or to sell. If the sensitivity of women were superior to that of men the self-interest of merchants would lead to their being always employed; but as the reverse is the case, the opposite supposition is likely to be the true one.

Ladies rarely distinguish the merits of wine at the dinner-table, and though custom allows them to preside at the breakfast-table, men think them on the whole to be far from successful makers of tea and coffee.

(1883, pp. 20–1)

Specifically Psychological texts on women are virtually non-existent before the 1890s. The three major relevant genres were the following:

1 works arising from the growing feminism controversy, e.g. J.S. Mill's pro-feminist *The Subjection of Women* (1869) and Alexander Walker's less well-known *Woman Physiologically Considered as to Mind, Morals, Marriage, Matrimonial Slavery, Infidelity and Divorce* (c.1850);
2 pious advice manuals such as Mrs Copley's promoting respectable bour-geois sex roles; and
3 semi-underground works (see Chapter 8) posing as sex education manuals or pseudo-medical books – one, *Aristotle's Masterpiece* (which had nothing to do with Aristotle), first appeared around 1684 and was continually being reprinted.

In 1901 an extraordinary German work appeared, translated into English as *Sex and Character* (1906). Its author, 21-year-old Otto Weininger, committed suicide two years later aged, we are told Adrian Molishly, '23 and a half'. Though hardly mainstream Psychology, it attracted wide acclaim and displayed precocious academic erudition. Weininger belonged in the late nineteenth-century *fin de siècle* neo-romantic camp (a reaction against positivism and materialism haunted by visions of decadence and decay) rather than the scientific one. His bizarre thesis is clearly expounded in Chapter IX, 'Male and Female Psychology'. Women quite simply have no soul or ego, existing at a totally different level of consciousness to males. Being incapable of genius, logical thought and significant creative achievement, and possessing neither free will nor genuine morality, when they display such qualities women are merely imitating men. Mother and prostitute are the two forms to which female character always tends. This is embedded in, and emerges from, a complex metaphysical system into which, mercifully, we need not enter. The following is one quote from among many astonishing passages:

Woman's thought is a sliding and gliding through subjects, a superficial tasting of things that a man, who studies the depths, would scarcely notice; it is an extravagant and dainty method of skimming which has no grasp of accuracy. A woman's thought is superficial, and touch is the most highly developed of the female senses, the most notable characteristic of the woman which she can bring to a high state by her unaided efforts. Touch necessitates a limiting of interest to superficialities ... . When a woman 'understands' a man ... she is simply, so to speak, tasting ... what he has thought about her.

(p. 191)

Weininger's near pathological misogyny was ironically destined to provide Greer (1970) with a telling target and point of reference. Curiously, he consulted Freud while writing the work and its appearance played a role in the split between Freud and his friend Fleiss. Most significant is surely the very fact that it was not laughed out of court, but hailed as a work of genius, containing the 'ripest wisdom' according to the publisher William Heinemann's prefatory note – who continued 'no thoughtful man will lay down this book without deep emotion and admiration; many, indeed, will close it with almost religious reverence' (p. viii).

If Psychological discussion of women was rare, physiological and psychiatric discussion was not. As well as Weininger's book, 1901 saw the publication of the German psychiatrist Moebius's *On the Physiological Imbecility of Woman*, advancing similar doctrines of greater female animality and poor self-control. The exposition of physiological differences, coupled with evolutionary theory, were regularly deployed to reinforce existing stereotypes (as also happened regarding race). Women's brains were, it seemed, smaller with less developed frontal lobes, hence their poorer reasoning and weaker wills. (I am keen to track down a paper I once encountered called 'The Missing 4 Ounces'.) Women, by being biologically tied to basic instinctual functions, especially reproduction and child-rearing, were simply less neurologically, hence psychologically, evolved than men. Decent male behaviour towards them should thus be patronising, protective, care-taking, tolerant of their irrationality and respectful of the intuitive emotional insights that their closer connection with nature bestowed – coupled with judicious intellectual distancing. Psychiatric evidence endorsed this image, women being especially prone to hysteria, widely believed to reflect a less well-integrated nervous system. Ellenberger (1970) discloses, among much else, how psychiatrists like Charcot could get unwittingly drawn into playing sex-typical games with female patients throughout this period.

From a different direction, criminology, came the leading degenerationist C. Lombroso's *The Female Offender* (1895) written with fellow Italian William Ferrero. Like Lombroso's other work this pays great attention to physiognomy. Female criminals are hairier, have more warts, less symmetric faces and weightier jaws than their law-abiding sisters – the work containing many mugshots to 'prove' it. This book is valuable on two counts: first, as illustrating how deeply, yet naively, sexual stereotyping permeated supposedly 'scientific' work, and second, as a source of numerous case histories providing a grim picture of the plights in which women could find themselves. Quite counter to Lombroso's intentions it enables us to redeem some forgotten women from oblivion. As far as stereotyping is concerned, here are a couple of quotes illustrating the belief that women are capable of worse immorality than men. On 'crimes of passion':

> often premeditation in the woman is longer than in the man; it is also colder and more cunning, so that the crime is executed with an ability and a gloating which in the deed of pure passion are psychologically impossible. Nor does sincere penitence always follow the offence; on the contrary, there is often exultation; and rarely does the offender commit suicide.
>
> (p. 147)

On habitual criminals:

> there is among them a small proportion whose criminal propensities are more intense and more perverse than those of their male prototypes.... Another terrible point of superiority in the female born criminal over the male lies in the refined, diabolical cruelty with which she accomplishes her crime.
>
> (p. 148)

And one case:

> M. the daughter of an eccentric, unpractical mother, received a high literary but incomplete education, crowned by a university degree, which only unfitted her for real life. At twenty-three she found herself an orphan, ruined by family reverses .... After various vain efforts she accepted a post of teacher ... but was dismissed ... on its being discovered she was a Protestant. Then, alone in the world, without means of existence, and haunted by the memory of more happy days, she began buying articles of jewellery in shops, where she obtained credit in virtue of the former position of her family .... A series of such frauds finally brought her to prison, where she died before her trial, worn out by misery and shame.
>
> (pp. 205–6)

But it is in the setting of the doctor–patient relationship that women first receive intensive Psychological scrutiny around 1900, and nowhere more so than on Freud's couch. The views of psychiatrists, including Freud and Jung, nevertheless remain clearly related to those being expressed in contemporary literature and philosophy. Again Ellenberger summarises this well, demonstrating the close affinities between their ideas on feminine psychology and those of philosophers (especially Nietzsche) and neo-romantic novelists (many of whom they cited with approval). Not all shared the extreme views of Weininger and Moebius of course, but there was a common consensus that women were passive, receptive and less rational than men. This sometimes took the semi-mystical 'complementarity' form: male and female are complementary parts of a single whole – an idea underlying Jung's later anima and animus archetypes. Fascination with archetypal female roles, especially the mother, was widespread during this period (J.J. Bachofen's 1861 *Das Mutterrecht* (Mother Right) was widely cited by turn-of-the-century writers;

see Bachofen, 1967). Many males seem, at this time, quite genuinely unable to see women except through the lenses of such images. Sceptics really should read some of the original material. Feminist opposition to this was intense, with egalitarian views also being promoted by many socialist men, and it was this controversy that rendered the issue so highly charged.

Havelock Ellis's *Man and Woman* (1896), revised and reprinted up to 1914, is in this latter camp. This is far more sober than those texts mentioned so far, critically reviewing all the available data on sex differences (including physiology). Regarding brain size, he affirms that it is relative, not absolute, brain size that matters – and finds that when the body-weight/brain-size ratio is used, women emerge as having slightly larger brains (a finding that still stands and is typical for higher primates) – a fact, he notes, known since 1836. There are, however, further technical and logical difficulties which might serve to further underestimate female brain size (although nobody, he believes, has arrived at a satisfactory method of settling the question). A similar reversal of the assumption that women have smaller frontal lobes (traditional site of 'lofty intellectual processes') emerges from recent data; again they are equal or slightly superior to men – although there is actually no real reason to ascribe any 'specially exalted functions' to them.

While Ellis (quite erroneously) holds women's sense of smell to be inferior to that of men, their taste sense, contrary to Galton, is superior. He also finds fault with Lombroso, countering his findings of inferior female sensitivities to touch and pain with those of better-designed studies by the American psychologist Jastrow. On intellectual capacity he is, in 1896, somewhat more supportive of traditional views, but aware of how environmental factors and the inferior social position of women might be implicated. By 1914 he has changed tack, insisting that although there may be differences in kind, 'In all the ordinary affairs of life the intelligence of women, whatever sexual differences may exist, proceeds side by side with that of men' (1914 edn, p. 263). Ellis was a leading male supporter of feminism and sometimes curiously anticipates points made more recently:

> Men have had their revenge on Nature and on her protégé. While women have been largely absorbed in that sphere of sexuality which is Nature's, men have roamed the earth, sharpening their aptitudes and energies in perpetual conflict with Nature. It has thus come about that the subjugation of Nature by Man has often practically involved the subjugation, physical and mental, of women by men.
>
> (1896, p. 395)

And he sarcastically observes: 'Women, it is true, remain nearer than men to the infantile state; but, on the other hand, men approach more nearly than women to the ape-like and senile state' (1896, p. 394). Even more pertinently he comments: 'So long as maternity under certain conditions is practically counted as a criminal act, it cannot be said that the feminine element in life has yet been restored to due honour' (1896, p. 396).

Ellis, one of the most important Psychological writers on sex, represented a liberal empirically oriented position, highly critical and cautious regarding prevailing stereotypes. His was, however, rather a lone voice within Psychology during the first half of the century. Much more influential were the new psychoanalytic and Jungian accounts. Though steeped in late nineteenth-century ideas about women, both Freud and Jung develop more ambiguous and complex theories regarding psychological sex differences. They may, none the less, be considered traditional insofar as they tend to see these as universal and in some sense innate or inescapable, rather than culturally produced. Both were initially seen by most feminists as embodiments of the patriarchal attitude towards women, but the present picture is far less straightforward than this (see, for example, Appignanesi and Forrester, 1993). Concepts like 'penis envy' (in Freud's case) or 'mother archetype' (in Jung's) are easily taken from the full theoretical contexts providing their technical meanings and ridiculed. Freud departed further from tradition than Jung. The key to female psychology for Freud lies primarily, of course, in the distinctive features of the infant girl's family position, combined with her biology. To oversimplify grossly: unlike the male, the female is not required to shift her primary identification from the mother to the opposite sex parent; for this reason – coupled with her absence of a penis – the Oedipal phase during which the boy resolves incestuous and patricidal wishes and emerges identifying with the father (now internalised as his 'super-ego') takes a very different form. Although her incestuous desires for the father have, like a boy's for his mother, to be somehow resolved, this resolution is necessarily less clear-cut, given her original identification with the mother and the fact that she does not suffer the boy's intense castration anxiety – a threat emanating primarily (though not exclusively) from the father. One upshot is that within psychoanalytic thought it was possible to preserve the notion of women as less securely moral and insightful, and more reliant on uncritical conformity to received precepts handed down by male authority. She is also less pressurised to transcend the early stages; in Mitchell's summary:

> She can with impunity continue to love her father and hate her mother as a rival, especially as these emotions are 'desexualized' with the latency period. That her mother as rival is stronger than the little girl does not seem to matter much, because she has no absolute strength and the little girl has nothing to lose. But the little boy fears the father who is his rival for his mother's love, because the father is truly powerful and potent and the boy has just that potency to lose. So while the girl can linger secure in this phase of life, the boy must leave it quickly.

(1974, p. 97)

The Freudian woman remains, to a large degree, the traditional woman with many of her negative traits (though not less intelligent), but the universality of her plight is due less to biology as such than to the universality of the developmental psychodynamics that this entails, involving a particular patterning of family relationships and targeting of the sexual instinct. While the Freudian male continues to see women in terms, particularly, of the mother role, this is not due to the projection of some archetypal image but to the persistence of an inner *imago* of his own mother as a desired ideal. The woman too sees men through the *imago* of her father. This backtracks markedly from neo-romantic doctrines.

Jung remained more loyal to Romanticism. For him we are all psychologically androgynous, a female anima dominates the male unconscious and a male animus the female one. The great female sex-role archetypes (along with more numerous male equivalents) are universal psychic realities, underlying our individual identities. One task is to avoid becoming, as it were, 'possessed' by any one of them. In Jung's personality typology, females are more typically dominated by the 'feeling' and to some extent the 'intuition' functions than men, in whom 'thinking' and 'sensation' tend to prevail. Jung's notion of complementarity precluded overt judgements on the relative merits of the sexes, but he gave a green light to quasi-mystical exaltation of archetypal roles like earth mother, virgin, wise old woman and the like, which some feminists have eagerly exploited and revalued – not perhaps quite what Jung had in mind. One's impression is that he was an unregenerated romantic, in the everyday sense, regarding women. Kerr (1994) argues that Sabina Spielrein (who ironically became a Freudian) was the ultimate source of his anima concept. He had numerous relationships with female clients and colleagues, and surely he flattered them all mightily as avatars of the archetypal Sophia, goddess of wisdom. A woman engineer – with her he would have had trouble.

In the meantime, from *c*.1910 to 1939, mainstream Psychology seems to have paid the psychology of women little attention of any importance. Sex itself, however, was a topic of growing interest – in addition to Ellis there was a pioneering US study of women's sexual behaviour by Katherine Bement Davis (1929), a precursor of the famous Kinsey Report (1953). All the research was conducted by women and the findings helped begin to erode popular assumptions about the low extent of pre-marital female sexual activity, masturbation and such. Another source of relevant literature at this time was the contraception and birth-control campaign (which to some extent took over the energies of the suffragette movement), the leading British figure in which was the redoubtable Dr Marie Stopes.

It is only around the late 1940s and early 1950s that there are signs of a real awakening of Psychological concern with the position of women. Horney counters the notion of 'penis envy' with a corresponding 'womb envy' in males, the existentialist Simone de Beauvoir publishes *The Second Sex* (1949), and Betty Friedan's *The Feminine Mystique* (1963) follows soon after. Even so, as late as 1968 such works appeared (to this male at least) to represent feminism's last throes, not a new beginning. By 1970 'women's lib.' had, however, stormed the cultural centre-stage. One significant work from this first phase was Elaine Morgan (1972) which caused a furore in human-evolution circles by arguing that women too had played a central role, rather than male hunters making all the running.

The impact of the new feminism on Psychology was complex. Since the 1930s the US-based anthropological tradition of studying child-rearing had expanded into a broader investigation of cross-cultural differences in character and sex roles (Eleanor Maccoby being most eminent in the latter). The new feminism coincided with the wider academic dissemination of this information, especially on Social Psychology courses. The lesson was that there were huge cross-cultural differences in sex roles, although a few underlying trends did exist (e.g. women rarely fought as warriors) and developmental psychologists embarked on intensive research into the acquisition of sex roles in relation to child-rearing practices. The topic now under scrutiny underwent an important shift, paralleling events in the area of 'race' (see Chapter 16). Previously, insofar as Psychology considered women, it was with respect to their seemingly distinctive psychological characteristics – 'the psychology of women'. The new move was to consider the psychological and social sources of sexism and sex differences. It being more or less axiomatic at this point that one must assume that the sexes were *not* essentially different psychologically to any significant degree, then the agenda had to be to explore how, as a matter of fact, the *apparent* psychological differences are imposed (by culture, child-rearing and social psychological processes) on psychologically neutral biological traits.

A further move rapidly followed: existing modes of research and theorising are themselves distinctively masculine in character (see, for example, Sandra Harding, 1986). Something quite complex is going on here, with ramifications way beyond Psychology. With a mounting crisis of confidence in humanity's ability to manage its affairs, responsibility for this failure is naturally seen as resting with the most empowered section of the species, i.e. white males. In this context traditional female qualities such as greater emotionality or closeness to nature, hitherto patronisingly contained or denigrated, become revalued, while traditionally highly valued male rationality and objectivity are the very traits implicated in their failure. Philosophers are, in any case, increasingly questioning the positivist notion of 'objectivity'. For Psychology this problematises orthodox methodologies as *themselves* being one more arena of expression of male psychology in the subject-matter sense. But it is now also an open question how far, if at all, the 'feminine' virtues are necessarily distributed along biological gender lines: what is clearer is that their traditional cultural classification of psychological traits in this way backfires on the males largely responsible for creating and sustaining it. Instead of Psychology studying the psychology of women, we have an emerging 'women's Psychology' viewing Psychology as itself an expression of male psychology.

As an example of this, consider 'The One or the Other? Textual Analysis of Masculine Power and Feminist Empowerment' by Morawski and Steele (1991). Among many points in this complex paper is one occurring during a critique of a 1969 publication by the personality theorist Walter Mischel, who has already, it is shown, got carried away by a 'valve' metaphor. Having established the actuality of the mental 'reducing valve', Mischel off-handedly comments: 'When we observe a woman who seems hostile and fiercely independent some of the time but passive, dependent, and feminine on other occasions, our reducing valve usually makes us choose between the two syndromes.' Suddenly introducing women into a previously genderless text in this way produces a number of perturbations. First, and most obviously, it throws the reader's position into question. 'When we observe a woman' is a phrase requiring the reader to join the author in a typical male activity, 'girl watching' (p. 114). A few more quotes reveal how Mischel has imported into his apparently ungendered 'objective' account a whole fantasy about castrating 'ladies' and the superiority of traditional male values, typifying traditional Psychology's adoption of 'the male gaze'. One central lesson to be drawn is that empathising, non-objectifying, 'feminine' modes of enquiry can be just as useful, and often superior, to male ones, especially in the area of Psychological knowledge.

The current situation defies easy summarisation. First the notion that there *is* an essentially distinct 'psychology of women' is itself called into question, undermining the whole rationale for a sub-specialism, 'the psychology of women'. The issue then becomes a contingent one of how gender differences are produced, by whom and in whose interests, moving the question into the arena of social power relations. There is a risk here, however, that denial of essential differences becomes tantamount to saying that (still inferior) women can become like (still superior) men in the right circumstances. This is averted by an ironic return to much of the traditional stereotyping, in which the traditional evaluation of the classic sex-role traits is challenged, along with the notion that they are necessarily gender-exclusive. There can be no return to the older 'psychology of women' (in which men define a human normality from which women deviate), at least without a corresponding 'psychology of men'. But also note the continued tension here, as in many other areas, between the needs to positively affirm differences and to deny them. At present we are again in the middle of the story (we were never anywhere else). Numerous outstanding issues remain unresolved. In particular we still, I think, have not fully understood if and how psychology and biological gender are related. It is logically possible that there are in some sense 'essential' differences – at least in how psychological traits are distributed. The difficulty is our notorious inability to pay more than lip-service to the slogan 'equal but different'. The solutions are either to deny difference, or to decouple the evaluative connotations of psychological traits from biological gender identity.

Does this mean that all the things written on the topic prior to, say, 1950 are worthless? Certainly not. As Juliet Mitchell argued regarding psychoanalysis, they are themselves evidence, often highly revealing, for how gender relations are constructed and managed. We do not need to read texts on their author's own terms, and this chapter is, I acknowledge, no exception.

BIBLIOGRAPHY

Further reading

Appignanesi, L. and J. Forrester (1993) *Freud's Women*, London: Virago. Encyclopaedic study of the role of women in the history of psychoanalysis.
Chodorow, N. (1992) *Feminism and Psychoanalytic Theory*, London: Yale University Press.
Ellenberger, Henri F. (1970) *The Discovery of the Unconscious: The History and Evolution of Dynamic Psychiatry*, London: Allen Lane.
Matlin, M.W. (1993, 2nd edn) *The Psychology of Women*, New York: Harcourt Brace Jovanovich. The major current US textbook.
Mitchell, J. (1974) *Psychoanalysis and Feminism*, London: Allen Lane.
Morawski, J.G. (1994) *Practical Feminisms. Reconstructing Psychology*, Ann Arbor: University of Michigan Press.
Sayers, J. (1986) *Sexual Contradictions: Psychology, Psychoanalysis, and Feminism*, London: Tavistock.
Scarborough, E. and L. Furumoto (1987) *Untold Lives: The First Generation of American Women Psychologists*, New York: Columbia University Press.
Weisstein, N. (1993) 'Psychology Constructs the Female or the Fantasy Life of the Male Psychologist', plus commentaries, *Feminism and Psychology* 3(2):194–245. Revised and expanded version of her 1968 paper 'Kinder, Küche, Kirche as Scientific Law: Psychology Constructs the Female'.

References

Aristotle's Masterpiece. Usually published without dates or publisher as a small book in red cloth covers.
Bachofen, J.J. (1967) *Myth, Religion, and Mother Right: Selected Writings of J.J. Bachofen*, trans. R. Manheim, introduction by Joseph Campbell, London: Routledge & Kegan Paul. Contains extracts from *Das Mutterrecht*.
Beauvoir, S. de (1949, English edn 1960) *The Second Sex*, London: Jonathan Cape.
Bell, T. (1899) *Kalogynomia or the Laws of Female Beauty: Being the Elementary Principles of that Science*, London: Walpole Press ('for subscribers only').
Boucé, P.-G. (ed.) (1982) *Sexuality in Eighteenth Century Britain*, Manchester: Manchester University Press.
Copley, Mrs (*c*.1860) *The Young Wife; or, Hints to Married Daughters*, London: The Religious Tract Society.
Davis, K.B. (1929) *Factors in the Sex Life of Twenty-Two Hundred Women*, London: Harper.
Ellis, H. (1896, 5th rev. edn 1914) *Man and Woman: A Study of Human Secondary Sexual Characters*, London: Walter Scott.
Ellis, H. (1936) *Studies in the Psychology of Sex* (4 vols), New York: Random House.
Foucault, M. (1979) *The History of Sexuality, Vol. 1*, London: Allen Lane. Further volumes followed this.
Friedan, B. (1963, reprint 1965) *The Feminine Mystique*, Harmondsworth: Penguin.
Galton, F. (1883, reprint 1919) *Inquiries into Human Faculty and its Development*, London: Dent.
Greer, G. (1970) *The Female Eunuch*, London: MacGibbon & Kee.
Harding, S. (1986) *The Science Question in Feminism*, Milton Keynes: Open University Press.
Kerr, J. (1994) *A Most Dangerous Method: The Story of Jung, Freud, and Sabina Spielrein*, London: Sinclair-Stevenson.

Kinsey, A.C., W.B. Pomeroy, C.E. Martin and P.H. Gebhard (1953) *Sexual Behavior in the Human Female*, Philadelphia: Lippincott; London: Saunders.
Lombroso, C. and W. Ferrero (1895) *The Female Offender*, London: Fisher Unwin.
Maccoby, E.E. (ed.) (1967) *The Development of Sex Differences*, London: Tavistock.
Maccoby, E.E. and C.N. Jacklin (1974) *The Psychology of Sex Differences*, Stanford: Stanford University Press.
Miles, R. (1991) *The Rites of Man: Love, Sex and Death in the Making of the Male*, London: Grafton Books.
Mill, J.S. (1869) *The Subjection of Women*, London: Longmans Green, Reader & Dyer.
Millett, K. (1971) *Sexual Politics*, New York: Avon Books.
Moebius (1901) *Über den physiologischen Schwachsinn des Weibes* (On the Physiological Imbecility of Woman), Halle: Marhold. Ellenberger provides no initials.
Morawski, J.G. (ed.) (1988) *The Rise of Experimentation in American Psychology*, New Haven: Yale University Press. See especially her own 'Impossible Experiments and Practical Constructions: The Social Bases of Psychologists' Work', pp. 72–93.
Morawski, J.G. (1990) 'Toward the Unimagined: Feminism and Epistemology in Psychology', in R.T. Hare-Mustin and J. Maracek (eds) *Making a Difference*, New Haven: Yale University Press.
Morawski, J.G. and R.S. Steele (1991) 'The One or the Other? Textual Analysis of Masculine Power and Feminist Empowerment', *Theory & Psychology* 1(1):107–31.
Morgan, E. (1972, rev. edn 1985) *The Descent of Woman*, London: Souvenir Press.
Pearsall, R. (1969, reprint 1971 Penguin) *The Worm in the Bud: The World of Victorian Sexuality*, London: Weidenfeld & Nicolson.
Rowbotham, S. (1973) *Woman's Consciousness, Man's World*, Harmondsworth: Penguin.
Stone, L. (1977) *The Family, Sex and Marriage in England 1500–1800*, London: Weidenfeld & Nicolson.
Stopes, M. (1918) *Married Love: A New Contribution to the Solution of Sexual Difficulties*, London: Putnam. By 1931 this was into its twentieth edition.
Stopes, M. (1928) *Enduring Passion: Further New Contributions to the Solution of Sex Difficulties, Being the Continuation of Married Love*, London: Putnam.
Terman, L. and C.C. Miles (1936) *Sex and Personality: Studies in Masculinity and Femininity*, New York: McGraw-Hill.
Walker, A. (c.1850, reprint 1898) *Woman Physiologically Considered as to Mind, Morals, Marriage, Matrimonial Slavery, Infidelity and Divorce*, Birmingham: Edward Baker.
Warner, M. (1976, reprint 1985 Picador) *Alone of All Her Sex: The Myth and the Cult of the Virgin Mary*, London: Weidenfeld & Nicolson.
Weininger, O. (1906) *Sex and Character*, London: Heinemann.

Two earlier texts not discussed in the main text are the following:

Patrick, G.T.W. (1895) 'The Psychology of Women', *Popular Science Monthly* 47:209–25.
Woolley, H.T. (1910) 'Psychological Literature: A Review of the Recent Literature on the Psychology of Sex', *Psychological Bulletin* 7:335–42. A fierce attack on prevailing attitudes.

See also the journal *Signs* and, among many other writers, Erica Burman, Donna Haraway, Evelyn F. Keller, Celia Kitzinger, Carolyn Merchant, Paula Nicholson, Ann Oakley, Janet Radcliffe Richards and S.A. Shields. In recent years the psychology of lesbianism has emerged as a distinct field, and there is currently (1996) a controversy within the BPS over the formation of a 'Psychology of Lesbianism' section.

16 Psychology and 'race'

There is a vast historical, philosophical, political, sociological and anthropological literature on 'race', perhaps the most sensitive issue currently perturbing our culture (notoriously, in Psychology, in the 'race and IQ' debate). Here we consider only Psychology's involvements. Although (unlike 'racism') 'race' is not a psychological concept, it has always been seen as having a psychological dimension. Psychology, we will see, has both promoted and opposed racism. Before pursuing this I should make my position clear: I do not believe that the notion of innate psychological racial differences is meaningful. Current genetic understanding of human diversity is roughly as follows: there is a single human 'gene pool' containing numerous alleles for each genetically determined trait. Within this, sub-pools may, for mainly geographic reasons, become relatively isolated from the remainder for longer or shorter periods. These are less genetically diverse than the total pool, containing only a sample of the total number of alleles. During isolation some new mutations may occur, adding unique alleles to a group's repertoire – but these will never be *universal* within it. Circumstances may exert their own selection pressures on the frequency of distribution (e.g. hairiness genes may be favoured in cold climates) thereby rendering them more or less frequent than elsewhere. The upshot is that isolated groups may acquire a somewhat distinctive typical physical appearance (although not all group members will conform to this). If, however, we map the frequency of different alleles globally we find that they vary enormously. Blood groups provide one pattern, hair type another, earwax type a third, and so on – in other words the world population is carved up differently for different genes. This must presumably also apply to any genes determining psychological traits (if such there be) – *there is no reason to assume that they would correlate with those physical traits traditionally used to identify 'races'*. Moreover we never encounter genetic traits that are both unique to *and* universal within a particular group, while no group is ever 100 per cent isolated – there is always some genetic exchange with outside. Gene-pool composition constantly shifts in any case, both by chance and as conditions of life change.

'Races' as distinct biological entities with some essential character do not therefore exist. Shifting from physical to psychological, the situation becomes even more obscure since the linkage between the two is highly convoluted, involving the cultural meanings given to physical traits or genetically rooted behaviours. Strictly speaking, I would argue that psychology is a product of cultural construal of genetic traits with no essential psychological meaning of their own. To explore this here would take us too far afield, but one implication must be spelled out: the very concept of 'race' itself and the psychological meanings that have accreted to racial classifications and their associated physical traits are *themselves* products of modern European culture.

Concerning 'racism', D.T. Goldberg (1993) argues that we should avoid the trap of imagining this as a single, unitary phenomenon. Rather we must approach it pragmatically since it varies in character over time, culture and circumstance. He offers a definition which I think is acceptable, namely that 'racism' should be used for any practice that has as its effect, intended *or unintended,* the exclusion of a group from full access to the rights, responsibilities and opportunities enjoyed by the majority population. This needs qualifying somewhat to differentiate it from sexism, 'ablism' or homophobia but is, I feel, broadly adequate. What is especially interesting for us, however, is that the concept of 'racism' as, by definition, a 'bad thing' and a psychological phenomenon – a psychological property that some people possess – was largely created by psychologists. This is ironic because over time the adequacy of seeing it as a purely psychological phenomenon has been increasingly challenged.

In what follows I can only sketch the main features of a story beginning in the mid-nineteenth century. Evolutionary theory provided an apparently scientific rationale for racial inequality, a doctrine now called 'scientific racism'. 'Races' formed an evolutionary hierarchy with Europeans at the top and, for example, indigenous Australians, South African 'bushmen' and South American Indians at the bottom. Intermediate rankings varied but Africans were always low, while Chinese and Indians jostled for silver and bronze medal placings, as it were. Much could be said about this but a few points must suffice here:

1 Physically the human evolutionary process was widely held to have finished and Europeans to have 'won'.
2 'Civilisation' was seen as a sort of natural phenomenon – the pinnacle of evolutionary development. European culture's superiority was not therefore seen as *cultural* but as *natural.* The white European was, by virtue of his (definitely!) evolutionary superiority, the vehicle by which this essentially *natural* progression had been accomplished.
3 'Lower races' were thus in diverse states of 'arrested development', in evolutionary dead-ends from which escape was impossible without white aid, if at all (levels of optimism differed).
4 Though fervently promoting this image, anthropologists and biologists were actually unable to discover clear-cut criteria for identifying racial groups. Skin colour, skull shape, hair type and complicated physical anthropometric ratios all proved inadequate.

5 Finally, Victorian interest in race was as much devoted to identifying the different European races as non-white ones. History itself being widely seen as driven by racial competition, European nations were cast as representing different racial groups. While resulting in the most extraordinary muddle, this political dimension to the race issue persisted in Europe with eventually disastrous results.

Psychology's involvement begins with Galton. Galton acquired his contempt for non-Europeans during an expedition in his twenties to Southwest Africa (Namibia). Only later did he give this a scientific gloss. He is, up to a point, optimistic in the long term; some lower races at least are capable, under white guidance, of improvement – if not full equality with whites. He also attempted to quantify levels of racial intelligence, estimating the percentage in each race likely, on a thirteen-point scale, to be geniuses, or equivalent to the European average, and so on. While writing relatively little on the issue as such, Galton's scientific racism was fundamental to his evolutionary viewpoint, and although more immediate matters of domestic degeneration and eugenics dominated his work, sooner or later Psychology would, he foresaw, have to attend to nurturing and controlling the 'lower races'. Galton, one must stress, was a major player in the mid-nineteenth-century scene – not merely a follower of 'scientific racism', but among its leading architects. Theoretically, however, Herbert Spencer had more impact, especially in the United States. Of most importance was what we might call the 'Spencer hypothesis', that the amount of energy allocated to higher functions of reason and will was much greater in whites than in 'primitives'. Conversely the latter allocated proportionately more to basic psychophysical and instinctive functions, thereby *excelling* whites on things like RT, perceptual and auditory discrimination, rote memory and mimicry, while being more dominated by instincts, less capable of self-control and long-term planning, etc. This idea suggested some kinds of Psychological research. Two papers claiming to confirm Spencer appeared in the *Psychological Review* during the 1890s, one on RT and one on memory, comparing white, 'negro' and (in the RT case) American Indian performance. It was obviously a no-win situation for non-whites: superior performance confirmed the Spencer hypothesis, while inferior performance 'proved' them inferior anyway.

Psychologists' positions were not, however, entirely uniform, scientific racism providing some latitude for interpretation. At one extreme is Le Bon (1899) for whom heredity is the most important factor in human life, every race has its distinct soul, and the major races are virtually different species (harking back to the pre-evolutionary doctrine of 'polygenism', especially popular in France). G.S. Hall (1904), by contrast, argued that 'lower races' were not in a state of arrested development but of adolescence, and would eventually reach maturity. He roundly attacked European treatment of other 'races', lamenting the destruction of peoples and cultures in terms befitting the anti-Columbus literature which greeted the 1992 quincentenary. We should respect native cultures; the white civilising and christianising mission should be based on understanding and building upon existing beliefs and customs. Translated into practice, however, this apparently more enlightened, if extremely paternalistic, view provided a rationale for segregation, separate education for blacks and American Indians, and black disenfranchisement.

At the turn of the century two events occur of major importance for the study of 'race differences': the 1898 Cambridge anthropological expedition to the Torres Strait (between Australia and New Guinea) and research done at the 1904 St Louis Exposition by R.S. Woodworth and F.G. Bruner. The Cambridge expedition included three subsequent leaders of British Psychology: W.H.R. Rivers, C.S. Myers and William McDougall, all experienced in the new experimental Psychology. Their wide-ranging studies of psycho-physical performance, including visual perception (Rivers), hearing (Myers) and RTs (McDougall), disclosed *no* systematic superiority among Torres Strait islanders (Rivers, 1901). Inspired by this, Woodworth took advantage of the presence of large numbers of foreigners at the St Louis Exposition to further study differences in perception and hearing (Bruner doing the latter) as well as some other phenomena. Though not published until 1908 (Bruner) and 1910 (Woodworth) the general thrust of the results was soon widely known: the Spencer hypothesis again found no confirmation. These two sets of findings largely laid the notion of primitive superiority in basic functions to rest (at least in scientific circles) and little further research was undertaken on the question. Attention now turned to the higher functions, especially intelligence, but these had to await appropriate research techniques. By 1910 several of these were available, including the Binet intelligence test, 'race and IQ' research starting with Alice Strong (1913).

After this 'race Psychology' remained a strand in US Psychology until the mid-1930s. The context of the earliest work was the issue of 'negro education' and typically compared white and Afro-American children's performance. Although Northern black children performed better than those in the South they nevertheless always underperformed the white groups. In the South such results helped to justify continued educational segregation and restriction of black curricula to practical subjects like woodwork and gardening (e.g. Ferguson, 1916). This phase culminated with the 1917–18 Army group intelligence test data (see Chapter 11). While not directly contributing much themselves, many leading psychologists such as Terman, Yerkes and Thorndike initially supported race Psychology.

Another topic had now arisen upon which the Army tests were also seen as bearing – the poor quality of southern European immigrants. This was bolstered by the rise of eugenics and what was then called 'nordicism' – belief in north European superiority, promoted in particular by Madison Grant's best-seller *The Passing of the Great Race* (1916). The army results revealed both dramatic Afro-American and, to a lesser but still considerable extent, southern European underperformance and received their most influential evaluation in C.C. Brigham (1923), which accepted Grant's nordicism and was adamantly racialist in tone. Along with smaller-scale studies of European 'race differences' this fuelled the immigration control campaign, and helped to ensure the passing of the Immigration Restriction Law (1924). As far as Afro-Americans were concerned, it was spotted fairly early that some northern 'negroes' actually outperformed whites from some Southern states, triggering a controversy that persisted until the 1940s (and still actually rumbles on; see, for example, Galloway, 1993). Until the early 1920s scientific racism, minus the 'Spencer hypothesis', provided the main theoretical framework for race-difference research.

The Army tests have received most historical attention, but race Psychology's concerns extended far beyond this. While Afro-Americans remained the largest single group studied, by 1930 they only constituted about 20 per cent of non-native white American subjects, alongside Japanese, Italians, Zulus, Jews and American Indians, etc. And although intelligence was the main topic studied, research also considered, for example, colour preferences, 'will temperament', fatigue proneness, 'social efficiency' and mental illness. Two psychologists in particular adopted this field as their speciality: T.R. Garth, who mostly studied American Indians and Mexicans, and S.D. Porteus, a Honolulu-based Australian immigrant who studied Hawaii's several 'racial' groups (Japanese, Chinese, native Hawaiian, Portuguese, Filipino and various 'mixed-race' permutations). There were, however, numerous one-off studies and several other psychologists devoted much effort to race-difference research. J. Peterson, for example, undertook several large-scale pieces of research, becoming the principal expert on 'negro intelligence'.

Opposition and criticism, never entirely absent, escalated during the 1920s, first in the popular liberal press and black magazines, but increasingly within the Psychological literature. By 1930 race Psychology was under extreme pressure. First, those studying the topic shared contemporary US Psychology's aspirations towards scientific credibility and were thus very sensitive to methodological criticisms. As a result many became increasingly conscious of the difficulties in unambiguously establishing the existence of innate racial differences. Some, like Brigham himself, totally recanted their earlier positions, while others became more qualified and cautious in interpreting their results. Only a small handful (such as Porteus) held firm beyond the mid-1930s. Internally, its own scientific rigour was sapping the race-differences project at the heart of race Psychology. Externally, however, the assault also intensified on several fronts after 1928. Thoroughgoing attacks on its methods and interpretations achieve more prominence, a major figure being the social psychologist Otto Klineberg. On the sociology/Psychology border-line there was growing interest in race prejudice and attitudes. This in effect reversed the logic of the entire problem: instead of the distinct psychological character of different races, it is the need to see races as psychologically distinct in the first place that needs explaining. On the anthropology border-line (incorporating some psychoanalytic thinkers) the 'culture and personality school' is crystallising. (Mead, 1928, may perhaps be taken as its starting point although it really originates at the beginning of the century when Franz Boas, Mead's teacher and leading US anthropologist, abandoned race in favour of culture.) Meanwhile growing numbers of Psychology graduates (including some non-whites) are working in the field as social workers, educationalists, clinicians and the like. The race-differences issue simply had no relevance to the practical issues that they faced, and after *c*.1930 we find a steep rise in the number of atheoretical applied papers being published (often intra-racial) on such topics as dealing with clients from ethnic minorities, factors affecting children's self-esteem and so on (there is some overlap here with the prejudice studies). With Klineberg's *Race Differences* (1935) constituting its funeral service, race Psychology was to all intents and purposes dead, while the contemporary political and ideological climate was increasingly hostile in view of the rise of Nazi anti-semitism. Garth, race Psychology's leading advocate, unequivocally changed sides.

The race Psychology phase served a curious function for Psychology, and for wider cultural thinking regarding 'race'. Rather than being a simple manifestation of racism, it was more a process in which the debates between supporters and critics collectively emancipated the discipline from theoretical commitment to racism and enabled it, in effect, to *create* the concept of 'racism' (a word first used in the 1930s). While not the only factor, Psychology's scientific failure to find race differences enabled it to *discover* 'racism'. Before *c*.1930 'racialist' doctrines and theories were acceptable intellectual positions, controversial perhaps but not seen as necessarily having ethical implications. Scientific racism's legacy of respectability took some time to dispel. The controversy within Psychology, in which most participants acted in good faith, finally enabled most psychologists, including erstwhile race psychologists, to see (a) that race differences were proving extraordinarily elusive and were possibly an illusion and (b) that, given this, fervent belief in such differences must (as they saw it) be irrational and, *ipso facto*, a form of psychopathology (and by the late 1930s the discipline had a number of conceptual resources for elaborating on this, including psychoanalysis). While not intended as such, race Psychology served as a self-emancipatory exercise via which the unconscious racism initially motivating it was forced to the surface and consciously recognised.

This process saw the first formulation of numerous criticisms of race-differences research which have largely persisted to the present (although more have been added). I will now outline these and suggest why the responses to them were inadequate. The arguments were both methodological and theoretical (or conceptual).

1 Differences may be accounted for by non-hereditary factors. Typical responses were: (a) psychological race differences must be the default assumption in the light of evolutionary theory and by analogy with physical differences; (b) current socio-economic status itself reflects ability; (c) environmental factors can be controlled for in designing research. The first

of these arguments had a high prima-facie plausibility – surely major physical differences would be accompanied by covert psychological ones? Technically, the key fallacy here is that, as explained earlier, the assumption that distribution of psychological traits systematically maps onto the physical traits traditionally defining racial identity is mistaken. This was seen somewhat hazily from fairly early on, but only became clear with advances in genetics from the mid-1930s. Klineberg (1935) saw the fallacy more simply as lying in the assumption (which he denied) that physical traits were of some, albeit covert, psychological significance. The 'status reflects intelligence' argument tended to be dropped as time went on, its flaws being fairly glaring (especially during the Depression), although it has recently re-emerged. Finally, optimism about the eliminability of environmental factors in research design progressively faded, this being in any case environmentalist behaviourism's heyday in the discipline at large. Although some persisted in thinking that it was logically feasible, most came to suspect that insoluble methodological paradoxes were involved..

2 Tests may be culturally biased. Usual response: bias can be offset by adopting non-verbal and performance-type tests. In the late 1920s doubts also arose about the value of group tests; individual tests (on which 'race differences' were generally smaller) might, it was felt, be more appropriate. There was, however, a poorly developed appreciation of the profundity of this problem among experimentalists before the mid-1930s. For social anthropologist critics, conversely, it appeared patently obvious, and as their views gained wider airing the problem of 'culture-fair' tests became more acute. It is still not entirely resolved and involves a paradox – you can only know that you have succeeded in designing a culture-fair test if it shows no differences; if it does show differences there is no way of knowing whether these are innate or culturally determined.

3 Overlap in distribution of scores demonstrates that there is no essential connection between 'race' and ability (or any other trait). Typical responses to this were: (a) the frequency of exceptional individuals determines a race's character and fortunes; (b) non-white high performers are those with some white 'blood' (the 'mulatto hypothesis'). The first was an old scientific racist tenet which faded during the early 1920s. The latter was empirically falsified – performance did not correlate with amount of white ancestry. The modern response is that significant mean differences between racial groups are scientific 'facts' and, notwithstanding overlap, they have socio-economic policy implications for attempts at enabling underperforming groups to achieve equality. This, however, still hinges on the false assumption that racial groups have an objective existence, with a fixed genetic character, in the first place.

4 The tester's own 'race' will have an 'experimenter effect' (as we now say) on performance. 'Experimenter effects' were largely ignored, though occasionally noted as a possible minor factor distorting the magnitude of differences in specific cases. They were not considered of fundamental

importance. Klineberg included 'rapport' as a factor affecting credibility of race-differences research but full appreciation of experimenter effects did not dawn on Psychology until the 1960s.

5 Sampling of non-white subjects may be unrepresentative. Some data, such as the US Army findings, were seen as overcoming this. Sampling was a perennial headache for race psychologists; however, the cumulative impact of repeated findings of differences similar in direction, if not degree, reassured them. In retrospect the variations in degree of difference may themselves be seen as weakening the nativist hypothesis: since large *within*-race differences were, it was usually agreed, environmentally caused, invoking heredity to account for sometimes minimal *between*-race differences would appear superfluous. This argument was not, however, clearly developed prior to Klineberg (1935). One should add that if races are mythical entities anyway, the notion of fair sampling becomes irrelevant – there is nothing to be sampled.

6 The concept of 'race' has no clear scientific biological meaning. The usual response was that 'race' might be theoretically problematic, but this did not affect the current reality of the existence of identifiably distinct peoples possessing unique and ineradicable innate traits resulting from millennia of reproductive isolation. This in part reflected an exaggerated view of the extent and duration of episodes of reproductive isolation and in part an old-fashioned awe of big numbers when applied to years. For relatively slow-breeding species like humans even a few thousand years' reproductive isolation (rare anyway, and probably never complete) amounts to little against a species history now estimated at *c.*150,000 years (for anatomically modern *Homo sapiens*).

7 'Racial' levels of performance can change over time, therefore current underperformance may be transient (Garth called this 'race mobility'). This was often simply rejected; evidence for 'race mobility' really reflected genetic changes resulting from out-breeding and racial contact (e.g. by the Greeks following the classic age). Even if it did occur it was on a time-scale too long to take into account realistically. It is perhaps necessary to differentiate this issue from the previous one. 'Race mobility' (an obsolete expression) really referred to the possibility of rapid (and reversible) changes to a gene pool's composition when new environmental circumstances alter the selection vectors. The previous issue, however, relates to an irreversible process of quasi-speciation involving mutation events and long-sustained idiosyncratic selection pressures. Acceptance of the former as a source of fluctuations in 'racial' performance does not entail acceptance of the latter as a source of racial sub-species. The deeper implication that this 'race mobility' subverts the heredity/environment distinction itself does not seem to have been drawn (and often remains unacknowledged to this day): in a nutshell, it means that heredity is itself environmentally determined.

8 The entire project was racist in motivation. People like Porteus responded that as scientists they were interested in finding the objective facts.

Sentimentally philanthropic 'race levelling' and racially biased 'race dogmatism' represented the poles between which they had to steer to find the truth. Versions of this are still used by the pro-differences camp in the 'race and IQ' controversy. Credibility of this evaporates when funding sources are identified (see below).

The baton now passed to those studying race prejudice. With the rise of Nazism, anti-semitism was naturally the primary focus of concern. Throughout the 1940s various publications on this, sometimes psychoanalytic in character, are appearing, but the best known and most influential was Adorno et al.'s *The Authoritarian Personality* (1950) (see Chapters 11 and 12). The pathologising of 'racism' now reached its apotheosis: it symptomatised a particular authoritarian personality type, driven to project its Oedipal fantasies onto out-groups as a result of distorted psychological development. As the 1950s progressed, US concerns shifted from anti-semitism towards a domestic agenda in which the civil rights movement was gathering momentum. While psychodynamic arguments persisted, they were clearly insufficient. Racism took more than one form. For those raised in racist cultures like South Africa or the Deep South, it was often no more than conformity to the values into which people had been reared, not a personal pathology. Racism, like apparent race differences, was culturally determined. As observed previously, Social Psychology's studies of prejudice were part of the intellectual wing of the civil rights movement itself. Black US psychologists like Kenneth and Mamie Clark had also begun to develop a 'black Psychology' strand within the discipline, rooted in the earlier applied genre mentioned above. By the mid–late 1960s President Johnson had enacted the appropriate legislation. One innovation for redressing Afro-American deprivation was the educational programme 'Head Start' aimed at boosting the educational performance of Afro-American children.

After three decades of relative quiescence, bar a few die-hards like Columbia University's Henry Garrett, the race-differences issue re-erupted with Arthur Jensen's 1969 report (in the prestigious *Harvard Educational Review*) on the success of the Head Start programme: 'How Much Can We Boost IQ and Scholastic Achievement?'. Jensen argued that Head Start had failed and that, notwithstanding the historical effect of environmental factors, Afro-American underperformance had a genetic basis. In the United Kingdom H.J. Eysenck took up the cudgels on his behalf. A replay of the 1930s match ensued, but on a much narrower issue: only intelligence was discussed and the debate was restricted to African/Afro-American performance. While some geneticists tightened up the counter-arguments, in some ways the controversy suffered by conflating issues of different kinds – theoretical (heritability of IQ being the principal red herring), methodological, political and moral arguments became inextricable. By the end of the 1970s it had simmered down only to receive further airing in the context of the sociobiology approach emerging in evolutionary biology. Many of the old arguments were still basically unanswered, while eminent geneticists (like R.C. Lewontin) and biologists (e.g. Stephen Jay Gould) produced new ones. Again the issue subsided, but remained undead. Recently J.P. Rushton (1994) and Herrnstein and Murray (1994) have resuscitated it once more. The publicity that the issue receives is grossly disproportionate to its importance within Psychology. It directly involves only a small minority of psychometricians, while for most psychologists it is simply not a meaningful topic of enquiry. A major source of funding for pro-differences research has been the New York-based Pioneer Fund, founded in 1937 by Wickliffe Draper, recipients of funding including Rushton ($656,672 1982–92), Richard Lynn ($388,187) and Jensen ($108,994). One is bound to conclude that the persistence of this controversy owes more to domestic US politics than it does to anything else.

Elsewhere, Psychology continues to be concerned with racism and prejudice, but the terms of engagement have changed. As increasing numbers of blacks have entered Psychology the running is being made not by white academics but by those on the receiving end, racism and gender studies fusing in this respect (Mama, 1995). We currently face two dilemmas here. First, viewing racism as a psychological issue may divert attention from other levels of analysis which are actually more relevant. Ascribing problems to psychological flaws in human nature rather than economic policies or institutional and social structures can let those responsible off the hook. Psychologists are sometimes too prone to being lured into playing this role. Second, 'race' is a myth, but identification with one's ethnic or cultural group (still inescapably racially characterised in Western culture, whatever the labels) is a central and necessary tactic in achieving liberatory aims. Imposed categories have to be adopted, redefined and revalued by those labelled as belonging to them before they can be transcended. How we resolve this dilemma is not something with which I can deal here, even if I knew how, which I do not.

To conclude, Psychology has both promoted and opposed racist policies and attitudes – more often, on balance, the latter. It should be stressed that the preceding sketch omits some interesting facets of the story, for example the inter-war mainland European fascination with the notion of 'primitive mind' (expounded by Lévy-Bruhl) and its relationship to Freudian and especially Jungian theorising about the unconscious. I have also had to leave undiscussed the Nazi version of race Psychology promulgated by, among others, E.R. Jaensch, L.F. Clauss and B. Petermann. Here I have suggested that the 1910–35 race Psychology phase was particularly significant in that it constituted the very process by which Psychology emancipated itself from scientific racism and discovered, and helped to identify, 'racism' in the current sense.

This is of course far from claiming that everything in the contemporary Psychological garden is rosy (see, for example, Howitt and Owusu-Bempah, 1994). As a discipline, Psychology is, for the most part, clearly opposed to racism. Eliminating racism at the level of organisational and disciplinary practice is rather harder. Insofar as racism continues to operate (wittingly or not) in the institutions and organisations within, and for which, psychologists work, the task will remain unfinished. Moreover, white psychologists have still not entirely succeeded in abandoning expressions and assumptions with racist, or at least eurocentric, connotations. The term 'tribal', for example, is currently causing some difficulty since it is most often used of non-European and primate groups, whereas 'clan' and 'nation' are typically used in European contexts. It would be churlish to deny that a vast sea-change has occurred since 1960, but in the mid-1990s cultural climate the 'race-differences' issue shows depressingly few signs of abating, for all the efforts of most professional psychologists.

ADDITIONAL POINTS

If the treatment of the 'race and IQ' controversy in this chapter seems to be rather peremptory this is because its cultural visibility is, in my judgement, genuinely disproportionate to its seriousness as a live issue *within* the discipline itself. See below for basic references on the issue.

There is a notion abroad that 'ethnic' is related to 'heathen', leading some to object to its use in phrases such as 'ethnic minority'. The second edition of the *Oxford English Dictionary* notes this belief and rejects it.

BIBLIOGRAPHY

Further reading

No comprehensive history of this topic is currently available.

Barkan, E. (1992) *The Retreat of Scientific Racism: Changing Concepts of Race in Britain and the United States between the World Wars*, Cambridge: Cambridge University Press. Helpful, but deals primarily with biology and anthropology.
Biddis, M.D. (ed.) (1979) *Images of Race*, Leicester: Leicester University Press. Extracts from British writers 1864–80.
Goldberg, D.T. (1993) *Racist Culture: Philosophy and the Politics of Meaning*, Oxford: Blackwell. Good, but stylistically difficult.
Howitt, D. and J. Owusu-Bempah (1994) *The Racism of Psychology: Time for a Change*, New York & London: Harvester Wheatsheaf.
Kovel, J. (1970, new edn 1988) *White Racism: A Psychohistory*, London: Allen Lane.
Mama, A. (1995) *Beyond the Masks: Race, Gender and Subjectivity*, London: Routledge.
Richards, G. (forthcoming) *'Race', Racism and Psychology*, London: Routledge. Intended to fill the aforementioned gap.
Samelson, F. (1978) 'From Race Psychology to Studies in Prejudice', *Journal of the History of the Behavioral Sciences* 14:265–78.
Stepan, N. (1982) *The Idea of Race in Science: Great Britain 1800–1960*, Hamden, Conn.: Archon Books.

Scientific racism and nineteenth-century background

Beddoe, J. (1885, reprint 1971) *The Races of Britain: A Contribution to the Anthropology of Western Europe*, London: Hutchinson.
Galton, F. (1869, reprint 1962) *Hereditary Genius*, London: Collins Fontana.

Hunt, James (1865) 'On the Negro's Place in Nature', in *Memoirs Read before the Anthropological Society of London 1863–4*, London: Trübner, pp. 1–64.

Le Bon, G. (1899) *The Psychology of Peoples*, London: Fisher Unwin.

Prichard, J. C. (1813, 3rd edn 1836) *Researches into the Physical History of Mankind* (2 vols), London: Sherwood, Gilbert & Piper.

Spencer, H. (1876) 'The Comparative Psychology of Man', reprinted in M.D. Biddis (ed.) (1979) *Images of Race*, Leicester: Leicester University Press, pp. 187–204.

Race Psychology and critics

Benedict, Ruth (1943) *Race and Racism*, London: Scientific Book Club.

Brigham, C.C. (1923) *A Study of American Intelligence*, Princeton: Princeton University Press.

Bruner, F.G. (1908) 'The Hearing of Primitive Peoples', *Archives of Psychology* 11, New York: Science Press.

Ferguson, George Oscar, Jr. (1916) 'The Psychology of the Negro: An Experimental Study', *Archives of Psychology* 36, New York: Science Press.

Garth, T.R. (1931) *Race Psychology*, New York: Whittlesey.

Hall, G.S. (1904) *Adolescence* (2 vols), New York: Appleton. See the last chapter of vol. 2.

Klineberg, O. (1935) *Race Differences*, New York: Harper.

McDougall, W. (1921) *Is America Safe for Democracy?* (UK edn entitled *National Welfare and National Decay*), London: Methuen.

Mayo, M.J. (1913) 'The Mental Capacity of the American Negro', *Archives of Psychology* 28, New York: Science Press.

Mead, M., T. Dobzhansky, E. Tobach and R.E. Light (eds) (1968) *Science and the Concept of Race*, New York: Columbia University Press.

Montagu, Ashley (1942, 5th edn 1974) *Man's Most Dangerous Myth: The Fallacy of Race*, Oxford: Oxford University Press.

Odum, H.W. (1910) *Social and Mental Traits of the Negro: Research into the Conditions of the Negro in Southern Towns*, New York: Columbia University Press.

Porteus, S.D. (with M.E. Babcock) (1926) *Race and Temperament*, Boston: Badger.

Rivers, W.H.R. (ed.) (1901, 1903) *Reports of the Cambridge Anthropological Expedition to Torres Straits, Vol. 2: Physiology and Psychology*, Cambridge: Cambridge University Press.

Strong, Alice M. (1913) 'Three Hundred and Fifty White and Colored Children Measured by the Binet–Simon Measuring Scale', *Pedagogical Seminary* 20:485–512.

Woodworth, R.S. (1910) 'Racial Differences in Mental Traits', *Science* N.S. 31:171–86.

Prejudice

A vast topic; these are some founding texts only:

Ackermann, N.W. and M. Jahoda (1950) *Anti-Semitism and Emotional Disorder: A Psychoanalytic Interpretation*, New York: Harper.

Adorno, T.W., E. Frenkel-Brunswik, D.J. Levinson and R.N. Sanford (1950) *The Authoritarian Personality* (2 vols), New York: Science Editions.

Benedict, R. (1943) *Race and Racism*, London: Scientific Book Club.

Bettelheim, B. and M. Janowitz (1950) *Dynamics of Prejudice: A Psychological and Sociological Study of Veterans*, New York: Harper & Brothers.

Dollard, N. (1937, reprint 1957) *Caste and Class in a Southern Town*, New York: Doubleday Anchor.

Fenichel, O. (1940) 'Psychoanalysis of Antisemitism', *American Imago* 1(2):24–39.

'Culture and personality' school

Benedict, R. (1935, reprint 1966) *Patterns of Culture*, London: Routledge & Kegan Paul.
Dennis, W. (1940) *The Hopi Child*, New York: Appleton-Century.
Erikson, E.H. (1950, rev. edn 1965) *Childhood and Society*, Harmondsworth: Penguin.
Kluckhohn, C. and H. Murray (eds) (1948, reprint 1949) *Personality in Nature, Society and Culture*, London: Cape.
Mead, M. (1928) *Coming of Age in Samoa*, New York: Morrow.

'Race and IQ' controversy

There is a vast amount on this; the following is a basic list only:

Pro-differences

Herrnstein, C. and R.J. Murray (1994) *The Bell Curve: Intelligence and Class Structure in American Life*, New York: Free Press.
Jensen, A. (1969) 'How Much Can We Boost IQ and Scholastic Achievement?', *Environment, Heredity, and Intelligence*, Harvard Educational Review, Reprint Series 2.
Rushton, J.P. (1994) *Race, Evolution and Behavior*, New York: Transaction.

Anti-differences

Fraser, S. (ed.) (1995) *The Bell Curve Wars: Race, Intelligence, and the Future of America*, New York: Basic Books.
Gould, S.J. (1981, reprint 1984) *The Mismeasure of Man*, London: Penguin.
Kamin, L.J. (1974) *The Science and Politics of I.Q.*, New York: Erlbaum.
Richards, G.D. (1984) 'Getting the Intelligence Controversy Knotted', *Bulletin of the British Psychological Society* 37:77–9.
Rose, S., L.J. Kamin and R.C. Lewontin (1984) *Not in Our Genes*, Harmondsworth: Penguin.

Other

Banton, M. (1967) *Race Relations*, London: Tavistock.
Banton, M. and J. Harwood (1975) *The Race Concept*, Newton Abbot: David & Charles.
Bolt, C. (1971) *Victorian Attitudes to Race*, London: Routledge & Kegan Paul.
Curtin, P.D. (1964) *The Image of Africa: British Ideas and Action, 1780–1850*, Madison, Wis.: The University of Wisconsin Press.
Galloway, F.J. (1993) 'Inferential Fragility and the 1917 Army Alpha: A New Look at the Robustness of Educational Quality Indices as Determinants of Interstate Black–White Score Differentials', *Journal of Negro Education* 63(2):251–66.
Grant, M. (1916) *The Passing of the Great Race*, New York: Scribner.
Haller, J.S., Jr. (1971) *Outcasts of Evolution: Scientific Attitudes of Racial Inferiority 1859–1900*, Urbana, Ill.: University of Illinois Press. See especially ch. 5 on Spencer influence.
Jordan, W.D. (1974) *The White Man's Burden: Historical Origins of Racism in the United States*, London: Oxford University Press.
Lorimer, D.A. (1978) *Colour, Class and the Victorians: English Attitudes to the Negro in the Mid-Nineteenth Century*, Leicester: Leicester University Press.

Owusu-Bempah, J. and D. Howitt (1994) 'Racism and the Psychological Textbook', *The Psychologist* 7(4):163–7. See also the correspondence in subsequent issues.

Shyllon, F.O. (1977) *Black People in Britain 1555–1833*, London: Oxford University Press.

Stocking, G.W., Jr. (1968) *Race, Culture and Evolution: Essays in the History of Anthropology*, New York: Free Press.

17 Psychology and war

Since 1914 Psychology has been practised in contexts dominated by war, either as a current, recent or prospective reality. Unsurprisingly then, this has left a deep imprint on the discipline. War presents Psychology with a dilemma. The majority, if not quite all, of modern psychologists accept that war is an evil pathology. This being so, their task should, ostensibly, be to diagnose its psychological roots. Such principled opposition to war is nevertheless offset by the fact that most (if again not quite all) psychologists, no less than anyone else, usually feel bound to support the war efforts of their host societies. Psychologists have been called upon increasingly to deploy their professional skills in such tasks as selection and training, propaganda and designing military technology. Perennially status-conscious, they have often welcomed the opportunities that war offers for forging links with other, 'harder' disciplines. Wartime provides abundant scientific funding and research opportunities, and Psychology, like other disciplines, has had few inhibitions in exploiting these. This does not imply cynicism; in the final analysis the psychologist's own fundamental identification is generally with national war aims. If the roots of the conflict appear to lie in the psychological character of the enemy, then the implicit dilemma between cure and combat is easily evaded. Since the First World War psychologists have also become clinically involved in the treatment of those suffering war-related mental disturbances of various kinds, primarily, though not exclusively, military personnel traumatised by combat, victims of 'shell-shock' or 'combat fatigue' (categories that were, of course, created by psychologists undertaking this work, although an ancestral condition, 'cannon-ball wind', was known from the early nineteenth century).

The involvements of Psychology with war can, therefore, initially be seen as of two basic kinds.

1 How the discipline has been shaped by its wartime roles and military tasks in general. This would include treating 'shell-shock' (in the United Kingdom) and the US Army intelligence tests during the First World War; continuing studies during the Second World War of 'combat fatigue'; research on perception and instrument design in the context of air warfare; involvements with training and selection; a long-standing interest in

propaganda; and post-Second World War social Psychological studies of leadership and group dynamics. By the Second World War a sub-discipline called 'military Psychology' had emerged in the United States (e.g. Meier, 1943), applying Psychology for military purposes. As Geuter (1992) shows, the demands of *Wehrmacht* Psychology in the 1930s were crucial in professionalising German Psychology, as were the 1917–18 Army tests for US Psychology (Samelson, 1979).

2 Attempts at diagnosing the psychological roots of war, accepting this as in some sense pathological. These have taken several approaches including traditional instinct theory (Wilfred Trotter, 1916), Freudian (Ernest Glover, 1933), Jungian (Anthony Stevens, 1990) and ethological (Konrad Lorenz, 1966), while the research on various psychological aspects of the effects of nuclear weapon deployment during the mid-1980s Cold War crisis can perhaps be included here. Two points about these should be made immediately. First, it may well be that seeking psychological explanations for war is inappropriate or at least inadequate, but psychologists have invariably concurred with John F. Kennedy's view that 'war begins in the hearts of men'. As we saw in the 'racism' case, Psychology risks being used to divert attention from economic or social–structural-level causes. If war arises from a tragic flaw in human nature 'we are all guilty', which translates in practice into 'nobody is really responsible'. Second, we are concerned here only with twentieth-century warfare, which clearly differs from earlier forms by its hi-tech genocidal and ecocidal character and increasing lack of demarcation between combatants and non-combatants in terms of exposure to risk. How far this can be explained in terms appropriate for understanding earlier and simpler modes of violent inter-social conflict is very much a point at issue. An important work fitting uneasily into either of these broad categories is Norman Dixon's *The Psychology of Military Incompetence* (1976), although in spirit it is nearer the present one.

Simply classifying war's significance for Psychology in this way is nevertheless insufficient to elucidate its more pervasive influence on the discipline. It suggests that this may be located in a number of discrete areas of research as a contextual 'boosting' factor as against other areas where it played no part. This is to seriously misrepresent the true situation; as Rose (1990) argues, war has deeply affected the role of Psychology in twentieth-century Western culture. War provides a hot-house environment in which virtually the entire range of Psychology's interests are both co-opted in the service of the national interest and, in the process, given specific orientations and social functions. These range from the needs to monitor and manage public and military morale via personality and ability assessment to the more technical applications of expertise on perception, vigilance, human–machine interaction and the like involved in developing high-tech military equipment. Developmental Psychology becomes involved in relation to nurseries, evacuation and child mental-health issues; Industrial Psychology is deployed in managing and organising munitions and military equipment production; psychiatrists and psychologists alike may find themselves engaged in psychological warfare, propaganda and morale-related tasks; while the treatment of psychologically traumatised service personnel promotes exploration of new therapeutic techniques.

Psychology's Second World War entanglements in particular can be seen to have largely determined its post-war character in areas as apparently distinct as the emergence of group psychotherapy, the rise of Cognitive Psychology, the flourishing of the 'culture and personality' school and the salience of attachment theory in Developmental Psychology. Since virtually all psychologists were drafted into war-related work in some way or another it is not surprising that this played a large role in their professional careers. For younger psychologists it tended to determine their initial research interests and areas of professional expertise, for older ones it provided new, well-funded opportunities for expanding their existing ones. To give but two examples: J.J. Gibson's wartime perception research with the Army Air Force was a major factor in leading him to rethink the nature of space perception, while it was at the Mill Hill Emergency Hospital, in the context of psychiatric treatment of soldiers, that H.J. Eysenck began formulating his two-factor personality theory and extending factor analysis beyond intelligence to personality.

In Rose's view the Second World War was crucial in Psychology's full emergence as a discipline centrally concerned with what he calls 'technologies of subjectivity' – that is, with devising technologies enabling the subjective realm to be rendered visible and quantifiable, 'inscribable and calculable', in the forms of graphs, scores, statistics and charts. While on this route already (First World War Army intelligence tests and less well-known US Army work by Dill Scott on assessment of specific abilities had marked the start of the process) it was the Second World War that brought it to fruition, exploiting and advancing the still relatively novel techniques of attitude scaling, factor analysis and personality measurement.

From this perspective the opening dilemma begins to blur, or at least shifts to the intra-psychic level. Even while being at war, psychologists (or many of them) are driven to ponder more intensely its psychological roots. This may express itself, as in psychodynamic approaches, by offering explanations in terms drawn from personality theory: the Nazi 'authoritarian' personality projecting or displacing unresolved Oedipal aggression, or, in the Jungian scheme of things, a collective projection of the 'shadow' archetype (e.g. by each of the Cold War blocs). Ethologists, on the other hand, have tended to view war as the activation of instinctive mechanisms such as 'territoriality'. At a different level there has been a whole sub-area in Social Psychology concerned with 'conflict resolution', drawing on empirical research into group dynamics, attitude formation and various mainstream theories of aggression like the 'frustration–aggression' hypothesis. Much of this does, however, beg the question – perhaps wars, modern ones at any rate, are *not* rooted in individual psychological processes but in socio-economic ones? While 'the hearts of men' may be involved, the purses of arms manufacturers cannot be ignored. This is not to deny that individual psychological factors can be utilised to motivate the 'national will'. Appropriate propaganda can easily trigger what are probably in some sense 'instinctive' reactions to defend the nation's womanhood, etc. (and 'what would you do if you saw a German raping your sister?' was the classic First World War question to conscientious objectors). This of course returns us to the Le Bon territory discussed in Chapter 12.

The technology of modern warfare curiously requires the very opposite of normal aggressive behaviour for its success: a bomber crew behaves almost identically to an airline flight crew except for some additional button-pressing. Can we really gain insight into, say, the development of the atom bomb, from studying the territorial behaviour of robins? Does this approach itself not seem a bit like a 'displacement' activity? Pub brawl-type aggression is actually physiologically limited; the adrenalin-loaded, high arousal state involved is necessarily short-lived. Firing artillery shells, by contrast, could be just like any other manual job. Can the one really shed light on the other? Cognitive factors are also involved: if the probability of being shot for desertion is perceived as higher than that of being killed in battle, then the latter becomes the rational choice. Second World War research also highlighted the importance of small-group dynamics in facilitating fighting 'morale', identification with comrades and group pressures to conform playing perhaps the major role in sustaining the 'fighting spirit' of combatants.

Some time during the Second World War Kenneth Craik wrote: 'War is a normal part of life; it has been in the past; those who say it ought to be unnecessary cannot prove their case from history' (1966, p. 176). As such it pervades all aspects of psychological life, and hence all areas of Psychology become relevant. But this is not to say that psychological factors are sufficient to explain why such a way of life is embarked upon. To answer this we must turn to more detailed examination of specific historical circumstances. Nevertheless it is hard to escape the feeling that there *was* some deeper collective psychological dynamic involved in the origins of each of this century's world wars. The First World War *does* in retrospect seem to be linked to the nineteenth century's 'beast within' model and the growing psychological insecurity of ruling class 'reason' touched on in previous chapters, while Nazism was clearly in some way rooted in the deeper psychological condition of the German people. In an attempt to get to grips with this latter, some psychologists have sought to identify widely shared pathogenic features of the 1900–20 German generations from a psychodynamic angle. As far as more recent wars are concerned, such as the Vietnam War, the psychological roots would seem more typically to lie not in human nature as a whole but in the specific psychologies of policy-makers and politicians; it is *their* perceptions of the global geopolitical situation and ideological assumptions that (via the power they enjoy to promote them) create the 'realities' in which war seems logical. In short, each war – whether international or civil – presents us with a unique blend of psychological (both individual and collective), economic and ideological or religious factors. When the latter are the more heavily weighted, the adequacy of psychological explanations is, at best, limited

To conclude, war has been the most far-reaching and insidious of all 'contextual' factors in its effects on Psychology, reflecting the fact that war has, after all, been the most universal psychological preoccupation of modern culture. War, real or prospective, has impinged directly or indirectly on all our biographies, and saturates our cultural lives from films to literature, poetry to technology. Any attempt to 'put Psychology in its place' must at some point confront the reality that whatever this 'place' is, it is located somewhere within the bloodiest century on record.

BIBLIOGRAPHY

Further reading

Bramson, L. and G.W. Goethals (eds) (1968, 2nd edn) *War: Studies from Psychology, Sociology, Anthropology*, Chicago: Chicago University Press.
Geuter, U. (1992) *The Professionalization of Psychology in Nazi Germany*, Cambridge: Cambridge University Press,
Rose, N. (1990) *Governing the Soul*, London: Routledge.

Additional references

The following is a small sample from a vast literature:

Bartlett, F.C. (1927) *Psychology and the Soldier*, Cambridge: Cambridge University Press.
Cantril, H. (ed.) (1950) *Tensions that Cause Wars*, Urbana, Ill.: University of Illinois Press.
Craik, K. (1966) *The Nature of Psychology: A Selection of Papers, Essays and Other Writings*, ed. Stephen L. Sherwood, Cambridge: Cambridge University Press.
Dixon, N.F. (1976, reprint 1994) *The Psychology of Military Incompetence*, London: Pimlico.
Durbin, E.F.M. and J. Bowlby (1939) *Personal Aggressiveness and War*, London: Kegan Paul.
Glover, E. (1933) *War, Sadism and Pacifism*, London: Allen & Unwin.
Grinker, R.R. and J.P. Spiegel (1945) *Men Under Stress*, Philadelphia, Pa.: Blakiston.
Lasswell, H.D. (1938) *Propaganda Technique in the World War*, New York: Peter Smith.
Lorenz, K. (1966) *On Aggression*, London: Methuen.
Meier, N.C. (1943) *Military Psychology*, New York: Harper.
Myers, C.S. (1940) *Shell-shock in France 1914–1918*, Cambridge: Cambridge University Press.
Samelson, F. (1979) 'Putting Psychology on the Map: Ideology and Intelligence Testing', in A.R. Buss (ed.) *Psychology in Social Context*, New York: Irvington.
Stevens, A. (1990) *The Roots of War: A Jungian Perspective*, New York: Paragon House.
Stone, M. (1985) 'Shell-shock and the Psychologists', in W.F. Bynum, Roy Porter and Michael Shepherd (eds) *The Anatomy of Madness: Essays in the History of Psychiatry*, vol.1, London: Tavistock.
Stouffer, S.A. et al. (1949–50) *The American Soldier* (4 vols), Princeton, N.J.: Princeton University Press.
Trotter, W. (1916) *Instincts of the Herd in Peace and War*, London: Fisher Unwin.
Watson, P. (1978) *War on the Mind*, London: Hutchinson.

Epilogue

In this book I have snaked back and forth over a variety of issues, throwing the odd opportunistic coil around some of them. In these final pages I wish to try to pull things together and see if a verdict on 'Psychology's place' can be reached.

A recurrent theme has been that Psychology eludes neat categorisation as an orthodox scientific discipline. Psychology indisputably adopts scientific research methods and derives theories from them, but a problem arises from the very nature of its subject matter: does the psychological realm exist as an objective 'natural' phenomenon amenable to scientific enquiry in the way that astronomical, chemical and biological realms exist? Moreover Psychology's goals, though often said to be 'the prediction and control of behaviour', patently extend beyond and in some cases conflict with this. In the orthodox sciences, however, prediction and (where feasible) control of their subject matter is of the essence. These difficulties largely arise from the 'reflexive' nature of Psychology as a direct, unmediated expression of its own subject matter. Put another way, Psychology consists of psychological discourse, but such discourse in itself represents 'the psychological' insofar as it is knowable and meaningful. When Psychology describes or explains psychology in novel ways it is actually engaged in a process of psychological change. As previously observed, to talk about oneself in a new way is to have changed oneself. One aspect of this 'status' issue was raised at the end of Chapter 8; the success or otherwise of Psychological theories and models is not determined by the court of strictly 'scientific' evaluation alone, but ultimately by the court of public opinion. Do we *like* or find useful the ways of talking about ourselves that psychologists propose? Naturally this is rarely a straight thumbs-up or thumbs-down verdict – people in certain professions or with certain problems will be more favourably inclined than others towards specific Psychological ideas. And some are better placed to fund the promotion of those they like than others.

But this is not the end of the story: modern culture has set as a general condition for all knowledge claims that they be 'scientific'. In this context, to be acceptable, Psychological work must be conducted in a scientific style, involving experiments and generating theories. That is, it must reflect the *scientific psychology* of twentieth-century humans (or those in Western and Western-dominated cultures at any rate). In other words, modernist humans tend to really think and operate in a 'scientific' way – construing their failures to do so as evidence of 'irrationality'. Thus the pressure is always to bring the psychological under the aegis of reason, including our emotions, feelings and perceptions. This dominance of 'scientific reason' is not uncontested, of course, and is increasingly under pressure as we near the millennium. Interestingly, though, much of this criticism is couched not as a critique of reason but of a too limited concept of reason, seeking not science's overthrow but its extension and loosening. Such tensions are much in evidence within Psychology itself, ranging as it does from highly positivist hard-line approaches to more intuitive non-experimental ones. That chronic pluralism of the discipline identified at the outset may indeed be understood as reflecting (though not fully representing) the psychological diversity of the population at large. In psychoanalysis, as we saw, Freud's apparent dethronement *of* reason *by* scientific reason presented a challenge still with us.

The 'reflexivity' concept may, however, offer us a way forward. Humans, collectively and individually, always face the challenge of making sense of their lives and experience. Unlike other creatures we have no 'essential' distinctively 'human' nature (though we may have legacies of ancestral pre-human natures): a cat, walrus or sheep has no worries about its identity, it just *is* a cat, walrus or sheep. This challenge was traditionally met at various levels from religious and cosmological systems via bodies of 'folk wisdom' in the form of stories and proverbs, down to the meanings embodied in everyday psychological language. When circumstances changed, so these systems of meaning adjusted. 'Human nature' is thus something that we have to continually recreate and rediscover, each generation in turn testing received wisdoms against its own experience. Since around 1800 the pace of historical change has meant that the gulf between each successive generation's experience has widened (this perhaps reached a peak in the mid-twentieth century). The rise of science and technology being a central feature of this flux, traditional wisdoms were seen as increasingly obsolete by those confronted with worlds radically different from those in response to which they were formulated.

This process of constant recreation of our 'human nature' (also known as being alive) is at the heart of the whole issue. How does it operate? To verge on tautology, we deploy the world of lived experience as a source of ideas for making sense of, giving meaning to, our individual lives. In doing this we, to varying degrees, supplement and/or replace traditional ideas that no longer seem relevant. What, then, is Psychology? The broadest answer is that *it is an institutionalisation of this process.* Why did it get institutionalised in this way? The answer to this is twofold. First, insofar as the 'raw material' for the process came increasingly from the realms of science and technology (as against the commonly accessible realms of nature and folk crafts, for example), expertise in such realms became necessary for the process to continue. Thus a discipline oriented to scientific and technological developments emerged, the goal of which was to explore their psychological meanings. This discipline is thus concerned with reflexively applying scientific discoveries about the external world (*and* the technologies that these yield) to human nature itself, to 'the psychological'. While never monopolising the process, inventing a discipline of Psychology was perhaps the only route by which it could be continued *vis-à-vis* the increasingly sophisticated and arcane phenomena discovered and created by modern science and technology. And as we saw, the event around which Psychology finally cohered as a unified discipline was the scientific acceptance of an evolutionary cosmology.

The second part of the answer is more specifically contextual. The mid-nineteenth-century expansion of urban industrial culture moulded the form that this reflexive process took. From the mid-eighteenth century 'human nature' was assuming a new social significance in the face of growing needs to manage such things as crime, madness and education. A century later this managerial need to understand human nature had greatly intensified. The new, city-centred, incipiently high-tech and heavily industrialised culture required management on an unprecedented scale. A multitude of new governmental agencies fed on statistical data and information on policy implementation. One aspect of this was a need to classify people for various purposes, and for this to be possible they had to be *rendered* classifiable. For example, whereas traditional village society could handle one or two mentally handicapped people within its informal community structure, in urban settings 'sub-normality' or 'idiocy' became a major issue; as education spread so did the needs for its bureaucratic monitoring and standardisation and concern with the education process itself, and so on. The world regarding which society's rulers and managers were recreating human nature was that of their own managerial and policy-making lives. (Further ramifications of this were discussed in Chapter 3.) It was not their own 'human nature' that they were having to make sense of, so much as that of everybody below them – indirectly making sense of their own by so doing. In this context the reflexivity of the enterprise, hitherto acknowledged by several philosophical writers, rapidly faded from view. The process became institutionalised in a form reflecting the psychological position and character of those institutionalising it.

We can thus see that while Psychology's place is the institutionalisation of something that the human race has always done, interpreting human nature in the light of its lived experience, its agendas, priorities and approaches have also been deeply affected by the historically specific managerial and social power interests of those implementing this institutionalisation – in a word, their own 'psychologies'. The discipline has, however, always included some for whom this was an insufficient response to the deeper task of sustaining meaning in human life. In Germany, for example, a variety of anti-Wundtian thinkers such as Dilthey and E. von Hartmann strove, during the earlier years of this century, to forge a new *Lebensphilosophie* ('philosophy of life') more satisfying than mainstream Psychology could offer, while Gestalt Psychology's desire to preserve meaning against reductionism was a central goal of their labours, as we saw in Chapter 6. (*Lebensphilosophie* was unfortunately co-opted by Nazi-era psychologists such as P. Lersch.) The twists and turns in the discipline's history may be partly understood as reflecting the various, somewhat erratic steps by which that initial hegemony was weakened and the range of 'lived experience' being fed into the process broadened. Thus in the last quarter-century or so the influx of women, blacks and uncloseted gays into Psychology has wreaked havoc with many assumptions, both theoretical and methodological, previously largely unquestioned (as discussed in Chapter 15, for example). One could say that the discipline has become more 'democratised' – something that both the cognitivist George Miller and the social constructionist Kenneth Gergen were advocating around 1970. Even so, while it may have extended beyond those original 'managerial' interests it has not abandoned them.

So, we now live in a world where, thanks to Psychology, our intelligences can be measured, our personalities 'tested', assessed and graphically profiled, our mental distresses variously diagnosed as anxiety states, neuroses and stress disorders, our attitudes quantified, the steepnesses of our learning curves praised, and our cognitive styles ascertained. In Nikolas Rose's terms, our 'subjectivities' have become 'inscribable and calculable'. It takes a leap of historical imagination to appreciate quite how bizarre all this would have seemed in, say, 1840, when at most one might have preened oneself on the size of one's phrenological 'organ of benevolence'.

If the 'place' of Psychology is to play the role outlined here, we are bound to reflect on the implications of this for our understanding of ourselves as psychologists. For a start there is the moral implication, alluded to elsewhere, that what we say about human nature really matters. If we are participating in this collective social process of maintaining and creating psychological meaning we cannot shrug our shoulders, disclaiming responsibility for how society 'misuses' our 'scientific' expertise. Authoritatively promoting the notion that humans are a kind of computer, for example, will make us see ourselves as such. This may be fine up to a point, but if we claim that they are *only* a kind of computer and that this claim has the status of a final scientific truth, we are unethically exceeding our authority. In some circumstances it might well enrich our self-understanding to utilise the computer image reflexively, but this should be as an expansion of our repertoire of psychological ideas, not as its wholesale replacement.

Finally, reinforcing this, it means that we are basically making the very odd claim that we are, in effect, professional human beings. Usually, of course, we delimit this – we are professional experts on dyslexia or perception or post-traumatic stress disorder or management training – but this does not dispel the oddness, if anything it heightens it. We are claiming livelihoods, salaries and careers as experts not even on the human condition as a whole (as a priest arguably does) but on one segment of it, as experts on talking, seeing or suffering. If we wish to continue to enjoy such roles we have to persuade our fellow humans that it is worth their while funding us. I suggest that we would, in the long run, be wiser to try to articulate the reflexive situation that we are in than continue the arch pretence that we are but simple humble scientists.

For me, Psychology should be about expanding, not reducing, possibilities; about enriching, not removing, meanings; about liberation, not finalisation. It should be a contribution to an active process of collective consciousness expansion, not a supposedly purely 'objective' process of expert mind-control and management. If this sounds grandiose, I would suggest that this is no more than what, without knowing it, it has *always* been, despite its attempts at being something else. Nobody can have the final word.

Name index

Subject index